NO EASY PEACE

PEACE

Liberating Anglicanism

*A collection of essays
in Memory of
William John Wolf*

Edited by
Carter Heyward and Sue Phillips

UNIVERSITY
PRESS OF
AMERICA

Lanham • New York • London

Copyright © 1992 by
University Press of America®, Inc.
4720 Boston Way
Lanham, Maryland 20706

3 Henrietta Street
London WC2E 8LU England

Library of Congress Cataloging-in-Publication Data

No easy peace : liberating Anglicanism : a collection of essays
in memory of William John Wolf / edited by Carter Heyward and
Sue Phillips.
p.   cm.
Includes bibliographical references.
1. Anglican Communion—Doctrines. 2. Liberalism (Religion)—
Anglican Communion. I. Heyward, Carter. II. Phillips, Sue,
1966–   . III. Wolf, William J.
BX5005.N6   1992   283—dc20   92–1115 CIP

ISBN 0–8191–8602–3 (cloth : alk. paper)
ISBN 0–8191–8603–1 (pbk. : alk. paper)

Co-published by arrangement with the
Episcopal Divinity School

 The paper used in this publication meets the minimum requirements of
American National Standard for Information Sciences—Permanence
of Paper for Printed Library Materials, ANSI Z39.48–1984.

ESSAYS

IN HONOR AND MEMORY OF

WILLIAM JOHN "BILL" WOLF
1918-1990

ACKNOWLEDGEMENTS

When this volume of essays was originally conceptualized in 1985, it was to be a project in honor of our beloved colleague, Bill Wolf. Now, many years later, we regret that this collection must be in his memory. Bill's wit, good humor, and theological genius illuminated the collection and writing of these essays right up to the time of his death. We deeply regret that he never saw No Easy Peace in its final form.

Many people contributed to this project during its lengthy formation. Robin Gorsline carried it through the early stages of compilation, offering valuable editorial insights. Gloria Delgadillo, Lena Lawrence, and Wally Dixon typed the manuscript. Fred Donovan and John Bosick offered encouragement and computer assistance. Suzanne Hiatt, Owen Thomas, and Fredrica Harris Thompsett have graciously provided administrative support for the project since its inception. The Episcopal Divinity School generously contributed financial assistance and staff support. Finally, we want to thank Eleanor Wolf for her patience and her enthusiasm for this volume.

C.H.
S.P.

Cambridge, Mass.
June, 1991

The mediation of the historical task of the creation of a new humanity assures that liberation from sin and community with God in solidarity with all humanity...does not fall into idealism and evasion. But at the same time, this mediation prevents these manifestations from becoming translated into any kind of Christian ideology of political action or a politico-religious messianism... It keeps us from any confusion of the Kingdom with any one historical stage, from any idolatry toward unavoidable ambiguous human achievement, from any absolutizing of revolution.

In the Bible Christ is presented as the one who brings liberation. Christ the Saviour liberates us from sin, which is the ultimate root of all disruption of friendship and of all injustice and oppression. Christ makes us truly free, that is to say, he enables us to live in communion with him; and this is the basis for all human community.

Gustavo Gutiérrez
A Theology of Liberation

NO EASY PEACE: LIBERATING ANGLICANISM

Contents

PREFACE

Carter Heyward

Word reached me late in the afternoon of June 6, 1990, that Bill Wolf had died earlier that day while he and his wife Eleanor were at their Heath, Massachusetts, home. In the company of a number of other families prominent in circles of modern Protestant theology, the Wolfs had spent their summers in the mountains of western Massachusetts, raising their kids, celebrating life in its many forms, and weathering crises that, over the past 45 years, have shaken the world and church as well as family and friendships. That Bill should die while reading, with his beloved spouse nearby, struck me as terribly right.

But I was also touched by an intense sadness. For in Bill Wolf's death, many of us lost not only a friend, but also one of a handful of churchmen of his race, class, and culture who genuinely believed in the revolutionary movements for justice in the world (and, too seldom, in the church) as sacred struggles in which a radically incarnate God is being born, again and again, in history.

In an even more personal way, Bill's death was, for me, a significant loss, for he was an older, gentle churchman who had respected and liked me in my strength. For a Christian woman to be affirmed in her strength by a male colleague happens rarely enough that it is noteworthy. It signals something special about the man. Bill Wolf knew that his strength was secured, not sapped, in relation to women and men who were uncompromising in the desire for a just and compassionate world. He seemed in no way diminished to be, from time to time, in the shadows of others' achievements. For Bill knew, I believe, and enjoyed knowing, that his own stature was growing in relation to those with whom he had cast his lot -- sisters and brothers within and beyond the church who were committed to helping usher in the reign of God now, not simply later.

It was sad, for all the contributers of this volume, that Bill died before we could finish it. But he was involved in its production almost to the end. In the spring, shortly before he died, Bill wrote an autobiographical essay for inclusion in the book, and he shared with several of us his excitement (and, coming from this modest man, amazement) that No Easy Peace was becoming a reality.

The idea for the book originated in the spring of 1986, a year after Bill's retirement from his position as the Howard Chandler Robbins Professor of Theology at the Episcopal Divinity School in Cambridge, Massachusetts.

Several of his faculty colleagues agreed that we wanted in some way to honor this remarkable person. Compiling a Festschrift -- "festive publication" -- in appreciation of Bill's work as a theologian, teacher, and priest of the church seemed especially appropriate, given Bill's own appreciation for the written theological word in communicating the love of God. It has taken longer (by two years) than we had anticipated, but by the early summer of 1990, we at last had a collection of essays representing different (though for the most part Episcopal) voices.

Bill was pleased that this volume does not pretend to represent all, or even most, perspectives in the Episcopal Church. It was never intended to appeal to all who are drawn to the study of Anglican theology or history. Like every book, this one has a bias. It has been compiled in an attempt to explore issues that are congruent with Bill Wolf's vision of an inclusive Kingdom of Christ. This vision led Bill, as it had his mentor, Frederick Denison Maurice a century earlier, to break rank with the "old boys' network," in which most mainline Christian theologians still today can shield themselves from the agendas of the Two-thirds World, women, people of color, the poor, gay men and lesbians, and other so-called "special interest" groups.

Many of the contributors to this book would identify ourselves as liberation theologians, but did Bill Wolf see himself this way? Bill knew himself best, I dare say, as a theological "liberal," at least in three senses: first, as an adherent to such theological principles as inclusivity, openmindedness, and freedom; second, and more specifically, as a custodian not merely of the liberalism within Anglicanism but -- in the lineage of Hooker, Maurice, and Temple -- of Anglicanism as a liberal theological tradition. Third, in the terms of a debate which roared among many Euroamerican Protestants while he was in graduate school in the 1930s and 1940s, Bill developed a stronger affinity for the "liberalism" of the late-nineteenth and early-twentieth centuries than for its "neo-orthodox" corrective, although he understood, appreciated, and employed the latter in his teaching and writing. Even in his earlier, more systematic reflections on revelation and the atonement, Bill was careful to affirm the world, science, and history as infused with, not contrary to, the Spirit of God. Because he saw this clearly, he was able to understand and welcome the dawn of liberation theology in the United States not as a "simply social," "purely political," or "merely Marxist" philosophy, but as a profoundly Christian movement.

As his own essay attests, Bill was drawn to and admired the liberation theology he encountered through the contributions of such luminaries as Gustavo Gutiérrez, James Cone, and his own neighbor and friend, Robert McAfee Brown. In his last years, Bill understood his own theology increasingly, I believe, to be motivated by and inseparable from a liberation theological commitment. This is the spirit in which we have compiled this volume.

The collection is ordered around topics and themes that were near and dear to Bill Wolf. Part One reflects Anglican theology-in-the-making today among progressive white Episcopalians, laity and clergy, men and women. If there is a single theme running throughout these essays, it is the incarnate, radically embodied character of the love of God. Though none of the five pieces focusses on christology, they bear witness, together and singly, to a god present in our lives -- sensual, hungry, intimate, and thirsty, able to love and be loved, touch and be touched, through our relationships with one another and with the larger world.

Drawing from feminist liberation theology and the relational psychology being shaped by the Stone Center at Wellesley College, Margaret Huff and I look at how the church may function as a creative, participatory body. Both David Gracie and Diana Scholl explore the contemporary significance of F.D. Maurice -- Gracie, by probing Maurice's radically sacramental understanding of peacemaking and justice, and Scholl in an imaginative letter from Maurice on the subjects of prayer and spirituality. In an update and assessment of the Myth of God Incarnate controversy in the Church of England -- with special attention to the 1987 publication of Brian Hebblethwaite's The Incarnation: Collected Essays in Christology -- Don Winslow offers an incarnational "principle" by which our christologies can be shaped as much by faith, risk, and innovation as by inherited dogmatic discourse. Frederica Harris Thompsett then presents "courageous" incarnation as a faithful opportunity, with roots in history, to live intimately as friends and lovers of God and one another.

In Part Two, the contributers help illuminate, from very different social locations, various components of the global crisis, especially racism, sexism, and capitalist exploitation. John Booty argues that the Christian tradition addresses the crisis by teaching us to care "for the wholeness of creation, serving the needs of all as we are in turn served by all." Susan Adams discusses "the challenge of partnership" to the mainline Christian churchs in Aotearoa (New Zealand) by both Maori people and women, especially Pakeha women (of European descent). Joanna Kadi analyzes classism in progressive social movements, and the myriad ways that race, class, and gender oppression affects the life and dreams of a Lebanese-Canadian woman. J. Antonio Ramos examines the opportunity of Latin American Christians, including Anglicans, to participate in liberation theological efforts toward authentic social and spiritual transformation.

Part Three presents issues of women, sex, and power as central and vital to the on-going reformation of the church itself. In a letter to an Anglican sister working for women's ordination in England, Suzanne Hiatt tells the story of the 1974 "Philadelphia Ordination" of women priests, and shows why it was, and is, controversial. Barbara Harris uncovers and reveals the "determination, perseverance, and creativity" of Black Anglican women who have "sought to serve the church over the last century." Owen Thomas examines ways in which feminist theology and Anglican theology might be mutually instructive, and asks whether the latter might "function as a bridge between feminist theology and traditional theologies." Anne Gilson attempts to "get at the roots" of the Episcopal Church's heterosexist policies in relation to lesbians and gay men. As a lesbian myself, I attempt to bear witness to the "sacred character of erotic power" and discuss coming out as a spiritual, as well as political, process. Finally, Corine Johnson presents, as a fundamental ethical and pastoral issue for churches, some connections between incest and what mainline (white) churches have taught about Jesus Christ.

In Part Four, the final section of essays, Bill Wolf's own autobiographical piece addresses his 45 years as a teacher, theologian, and priest of the church. This is followed by testimonies from two of his neighbors and friends in Heath -- a reflection by Robert McAfee Brown on his friendship with Bill and the homily given by Pamela Porter at Bill's funeral at the Evangelical Community Church in Heath on June 9, 1990.

As amply as the collection may represent many of Bill's concerns and passions (he was, for example, passionately committed, as his essay indicates, to the affirmation of "gayness and lesbianism" as needing the church's "strongest support"; and, as noted, he was a hearty ally of liberation theologies), certain issues which moved him and impacted his theology are not addressed in this book: the importance of the ecumenical movement, especially the Episcopal Church's role in it through the 1960s and early 1970s; the critical import of history as the arena of God's activity, and the ground of God's incarnation; and, finally, the role of literature -- historical novels in particular -- in sparking Bill's theological imagination.

His novel about Benedict Arnold was his primary writing project in retirement, a vehicle that brought his theological interests full-circle, back to a study of good, evil, and suffering, which, in more systematic fashion, had been central in his earliest works on revelation and atonement. Of his novel, Bill wrote, in his essay for this volume:

> Asked why a theologian should be interested in writing a novel, I usually reply that Benedict Arnold's is our story -- the story of the good, the

bad, and the ugly in each of us. Arnold still remains a mystery to me, but so does the reality of evil and suffering.

The systematician and the novelist, 45 years apart, wrestle with the same mystery which, no doubt, generated Bill Wolf's passion for justice in Latin America, in North America, in "the whole inhabited earth," and in the Episcopal Church.

Benedict Arnold was due to be published on May 31, 1990. It arrived in Heath on June 6. The book was taken immediately to the hospital where Bill had been rushed. He was by then gone, but in the realm we here do not know fully, he surely is finding the "wider audience" he had hoped to reach with his novel.

¡Presente!

Carter Heyward
June 1, 1991

PART ONE

**AN INCARNATIONAL SPIRITUALITY:
IMAGES OF FAITH, LOVE, WORK, AND THE
LEGACY OF F.D. MAURICE**

FOUNDATIONS FOR ANGLICAN ECCLESIOLOGY

Carter Heyward and Margaret C. Huff

As Episcopalians and feminist scholars and teachers (one of us in systematic theology, the other in pastoral psychology), we are attempting here to suggest a basis for an understanding of the church, its purpose and the way it "works" when it is working creatively. Our suggestions are shaped at the crossroads of three theological perspectives. Two of them -- feminist theology (especially feminist liberation theology) and liberation theology, are distinct contemporary movements with historical roots. The third is a synthesis of historical tendencies within Anglicanism which are significant for the contemporary church. We are referring here to Anglicanism's moorings in a theology of mystical "participation" (Richard Hooker) and "unity" (Frederick Denison Maurice). Carter Heyward has been exploring the common ground of these feminist, liberation, and Anglican visions of what and who we may be as people of God.

Another perspective that informs our work is the "self-in-relation" psychology being developed by feminist therapists and theorists at the Stone Center for Developmental Services and Studies at Wellesley College in Massachusetts. Margaret Huff has been examining ways in which feminist liberation theology/ethics and "self-in-relation" psychology can be mutually instructive.[1]

With several other feminist liberation theologians and psychologists, we have been meeting since January, 1988, to study points of identity, convergence and difference between theological and psychological understandings of living as selves-in-relation. This paper is an effort to construct a springboard into an ecclesiological understanding which would reflect a commitment to human well-being in its many aspects. This is not intended to be an ecclesiology per se. We are merely making suggestions toward the development of an ecclesiology.

At the outset we shall offer an understanding of sacred power (divine and human, in co-operation) as the power in right, mutual, relation. From there, we shall consider how such an understanding might contribute to a doctrine of the church as mutual participation and as community. We will conclude with brief reflections on our commitments as Christian people.

Sacred Power as Relational: God as the Doing of Justice

We begin on the assumption that a sound ecclesiology will be steeped in sound doctrines of God, humanity, and christology (in what sense divine and human realities are joined, in Christ's Body). So we are concerned here with theological, anthropological, and christological possibilities.

A basic motif in Anglican, feminist, and liberation theologies is that sacred power is relational power: God's power -- or God as power -- is inherently relational in its movement. God does not act alone; God acts in relation to creation. More basically, God is not alone.

It is wonderful that the inmost life of God should be communicated; but it would be a contradiction that it should not be communicated. We cannot think of a Being of perfect love as wrapped up in Himself [sic], as dwelling in the contemplation of His [sic] own excellence and perfection.[2]

Essentially and intrinsically, God is relational power: specifically, the power in right, or mutual, relation. Feminist, liberation, and a number of Anglican theologians have understood this relational metaphysics as the theological backdrop to our claim that justice -- as right, mutual, relation -- is normative for Christian theology, ethics, and life. As Desmond Tutu writes:

God created us, we believe, for interdependence because none of us is meant to be completely self-sufficient. We are meant to find our complement in others, and this is true for societies as well as individuals. God wants us to be members of the one family, the human family. All kinds of problems occur when we seek to disobey the fundamental law of our being.[3]

Far from being a modern issue, such a profoundly relational (hence, moral) theology is classical. In his writings on the Trinity, Augustine summed up the christological gist of this claim in his insight that the Holy Spirit is the love between the Father and the Son. From this perspective, both theological and anthropological, God is the power in the relation between one "person" and another.

Let us explore further the significance of this theological foundation, the relational matrix of our humanity, for our daily lives. From a psychological perspective, self-in-relation therapists and theorists recognize that women (and men) attain our senses of identity through differentiation within the context of relationships. Psychiatrist Jean Baker Miller writes,

From the moment of birth this internal representation is of a self which is in active interchange with other selves. Moreover, the kind of interaction has one central characteristic, and that is that people are attending to the infant -- most importantly attending to the infant's core of being, which means the infant's emotions -- and the infant is responding in the same way, i.e., to the other person's emotions. The beginning of mental representations of the self, then, is of a self whose core -- which is emotional -- is attended to by the other(s); and who begins to attend to the emotions of the other(s). Part of this internal image of oneself includes feeling the other's emotions and acting on the emotions coming from the other as they are in interplay with one's own emotions. This means that the beginnings of the concept of self are not those of a static and lone self being ministered to by another (incidentally, this construct has a strongly suggestive male flavor), but much more of a self inseparable from a dynamic interaction. And the central characteristic of that interaction is one of attending to each other's mental states and emotions.[4]

Later in the same paper, Miller states, "All growth occurs within · emotional connections, not separate from them" and "The only possibility of having any sense of self at all is built on this core process."[5] Miller's colleague, psychologist Janet Surrey, writes of distinguishing this understanding of women's development from the usual model of Separation-Individuation:

> I would like to propose a new construction: Relationship-Differentiation... By differentiation, I do not mean to suggest as a developmental goal the assertion of difference and separateness, rather I mean a dynamic process which encompasses increasing levels of complexity, structure, and articulation within the context of human bonds and attachments... I am not diminishing the significance of other lines of self-development (e.g., competence, agency, or initiative). I am implying that these other capacities are developed for women in the context of important relationships.[6]

Unlike its predecessor in relational psychology, object-relations theory, which holds that healthy development occurs through our separation from one another, self-in-relation psychology suggests that our mutually-empowering connectedness, in which the authenticity of each participant is honored and respected. Self-in-relation theory does not assume an undifferentiated unity, or sameness, into which all human beings are absorbed. Rather, we come to know who we are -- and who we are not -- through responsiveness, our own and others', in mutual relationships. Within and through these relationships, we become effective agents, empowered to act. As Janet Surrey writes:

I define psychological empowerment as: the motivation, freedom, and capacity to act purposefully, with the mobilization of the energies, resources, strengths, or powers of each person through a mutual, relational process. Personal empowerment can be viewed only through the larger lens of power through connections. [7]

We should note that the Stone Center theorists restrict their insights into development to that of women, since they are basing their theory on their clinical work with women. With them, however, we believe that this psychology has profound implications for men as well as women and can be recognized as important by those men who (miraculously) have not been overwhelmed by the aspiration to possess a "separate" and "individuated" self. Such a "self-possessed" individual character structure has become the apex of identity for the white Western male of social and economic privilege.

Our reading of Western theology, confirmed by living as white women in Western culture, leads us, with our psychologist sisters, to suspect that most white men with access to economic privilege do not experience themselves as intrinsically relational. Most white men have difficulty, we perceive, knowing that their identities are formed, constantly, by relational interaction. Such men of social and economic privilege, as well as other men and women who aspire to be like them, fail to see how profoundly their moral choices are shaped within the matrix of radically relational responsibilities not only to their own families and loved ones, but, moreover, to others elsewhere whom they may not know personally but whose lives are interwoven nonetheless with their own families and loved ones. We suspect also that because men of privilege -- and all who aspire to the privilege held by such men -- have learned to experience themselves as "on their own" and "competitive" with others for whatever is really worth having, these men experience others more as potential adversaries than as friends. [8]

With many women, the problem is not as much the opposite (e.g., women can be fiercely competitive, too) as it is the experience of ourselves as separated from one another, broken apart from our larger body of sisters and brothers. As women, we have been encouraged to _feel_ the connectedness and to know that we need one another. However, we daughters of twentieth century white western culture learn to experience ourselves as cut off from ourselves-in-relation -- often from men, but also from our mothers, our sisters, our children, and a relational matrix of strong friendship. The greatest blessing of the feminist movement, we believe, has been to empower us to reconnect and strengthen our network of friends and sisters.

We believe this reconnection and strengthening of the foundations of genuine friendship among women (and men who are in solidarity with us) may be at the very heart of an ecclesiology for our time and place in history. Such a possibility is rooted in the experience and vision of ourselves together, sisters and brothers with common purpose and affection in the midst of our differences. We are friends of one another, because we are friends of justice -- right, mutual relation -- and, as such, are friends of God, our power in right relation.[9]

By proposing the inherently relational basis of human being as it forms our feelings, thoughts, intuitions, and perceptions of ourselves and others, the self-in-relation psychology we have mentioned above has contributed to our theological understanding of sacred power, the power of God, as our power in right, mutual, relation, in the small and large "places" of our lives. As a theological possibility, the self-in-relation position contributes to an understanding of sacred power which takes seriously the "love commandments." God, or the power of love, is the power of right relation, righteousness, or justice. God is the doing of justice. God is not the power in wrong -- unjust, non-mutual, distorted -- relation. God is not the relationship itself; nor is God identifiable in a static way with any particular "person" or "party" in the relationship, although from time to time God's presence may be especially apparent in the relational presence of a particular person.

The significance of such a relational understanding of God, of humankind, and of other-than-human creatures as well, cannot be overstated. As moral philosopher John Macmurray, addressing this relational possibility a generation ago, wrote,

Persons...are constituted by their mutual relation to one another. "I" exist only as one element in the complex "You and I." We have to discover how this ultimate fact can be adequately thought, that is to say, symbolized in reflection.[10]

To "discover how this ultimate fact [the sacred power of relationality] can be adequately thought...[or] symbolized in reflection" is to learn how to reason together in such a way as to do justice not only in relation to one another, but also in relation to God. This radically social vision -- theological and anthropological as well -- provides a christological window through which we may glimpse right relation as mutual relation between Creator and creatures, in which both or all parties are more fully empowered in the relationship.

In Jesus' relation to God, Jesus grows with God in love. It is a relation in which each gives and receives and stands out as distinct from the other. Jesus is not God's little boy... Rather, Jesus is God's child who grows in relation to God and becomes God's friend in a voluntary and mutual relation. God is parent in that God is resource for Jesus' growth in power. But it may be equally appropriate (and I believe it is) to image God as Jesus' child, whose growth in the world Jesus facilitates.[11]

We believe it is important, at this juncture, to signal a danger in what we are saying about mutuality, right relation, justice and God. We believe, furthermore, that it is an especially "Anglican" danger -- to accept ideally, as goals, perhaps even as eschatological vision, such commitments as mutuality and justice and to embrace them rhetorically as images of divine will, without adequately realizing the cost, or what is involved in living our lives on the basis of such commitments.

In Western societies, it is hard to envision, much less live on the basis of, mutuality. It does not pay well -- financially, professionally, socially. The image of a church pledged to mutuality among its members and between itself and other bodies in the world is an image of a suffering church, no question. And that is what we're talking about at the root of this proposal. Genuine mutuality between and among persons creates justice and, as such, constitutes a commitment to justice-making within the church and beyond the church.

It might be useful to move a little further here into a discussion of what we mean by mutuality as a means of illuminating what we mean by justice, since everything we are proposing about the church is predicated upon Christian commitment to mutuality and justice as foundational to Christian purpose.

Consider the decision by the 1988 General Convention regarding "Episcopal visitors," in which Episcopalians were assured that they will not have to accept the ministrations of women bishops, a resolution much in keeping with the House of Bishops' "conscience clause" which, for over ten years, has served to "protect" Episcopalians from the ministry of women priests and deacons. What might mutuality mean in the context of such decisions as these?

In reaching a compromise between those who say they cannot accept women as bishops or priests and those who not only can, but do, (including those women who are priests), the elected leaders of the church believe that they are doing their best at preserving the unity of the denomination -- holding us together, in a tension of the via media. From this perspective, "mutuality" (between women ministers and the larger church body) seems to become that which serves everyone's interests to some extent. But, in fact, we propose that real mutuality cannot be established by seeking a lowest common denominator. Mutuality does not serve everyone's interests up to a point. Mutual relation finally serves everyone's interest fully insofar as it is rooted and nurtured in special relation to those who, historically, have been disempowered in the relation -- in this case, women in the church.

It is not enough for bishops or other church leaders to try to "take care" of women priests committed to their charge. Caretaking is not mutual. It is not empowering. Empowerment can never be a unilateral dynamic. A women grabs her son and pulls him away from a hot oven. She then takes time to help him discover what "hot" is. The rescue action is caretaking; the helping him learn is caring. To try to protect women from hostile church people may involve some caretaking (the most helpful being to encourage women to respect and take care of ourselves and one another). In profoundly sexist contexts such as Christian churches, however, genuinely caring for women -- priests, bishops, deacons, laywomen, little girls, older women, mothers, daughters, sisters, spouses, lovers, and friends -- involves following women's lead as we attempt to name and claim our power in relation, which is in fact our God. Only in such a dynamic relational context, in which men listen to women and take women's lives as seriously as all of us have been taught to take the lives of men to whom we have given spiritual power over us, can we discover what it might mean for women and men to be in right mutual relationship within the church.

The only way a genuinely mutual decision could be made toward creating a just and compassionate, creative and liberating, relationship between women clergy and the larger church would be for bishops and other elected leaders of the church to follow the lead of ordained (and other) women in charting our relational movement with our parishes, schools, dioceses, provinces, sister and brother Episcopalians. Mutuality is a relational movement, not a static state. A commitment to mutuality constitutes a shared willingness to be touched and transformed by what we are able to bring to the relationship and by what the relationship brings to us.

In a mutual relationship, all of us learn, grow, and change -- not just traditional Episcopalians who are leery of the ministries of ordained women. Women, ordained and lay, have much to learn as well as to teach, much to receive as well as to give. But right, mutual, relation is not founded upon a bookkeeper's quid pro quo reciprocity. In any justice-making relationship, the empowering movement -- movement to empower -- is toward those who historically have been disempowered in the relationship.

It is appropriate, therefore, that, in any sexist situation, those with power commit themselves to the empowerment of women and in a racist situation, we commit ourselves to the empowerment of people of color. For Anglicans, the via media, or middle way, needs to be understood, clearly, not as the way of compromise. Rather, the via media "is a way of engaging in dialogue. . . a willingness to be touched and changed, an ability to speak one's mind"[12] To be people of "the middle way" is a profoundly mutual way of being, because it is an open and compassionate way of being. In order to be open, or compassionate, in any well-seasoned, mature way we must have a point of view. To be people of the via media, we must stand somewhere rather than in-between-everywhere, which is to stand nowhere.

To live in mutual relation -- to do what is just -- we must stand with those who have been oppressed, victims of injustice, violence, battering, abuse, trivialization. Standing with them (sometimes being them ourselves), we must move as courageously as we can, and as cautiously as we must, into shaping a model of justice which respects the dignity and well-being of those who have perpetuated the violence and held the unjust power in place, but not at the cost of the dignity and well-being of the oppressed, victimized, battered, abused, trivialized. We propose that this fundamental commitment to mutuality as justice underlies our capacity to live as God's people in this world and, as such, is morally and pastorally foundational to an ecclesiology.

We turn now to how we might envision the church embodying our commitment to the justice, or caring, that is possible only where there is movement among us in and toward mutual relation.

One Whole Catholic Church: Mystical Body

Prior even to the "catholicity," or universality, of the church is the early Christian vision of the universality of the goodness of God's whole realm. As Irenaeus of Lyons wrote in the second century of the Common Era;

> All men [sic] are of the same nature, able both to hold fast and to do what is good; and, on the other hand, having also the power to cast it from them and not to do it. With God there are simultaneously exhibited power, wisdom, and goodness. His [sic] power and goodness appear in this, that of His [sic] own will He [sic] called into being and fashioned things having no previous existence; His [sic] wisdom is shown in His [sic] having made created things parts of one harmonious whole... "[13]

Contending against the radically dualistic Gnostics, Irenaeus struck an antidualistic chord with which the church historically has tended to have a disharmonious relationship. For Irenaeus, God is involved thoroughly in human and other creaturely life; God is involved in the very fabric of our daily lives. The eschatological meaning of this divine involvement in human affairs is that even now we are in process of redemption. God is with us.

This theological tendency -- toward affirming a radically incarnate God -- can be distorted to justify human passivity in relation to the problems of the world. If God is working out God's purpose, why not sit back and let God do it? Such reasoning, however, misses the radicality of divine involvement with us. We cannot just sit back and let God do it because our lives bear up God in the world. We are responsible for "godding."[14] As Dorothee Soelle has noted, "Our hands are God's hands in the world."

Interpreted from the lively moral posture of Soelle or of Frederick Denison Maurice, the "unity" of divine-human life is the very essence of redemptive movement. At the heart of such an "activist" faith in the unity of God and humankind is the experience and vision of one mystical body, fully human and fully divine, which Christians call "Christ." This mystical commitment, from a biblical perspective, is both Pauline and Johannine. It draws on Paul's emphasis on the oneness of the Body with its many members, and on John's vision of the coinherence of the members -- not only the human members, but divine as well.

To commit comes from the Latin, committere, meaning to connect, or entrust. Commitment is an act of committing to a charge or trust, and the state of being obligated or emotionally impelled. It is something you do and something you are. The popular Anglican pull toward the Fourth Gospel is, we suspect, a relational "intuition" of the intrinsic connectedness between all that lives, breathes, and has its being in the universe. In our natural condition -- in our human, non-human, and divine being -- we are committed to one another.

We are connected with the divine and entrust our being to God. The lines of connection are not one-way, however. God entrusts God's being to us. Commitment is not synonymous with obedience. In fact, commitment may require disobedience; prophets usually have been disobedient to civil and/or ecclesial authority. Nor is commitment identical to single-purposeness, which often leads to arrogant zealotry. Commitment is not essentially dualistic and exclusivist, since our connections can be multiple and inclusive. Living a committed, sacramental life strengthens and enriches all of our commitments. In turn, additional commitments may strengthen and enrich our initial or primary commitment. Commitments which are life-giving encourage us to seek, not forsake: other commitments are a way of expanding and sharing that which gives life.

The mystical dimension of the Johannine vision of relational commitment is in the author's recognition that coinherence -- or mutuality -- is between divine and human, not only human and human, members of the Body. This mystical emphasis undergirds the focus in Anglicanism on the sacramental faith that our lives reflect, reveal, and in some sense "call forth" or "generate" the life of God. In breaking bread, whether during the Service of Holy Communion or at the family table, we participate in blessing and serving a food that is holy because it is shared. The sharing is not just among the humans who partake of the bread, nor among the humans and the dogs who receive the crumbs, but also a sharing of the plants, the farmers' skills, the millers' talents, and the bakers' gifts, and the sacred source of the rain and sun.

To this point there is nothing distinctly Anglican about what we have discussed. We are speaking here of what is, essentially catholic, we believe, whether Anglican, Roman, Orthodox, or Protestant. Attempting to "anglican-ize" such a catholicism, such liturgists and divines as Thomas Cranmer and Richard Hooker worked carefully so as not to lose the mystical and sacramental character of the newly established church in England. Much more than the Roman polity which they were "protesting," these Anglican theologians stressed the participatory character of the whole people of God.

Writing in the second half of the sixteenth century, Hooker constructed a doctrine of participation as the means whereby we are the Body of Christ, the church as we are meant by God to be, coinhered with/in one another and also with/in God. In the Fifth Book of his Ecclesiastical Polity, Hooker addresses our "participation in divine nature" (2 Peter 1:4):

> We are...in God through Christ eternally according to that intent and purpose whereby we were chosen to be made his [sic] in this present world before the world itself was made, we are in God through the knowledge which is had of us, and the love which is borne towards us from everlasting... For his [sic] Church he [sic] knoweth and loveth, so that they which are in the Church are thereby known to be in him [sic].[15]

The implications of Hooker's doctrine of participation are far reaching. This preeminent Anglican father was non-dualistic and non-monistic in his radically Chalcedonian understanding of our relationship to God and one another: <u>We humans are neither fundamentally opposite to nor separate from God</u>. <u>Neither are we identical to nor to be confused with God</u>. <u>We are neither God nor are we unGod(ly)</u>. We are in relation to God much as we are to one another. Together, in relation, we participate in giving our Body its life, purpose, and shape.

It is as participants, with God and one another, that we embody the divine -- make God incarnate. In this way, we live empowered, empowering lives, resources of the Sacred with and for one another. Our intentional participation -- commitment -- grows out of our recognition of the connections between and among ourselves in relation to one another, other earth creatures, and our sacred wellspring. This then is a foundation for a relational ecclesiology.

A caveat should be noted here. Commitments, like relationships, can be distorted. They can be, or can become, unjust, in which case, they are destructive. If a commitment is life-sapping, it needs to be assessed as honestly as possible to see if it can be changed into a life-giving, constructive relationship. Sometimes friendship, sometimes a re-energized faith or new understanding, sometimes new ways of working or playing can bring about such transformation. If, however, such transformation is not possible or in some cases is not desired, then the commitment needs to be abrogated. This is exactly what is happening among many women, and many gay and lesbian people, who, in good faith, have left the church which they experienced as viciously sexist and heterosexist.

Church as Mutual Participation

For Hooker, "participation" was the key to understanding the church. In his social and historical context, Hooker viewed "participation" as a sacramental means, both visible and invisible, of human involvement with divinity. So closely are we related to God, and God to us (a christological perception), that our participation "with" God and one another might better be imaged as our participation "in" God and one another. This is an interpretation of the basic Johannine theme of our mystical unity, in Christ. It should not be read as a doctrine of "sameness." To participate is not to be merged or mingled with, to the effect of losing one's particularity.

Consider the following description of mutually empowering relation as descriptive also of our "mutual participation" as members of creation, and, more specifically, as members of that group of humanity which identifies itself as the Body of Christ -- the church:

In [mutually empowering relationships], both [or all] people feel able to have an impact on each other and on the movement or "flow" of the interaction. Each feels "heard" and "responded to" and able to "hear," "validate," and "respond to" the other. Each feels empowered through creating and sustaining a context which leads to increased awareness and understanding. Further, through this process, each participant feels enlarged, able to "see" more clearly, and energized to move into action. The capacity to be "moved," and to respond, and to "move" the other, represent the fundamental core of relational empowerment. [16]

Noteworthy from an eccesiological perspective is the sense of <u>movement</u> in mutually empowering relations or mutual <u>participation</u>. To participate with one another as sisters and brothers in the church is not a static or unchanging way of being in relation. Rather "each person is changed through the interaction." [17] Moreover, as Janet Surrey writes,

The movement of relationship creates an energy, momentum, or power that is experienced as beyond the individual, yet available to the individual. [All] participants gain new energy and new awareness as each has risked change and growth through the encounter. [No one person] is in control; instead, <u>each is enlarged and feels empowered, energized, and more real... This...movement of relationship, then, transfers to action in other realms as [the people] become increasingly response/able and empowered to act.</u>[18]

To be "enlarged, empowered, energized, and more real." What a description of sacramental participation in the church! Surrey is speaking not only of emotional responses between two people in a mutually empowering relationship. As she acknowledges elsewhere, she is concerned with the politics and spirituality of our lives. Her interest in mutuality is more than academic or clinical. Like her feminist liberation theological sisters, Surrey is aware that the survival of the planet depends upon our capacities, as church and as people in general, to generate radical mutuality among ourselves, thereby becoming empowered to do justice, and to <u>be</u> justice, for all.

With reference, for example, to workshops designed to empower women to speak out for nuclear disarmament, Surrey writes:

From the expressions of helpless rage, despair and confusion, the group builds together a sense of urgency and shared responsibility: We must do something.

Negative effects of helplessness, anger, fear, and confusion become transformed into the energy of positive movement.... The "I" is enhanced as the "we" emerges. Through building the "we" -- seeing together through creating an enlarged vision, participants transform their personal self-doubt and confusion into clarity and conviction. The sense of powerlessness of the individual is supplanted by the experience of relational power.[19]

"The 'I' is enhanced as the 'we' emerges." This is a basic affirmation of feminist liberation, and other liberation, theology. Its roots are in a socialistic anthropology with profoundly relational theological implications. The affirmation is essential to understanding our "participation" as church. We argue that this affirmation is more Anglican (at least more "Hookerian") than Catholic in a sectarian sense (e.g., Roman, Orthodox, or Anglo-Catholic). Hooker and others emphasized the vitality of the whole church's participation, not just the special role of bishops and other clergy, in God's redemptive movement.

This leads to the question of how a church might be organized so as to enhance the mutual participation of its members as well as the mutuality of the whole people in relation to God. We are not prepared at this point, nor do we intend, to address the issue of 'orders,' hierarchically arranged in terms of ecclesiastical authority. We will suggest only that hierarchical arrangements among adults do not tend to foster mutual empowerment. Even between adults and children, to organize power around fixed locations of "authority," "obedience," and "discipline" is to impede mutually empowering relation and thereby diminish the possibilities of anyone (children or adults) experiencing themselves as "enlarged, empowered, energized, and more real."

Essential to the capacity to believe in the sacred power of mutual participation is the gift of imagination -- or what Dorothee Soelle calls phantasie, a blend of imagination and intuition. Only with phantasie can we actually envision the creative, liberating power in mutuality as God's power to act in history. Our phantasie enables us to look beyond ourselves in our own small locations in time and space and "see sacredly" that our lives and relationships, our commitments and vocations, are connected with those of others who have gone before us, who will come after us, and who go with us now. Our phantasie draws us beyond ourselves and, in so doing, moves us more fully into ourselves as we are meant to be.

Phantasie is a divine gift, available to all who yearn to see, through the eyes of the divine, a glimpse of the realm of God -- which is an image of

ourselves, in right mutual relation amidst our variations and differences, as
community: with one another, together, in unity.

Church as Community

We turn to Frederick Denison Maurice for an understanding of spiritual
"unity" and of "community" as its human organization. Maurice undertook the
theological task of reconciliation, attempting to draw people together from
different religious (and secular) traditions and commitments, in dialogue, as a
means of exploring possibilities of unity of faith and witness. Maurice
understood that unity is no simple matter.

He saw that unity is not a matter of reducing differences to a lowest
common denominator. Not a matter of merging into sameness. Not a matter
of the weaker being subsumed into the identity of the stronger. Unity, for
Maurice, was rather the effect of relating honestly and openly amidst diversity
of experience and opinion. Genuine unity, he realized, was predicated upon the
ability of all participants in community to learn and grow within the relational
context.

This "relational hermeneutic of inclusivity" (our term) caused Maurice
problems with Dr. Jelf, his superior at King's College, London, where Maurice
taught. Dr. Jelf rejected Maurice's claim that all persons can, and in all
likelihood will, be saved by God, rather than that some would be cast into
eternal damnation. The possibility of such far-reaching unity among human
beings, and between humanity and God, would weaken the church's authority
to separate good from evil, right from wrong, in from out, and thus diminish
the church's authority, reasoned Dr. Jelf and his colleagues in their decision to
remove Maurice from his teaching post.

We are reminded of the Roman church's inhibitions and punishments of
such theologians as Leonardo Boff, Charles Curran, and John McNeill for
teaching theology and ethics which do not fall squarely in line with those of the
official magisterium. We think also of the Vatican's threats against the nuns
who signed the "right to dissent" advertisement in the New York Times.

In our own church, we think of the usually less dramatic forms of
ecclesial disapproval which meet the teachings and actions of those Episcopalians who suggest that our unity may be steeped in our diversity -- of color,
class, gender, culture, sexual preference -- and, moreover, that without such
diversity, there can be no real unity. This is because our common ground can
be recognized and welcomed only inasmuch as our particular experiences inform

and help give it shape. There can be no unity when one person, party, or sect (in the case of religious organizations) is setting the agenda. Unity is born out of difference, diversity, particularity, and commitments.

So too is community. The church as community is the mystical Body (for Maurice, the Kingdom of Christ) in which an infinitely varied people live together in the world and act together, sometimes in institutional form, on behalf of the loving God who has revealed Himself (sic) in Christ as our neighbor, our brother and sister. We do not have to believe the same things, or even be Christian for that matter, to participate in building the Kingdom of Christ. Unitarians, Trinitarians, Jews, and others work together in this task insofar as we love ourselves and others in God's world.

Maurice's comprehension of the church as community was rooted in his belief in Christ as the Spirit which makes us one, the Power which moves us into community -- and has from the beginning. Community-building is Christ's goal -- to heal our brokenness, mend our divisions, bring us together, all the while honoring our differences and variations.   Christ is the Spirit which discerns and lifts up the truth or goodness in each particularity, leaving no one outside the sacred realm in which truth and goodness are (and shall be) more fully manifest -- that is, as they are generated in mutual relationship, each one of us respecting and learning from the other.

Maurice was, in this sense, a reconciler: a community builder. He was also a prophet. He was prophetic because he valued the dignity and worth of every person and group enough to take each seriously. Maurice's doctrine of the universal church was that of an inclusive, expansive community of various sorts (not necessarily Christian) joined together in active involvement on behalf of human well-being.

Interestingly, Maurice's commitment to the polity of the Church of England seems to have been more "doctrinaire" and rigid than his constructive theology. Behind this discrepancy may have been the split in Maurice between the theological prophet/visionary and the Anglican priest. This is a common and difficult split, still among (and within) professional theologians and church leaders who are open to new understandings and are committed to working within the institutional church.

In order to live creatively in this tension -- in the pull between ecclesial loyalties and spiritual movement in relation to the larger world/church -- participants in Christian community must be clear about our commitments.

Commitments: Some Questions

We have suggested that living as selves-in-relation, in community, as participants in the Body of Christ, involves commitment -- intentionally connecting with, and entrusting ourselves, to one another. The church cannot function faithfully simply as a conglomerate of individuals who drift together or float alongside each other's lives because each likes the stained glass, the priest's charisma, or justice. Even if we land in the same parish because we like the rector's sermons, we need more than this common attraction to help us become a participatory church community. We need to become clear about our own commitments -- on what basis we are connecting with, and entrusting ourselves to, one another. In this brief conclusion, we can only list several of the questions which seem to us important about our commitments as participants in the church.

(1) What are our primary commitments, and how do we experience the connections and conflicts between and among them? For example, many of us are committed to a family which includes a "significant other" or spouse, children, parents, other relatives or friends, and pets. Most of us must earn a living, and we work at jobs which hold more or less meaning for our lives. Most of us have avocational interests and commitments -- e.g., to painting, poetry, politics, writing, cooking, justice-work, service of one form or another, sports. Most of us have a commitment to prayer and meditation, and to taking care of ourselves physically, emotionally, intellectually, and spiritually.

Any of these commitments may be primary for us at any given time in our lives. In some cases (such as with a spouse or children), the primary commitment is for an extended period of time, perhaps forever, but, in the here and now, few of us have only one basic commitment. Only insofar as we are able to be clear and honest with ourselves about what generates our passion and love can we be honest with one another. Strong, creative community is founded upon our ability and willingness to be honest and clear about our primary commitments.

(2) How do our commitments "participate" in the shaping of the primary commitments of the church community? And vice-versa -- How does the church help shape our primary commitments? These are chicken and egg questions, since the mutual shaping of individual and community is an ongoing, dialectical process. Only Susan, a battered wife, can say in what ways her commitment to take care of herself and her children is supported, or not, by the church to which she belongs. And only the members of that parish can testify to ways in which their community (or lack of community) has contributed to

Susan's well-being, or to her battering, and to ways in which Susan's situation may be sharpening their awareness of the proximity and proportions of domestic violence.

A creative church community plays a major role in shaping our personal commitments and to help us make connections between our own commitments, as well as between our commitments and those of others. An open, growing church community is always in the process of being shaped by its members' clearest and strongest commitments.

(3) What primary role can (and should) the church community play in supporting its members in making meaningful commitments in our love and work? In both arenas, many of us are frustrated and feel unsupported in our search for meaningful loving relationships and for purposeful, interesting work. Ordained leaders in the contemporary church often are singularly unhelpful to people who are suffering crises in either our love or work -- in the first instance, by preaching sanctimonious piety about marriage, monogamy, and sexual sinfulness; in the second, by preaching patience in the face of the actual economic conditions and abusive dynamics in which women and men labor and live stress-filled lives. The effect of these "spiritualizing" responses is to trivialize the concrete reality of our lives. Since love and work constitute, for most of us, the arenas of our primary commitments, we who are the church community must learn to take seriously these critical dimensions of our own lives and those of others. Otherwise, the church increasingly will have no creative, liberating significance for men, women, and children who are honest with and about themselves.

(4) What does it really involve to live as a religious community, as those who choose to commit ourselves to a common purpose with one another? The broadest and largest religious community is the church, and the church is the laity. None of us ceases to be laity just because of ordination.

We're in this church together. As churchpeople, we have an opportunity not to seek the lowest common denominator of our possibilities, nor to run roughshod over one another without concern for our mutual well-being. Our call is to seek justice, love mercy, and walk humbly with our God. This sacred power calls us into being and invites us to shape ourselves as a people, ourselves as we are meant to be, together, ourselves as an incarnation of the spirit that is fully human and fully divine.

NOTES

1. Margaret C. Huff, "The Interdependent Self: An Integrated Concept from Feminist Theology and Feminist Psychology," in Philosophy and Theology, vol. II, no. 2, 1987.

2. Frederick Denison Maurice, Theological Essays (London: J. Clarke, 1957), p. 291.

3. Desmond Tutu, "The Theologian and the Gospel of Freedom," The Trial of Faith: Theology and the Church Today, ed. Peter Eaton (Wilton, Conn.: Morehouse-Barlow Co., 1988).

4. Jean Baker Miller, "The Development of Women's Sense of Self," (Wellesley, Mass.: Stone Center for Developmental Services and Studies, Wellesley College, 1984), pp. 3-4.

5. Ibid., p. 4.

6. Janet L. Surrey et. al., "Women and Empathy: Implications for Psychological Development and Psychotherapy," Work in Progress, no. 82-02 (Wellesley, Mass.: Stone Center for Developmental Services and Studies, Wellesley College, 1983), p. 7.

7. Janet L. Surrey, "Relationship Empowerment," Work in Progress, no. 30 (Wellesley, Mass.: Stone Center for Developmental Services and Studies, Wellesley College, 1987), p. 3.

8. Huff, p. 88.

9. Carter Heyward, The Redemption of God: A Theology of Mutual Relation (Washington, D.C.: University Press of America, 1982).

10. John Macmurray, The Form of the Personal (London: Faber and Faber, 1957), p. 24.

11. Heyward, p. 38.

12. Heyward, p. 13.

13. Irenaeus of Lyons, Adversus Haereses (IV, c. 37, 38).

14. See Heyward, The Redemption of God and Virginia R. Mollenkott, Godding: Human Responsibility and the Bible (New York: Crossroad, 1987).

15. Richard Hooker, Ecclesiastical Polity (Book V, 56.6).

16. Surrey, pp. 6-7.

17. Ibid., p. 7.

18. Ibid.

19. Ibid., pp. 15-16.

CALLING THE EPISCOPAL CHURCH TOWARDS PEACEMAKING: HINTS FROM F.D. MAURICE AND THE SERMON ON THE MOUNT

David McI. Gracie

Imagine a courtroom with 30 defendants seated towards the front. Those on trial are of varying ages and religious backgrounds. Each has been charged with trespassing for sitting on a railway track to block a train carrying ammunition for shipment to Vietnam.

As the judge enters the courtroom, some of the defendants rise to their feet; others refuse to stand. Among those seated are Quakers, members of the Society of Friends, who will continue their distinctive witness by refusing to place their hands on a Bible to swear to tell the truth. The judge makes no issue of their behavior; they are allowed to 'affirm' instead of swearing, and the trial proceeds.

Part of my calling, as an Episcopal priest and campus minister, is a commitment to working for peace. I have been involved in many public demonstrations against war, from the days of Vietnam to the present. In every act of non-violent civil disobedience -- sitting in doorways or on a railroad track -- the company of witnesses for peace has included Quakers. This Anglican peace activist finds much in common with his Quaker sisters and brothers. Yet, the fact that some of them remain seated in a court, while I and others stand, has caused me to reflect upon the differences between our two Christian traditions.

To think of these differences is to think of the nineteenth century English Anglican theologian, Frederick Denison Maurice, who taught his theology in terms of the contrasts between the Quaker and Anglican ways. Maurice, while a devoted Anglican, also appreciated aspects of Quakerism -- especially the Quakers' strong adherence to principle. Maurice's classic work, The Kingdom of Christ, bears the subtitle, Hints to a Quaker Respecting the Principles, Constitution, and Ordinances of the Catholic Church. Re-reading The Kingdom of Christ, I find these hints helpful in understanding our place as Episcopalians in the ongoing peace movement in this country, a movement so often led and inspired by members of the Society of Friends.[1]

I propose here to briefly review Maurice's exegesis of the Sermon on the Mount, found in Volume II of The Kingdom of Christ, and then to consider what may be the unique character of the peace witness of those of us who stand when the judge enters the courtroom.

When he exegeted the fifth chapter of Matthew, Maurice entered territory considered special by the Quakers. They believed that in this text

Christ made the case for pacifism, and drew a clear distinction between the kingdoms of this world with their human laws and God's realm with its divine law. Maurice does not agree with their interpretation. While his exegesis is sometimes strained and his conclusions sometimes startling, Maurice offers valuable insights for Anglicans concerned with witnessing for peace and justice.

Maurice focuses on Matthew 5:21-48. These are the passages which read: "Ye have heard that it hath been said by them of old time... But I say unto you.... " He finds the key to their interpretation in the verses which directly precede them (vv. 17-20), verses which present the proposition which makes the rest clear for him:

> Think not that I am come to destroy the law, or the prophets: I am not come to destroy, but to fulfill. For verily I say unto you, till heaven and earth pass, one jot or one tittle shall in no wise pass from the law, till all be fulfilled. (Matthew, vv. 17-18)

Maurice comments:

> Till heaven and earth have passed away, till the whole existing economy of things has ceased, so long as there is any evil to be prevented in it, so long as there is flesh in any man which is not subject to the will of God -- so long as law in its outward character must exist; and he is least in the kingdom of heaven, he has least spiritual intuition, who shall try to abridge it of its precepts or its terror.[2]

The Quaker, according to Maurice, is a dispensationalist who believes that, in the Sermon on the Mount, Christ is stating the maxims of a previous dispensation only to replace them by the rules for a new age. For Maurice, such a view contradicts the meaning of verses 17-20.

> Everything would seem to show that Christ came to confirm rules existing before: to show the ground, the inward righteousness, of these rules; and to lead those who were willing to be... disciples into the possession and enjoyment of it.[3]

There is not a lower and a higher standard given to us by God, but one universal standard. Therefore,

> the righteousness which exceeds that of the scribes and Pharisees is one which is spiritual and not literal, the conformity of the life and character to the original mould after which all outward laws are fashioned -- the pattern on the Mount.[4]

The "original mould" and "pattern on the Mount" lead us to the Letter to the Hebrews, an epistle much loved by Maurice. The biblical truth Maurice is setting before us here finds its clearest expression in that epistle. The One who gave the law of old is "the same yesterday, today and forever" (Hebrews 13:8). Maurice puts it this way:

> He says, It has been said by them of old time -- that is, in other words, I...Jesus Christ, said in old time, for it was he who gave the law, he was King then, he is now.[5]

So, according to Maurice's reading, the "I say unto you" sayings do not displace but rather support, illumine and undergird what was said "by them of old time."

> [We must not] permit ourselves to imagine that his work was to substitute one formal precept for another, and not rather to stanch the fountain of evil in the heart, whence had proceeded all those crimes against which the outward law was the true and permanent witness.[6]

How Maurice manages to give such a reading to each of these passages would make a fascinating study, but it is only his treatment of those passages that have been most used by Quakers and other Christian pacifists, namely verses 38-45, that are under review here. Indeed, while he attempts to undo the Quaker argument from scripture, Maurice explores for us the possibility of a broad avenue of action for peace which goes well beyond that of most Anglicans, although it is always an avenue of law and respect for law.

We begin with verses 38 and 39, which state:

> Ye have heard that it hath been said, An eye for an eye, and a tooth for a tooth: But I say unto you, That ye resist not evil: but whosoever shall smite thee on thy right cheek, turn to him the other also.

Maurice's commentary at this point is shocking to our contemporary sensibilities, because he wholeheartedly affirms the principle of "an eye for an eye and a tooth for a tooth."

> [It is] a principle which lies at the foundation of a state... It is a righteous principle, I had almost called it the righteous principle; for it is that which presents to us the most complete image of the order and moral government of the world... Vengeance must be somewhere -- 'It is mine,' saith the Lord; and the state is that which teaches each man

that there is a Lord, an invisible ruler, and judge, and governor over him, whose authority he is bound to acknowledge, and upon whose authority every act of private vengeance is an infringement.[7]

Maurice believes that the law gives us "an apprehension of the system of retribution which is established in the universe," a system presided over by a judge.[8] He maintains that if we regard God only as the renewer and sanctifier of our lives, we sacrifice our belief in God's personality, which is dependent on our understanding God as judge. Yet law has its clear limits. Law can make it inconvenient for someone to attempt private vengeance, but law cannot remove the person's desire for vengeance. According to Maurice, the Gospel is given to us to "exterminate that same selfish principle out of the mind and heart."[9] The injunction to turn the other cheek is to be read in that light; but the patient endurance of wrongs to which it calls us is intended to help others observe the law more fully, and to hold it in "cheerful reverence."

The admonition, "resist not evil" is read by Maurice as a principle, not as a new rule. It means for him that we should not resist evil for any selfish purpose -- a clear call to unselfish obedience of the law as an essential principle of faithful living. As a result, we will resist lawlessness. For if we pattern ourselves after Christ, we will remember that Christ's life of perfect obedience was a "a constant resistance to evil."[10] In fact, Maurice's example of the proper sort of resistance is one of civil disobedience. "When Hampden resisted ship-money, I think he complied far better with our Lord's precept than if he had paid the tax."[11] In short, tax resistance is in conformity with the Sermon on the Mount.

Such civil disobedience is offered, properly, because of love for the law. "It is most ridiculous to affirm that the most opposite methods may not at times be necessary to uphold [the dignity of the law]."[12] How do we choose the correct method, then? Sounding just like a Quaker, Maurice tells us to rely on individual conscience, "guided by the Spirit of God, and seeking light from the Word of God."[13]

We come next to the locus classicus for pacifist doctrine:

Ye have heard that it hath been said, Thou shalt love thy neighbor, and hate thine enemy. But I say unto you, Love your enemies, bless them that curse you, do good to them that hate you, and pray for them which despitefully use you, and persecute you. That ye may be the children of your Father which is in heaven; for he maketh his sun to rise on the evil and on the good, and sendeth rain on the just and on the unjust. (vv. 43-45)

Love for our enemies, we would think, must surely be inconsistent with the hatred of enemies against which it is counterposed. Not for Maurice!

The words, then, 'Thou shalt love thy neighbor and hate thine enemy,' are not destroyed but fulfilled by the words, 'Love your enemies, bless them that curse you...'[14]

A reading and analysis of the whole of Maurice's discussion is necessary to fully appreciate what Maurice is attempting to say here. I will review briefly only one aspect: his positive understanding of the hatred of evil. He maintains that we cannot love good without hating evil, and this hatred of evil is without meaning unless it leads to actions for resisting and extinguishing evil. For the state, this can mean acts of war.

God's spirit, Maurice confesses, is the spirit of universal love, and yet he reminds us that the God who sends rain and sunshine on all "sends also plagues and pestilences."[15] His teaching at this point is a very broad hint about the nature of God the Redeemer who does not cease at the same time to be God the Judge. And it is to the Hebrew Scriptures that Maurice turns for his understanding of the nation that exists under this redeeming and judging God. The nation, so conceived, has a duty to resist and oppose its enemies.

He requires of his chosen people that they should feel as he feels...to maintain the principles of order and truth; to be avenged of those who violate them; not to shrink from the sacrifice of individual life, sacred and awful as it is, for the sake of maintaining that without which life is a mere miserable lie.[16]

Maurice believed that this divinely inspired mission for the chosen people was true as much for 19th century England as it was for ancient Israel -- true "so long as the nation was a nation, so long as it owned God and God owned it."[17] However, there was no guarantee of the continuation of that relationship. He refers to the time in the days of the prophet Jeremiah when Israel had ceased to be a witness for God; then

to resist the invader was merely to assert the continuation of a self-willed power, which had thrown off the divine yoke; [then] allegiance was dissolved, society at an end.[18]

Here are limits not only to the state's right to make war, but to its right to claim our allegiance at all.

At the conclusion of his review of the Sermon on the Mount, Maurice has some praise for the Quakers.   However, he does not voice that praise until he has first criticized what he calls their "negative testimony," namely the way in which their teaching about war and peace may encourage cowardice in some, a sense of disrespect for the nation, and an attitude that the army can behave only murderously.   His praise is for their "positive witness," and he encourages us all to share in it.

> Everyone who lets the world see that selfishness is not his law, that he can obey a principle, that the arm of God is more to be trusted than the arm of flesh, will certainly do good.   But there is nothing to hinder the Catholic Church from bearing such testimonies; many in all ages have borne them.[19]

What hinders us today, then?   Why have we so often been in the position of giving not even a hint to the Quakers, but rather of taking our lead consistently from them -- whether on the railroad tracks or in the halls of Congress?   We can be grateful for all we have learned from the Society of Friends about alternatives to violence in this war-weary world, but what is the stamp of our own peace witness?

I would argue our own witness is neither philosophically anarchist nor theologically pacifist.   Our witness should be consistent with the Anglican emphasis on the high calling of the state and the rule of law.   "Lord, keep this nation under your care," we continually pray.   "Lord, save the state" perhaps said it better.   Whatever the wording, we need to remember that it is an armed state for which we pray.   Tertullian, in his Apology, testified of the early church that it prayed for the empire by asking "for brave armies, a faithful senate, a virtuous people, the world at rest."[20]   We ask for the same.

In the Prayer Book, the prayer for the armed forces is now followed directly by a prayer for those who suffer for the sake of conscience.   This telling juxtaposition suggests that the proper question is not whether the state should be armed but what it is doing with its arms.   Is it using them to keep the peace or to engage in aggression?   When it is the latter there is nothing to prevent us from joining the ranks of those who make their witness of conscience, "that our society may be cleansed and strengthened."[21]

Vigorous opposition to illegal or immoral actions of government is to be expected from those who pledge at their baptism "to strive for justice and peace among all people."   Our society and our church would be much healthier if those Christians who value law and order would display a higher degree of sensitivity toward governmental disregard for law and violation of the established standards of international order.

There are concrete instances of faithful resistance for the sake of conscience which can serve to guide us on our path of civil disobedience and peacemaking in an Anglican mode. For example, in the concluding years of the Vietnam War, several of us on the staff of the Diocese of Pennsylvania refused to pay a portion of our federal income taxes. We sought to question the war's legality. As an undeclared war, a war of aggression and a war waged excessively against civilians, we believed it violated both the United States Constitution and international law.

Of course, the federal courts were refusing, almost totally, to rule on suits which raised these issues. The government responded to our tax refusal with an IRS order to the diocese to garnishee our wages. Diocesan Council responded favorably to a request to refuse the order, on the grounds that the church which helped form our conscience ought not be compelled by government to force us to violate it. The council saw an issue of religious freedom and was willing to test the issue in federal court.

Predictably, the federal judge did not see religious freedom issues and ruled for the IRS. By that time, however, the war had ended and we paid our back taxes. Despite this outcome, the council had acted honorably and faithfully to provide space to continue the civil disobedience, and to place the protest within the framework of the law.

A more contemporary example occurred when, in early 1987, Bishop H. Coleman McGehee, Jr., of Michigan, himself a former Virginia assistant state attorney general, filed a friend of the court brief with the Michigan Supreme Court on behalf of protesters who had committed civil disobedience at a plant which manufactures engines for cruise missiles. Bishop McGehee was joined by a Methodist and a Roman Catholic bishop. Their brief objected to the fact that the 30 protestors, arrested for trespass, were being held in jail -- some for months -- until they promised never again to commit civil disobedience at that plant!

In October of that same year the Michigan Supreme Court resolved the issue by ruling that jailing individuals for refusing to make promises about future conduct was wrong. Bishop McGehee publicly applauded the decision and commended the protestors who had gone to jail for refusing to compromise on a matter of conscience. The bishop was not only a friend in court; he also had joined the demonstrators in a vigil at the plant.[22]

These two examples illustrate an approach to peacemaking within the Anglican tradition represented by F.D. Maurice.[23] In these instances, opposition to war and to the nuclear arms race was not based on any doctrines of human perfectionism or a new dispensation. Instead, those involved attempted to discern the pattern of God's rule as reflected in the laws of nations and our own country and act accordingly.

After two "world wars," the war in the Persian Gulf, and many other armed conflicts in this century, as well the foreboding omnipresence of the nuclear arms race, we can never again share Maurice's sense of nations being chosen of God to take vengeance on evildoers. We -- our own nation as well as others -- have too often transgressed the limits he found marked out in Jeremiah, acting like "a self-willed power, which had thrown off the divine yoke."[24] However, awareness of our own national faithlessness ought not lead to an abandonment of prayers that through obedience to God's law our government may secure "justice and peace at home... [and] show forth [God's] praise among the nations of the earth."[25]

Such a prayer must remain on our lips and in our hearts even as we resist our country's present lawlessness, through invasions and proxy wars, in Central America, and as we condemn the stockpiling of nuclear weapons which threaten the entire created order. Our prayer and our resistance stem from the same root, and from deeply conservative instincts: a desire to conserve the world, to save the state, to reflect more clearly in society "the pattern on the Mount."[26]

Thus we stand when the judge enters the courtroom. We respect the witness of our sisters and brothers who remain seated, but we try to witness in our own way to a faith in God who is both redeemer and judge. We still hope and pray that God's judgments may be carried out by this state, and not against it in consuming fire.

NOTES

1.   During my seminary studies at the Episcopal Theological School -- well before I had any extended dealings with Quakers, and certainly before I stood trial or went to jail with them -- Bill Wolf taught me to appreciate Maurice.

In those days, the sexist language of Maurice caused me no trouble; today, his language grates, sometimes harshly. However, as the editors of this work and I have struggled to 'clean up' his language we have made him more inaccessible than ever! So, we have left the sexist language and patriarchal thought patterns intact. We hope that doing so will contribute to a better understanding of Maurice, and a keener appreciation of the benefits and limits of his thought for us today.

2.   Frederick Denison Maurice, The Kingdom of Christ or Hints to a Quaker Respecting the Principles, Constitution and Ordinances of the Catholic Church (London: SCM Press Ltd, 1958), Vol. II, p. 207.

3.   Ibid., p. 207.

4.   Ibid., p. 208.

5.   Ibid., p. 217.

6.   Ibid., p. 211.

7.   Ibid., p. 222.

8.   Ibid., p. 222.

9.   Ibid., p. 224.

10.   Ibid., p. 225.

11.   Ibid., p. 225. John Hampden (c. 1595-1643) refused to pay a tax levied by King Charles I in 1637. This levy, made without the consent of Parliament, was one of the causes of the Great Rebellion.

12.   Ibid., p. 225.

13.   Ibid., p. 225.

14.   Ibid., p. 232.

12. Ibid., p. 225.

13. Ibid., p. 225.

14. Ibid., p. 232.

15. Ibid., p. 230.

16. Ibid., p. 228.

17. Ibid., p. 229.

18. Ibid., p. 229.

19. Ibid., p. 232.

20. Apology 30, The Ante-Nicene Fathers, ed. Roberts and Donaldson (Grand Rapids: Eerdmans, 1969), Vol. III, p. 42. See the discussion of such prayers of the early church in Adolph Harnack, Militia Christi, trans. David Gracie (Philadelphia: Fortress Press, 1981), p. 106.

21. Book of Common Prayer, p. 823.

22. H. Coleman McGehee, Jr., "The Bishop's Commentary," the Diocese of Michigan, Detroit, Michigan, October 1987.

23. The question raised by Cotesworth Pinckney Lewis in his sermon before President Johnson in Williamsburg, Virginia, on November 12, 1967, serves as another example. Far short of civil disobedience, Lewis' simple questioning of the legality and morality of the war in Indochina had a telling effect. See the account in John Booty, The Episcopal Church in Crisis (Cambridge, Massachusetts: Cowley Publications, 1988), pp. 75-77.

24. Kingdom, p. 229.

25. Book of Common Prayer, p. 820.

26. Kingdom, p. 208.

F. D. MAURICE AND THE LIFE OF PRAYER:
AN IMAGINATIVE INTERPRETATION

Diana Scholl

F.D. Maurice took God seriously. What intrigues me is how Maurice understood this most basic relationship of his life. The question for me is not what Maurice knew about God -- his theology -- but how Maurice experienced God -- his spirituality. In Maurice's writing we often see the results of his I-Thou relationship with God, but I wanted to learn if he ever wrote about the encounter itself. Can we glean from his writings either descriptions of Maurice's prayer life or evocations of the aura of his experience of prayer? If we can understand even partially this most intimate aspect of his life, we can deepen our insights into his thought and his contributions to the life of Christianity.

Although Maurice would agree that there is a difference between intellectual knowledge and experience as modes of approach to a question, he would also concur that there is a danger of a false dichotomy. There is no way to distinguish cleanly Maurice's theology from his spirituality -- each creates and informs the other. As Maurice himself affirmed, what he knew about God was inseparable from how he experienced God. He believed that this is true for any honest, creative theologian. But Maurice told us little specifically about spirituality as formative experience.

Surely, one reason Maurice did not speak more personally of his experience of God was that he was a white male theologian in Victorian England. His writing reflects a "gentlemanly" constraint that keeps even his most personal letters theoretical and expository. Even when addressing matters of personal concern, most of what he wrote was traditionally structured theological discourse. But there was probably another reason for Maurice's withholding of reflections on his spirituality. In his study of Maurice on prayer, John Orens warns that there is little in Maurice's writing on methods of prayer or spiritual advice of any kind. He notes that the very idea of spiritual direction was distressing to Maurice. I suspect the reason Maurice was troubled about spiritual direction was the high probability that the "director" would succumb to spiritual pride and thereby damage both persons. Maurice believed that no one is above and beyond or better than anyone else in the body of Christ. He believed that we find our way together.

Orens suggests that Maurice's strong reaction against the individualistic piety of his time came close to disregarding the validity and appropriateness of individuals' prayers. This, however, seems to me a bit unfair to Maurice. Although we have no record of the content of his prayers, we know that Maurice had a very intense personal intimacy with God.

In order to pursue my interest in Maurice's spirituality, I had to read as widely as possible and use all of my intuitive senses to discern the spiritual energies guiding and manifesting themselves in Maurice's life. My work led me into the realization that prayer was not just the basis of F.D. Maurice's theology. It was the basis of all his knowledge, the foundation of his experience, the ground upon which he lived his personal life with all of its travail and beauty. As Maurice called himself a "digger," so too must we dig to perceive the life of the Spirit in his work. We must read his words and feel his emotions as signs of God's active presence in his life. For Maurice was a man of deep feeling with a strong experience of profound connectedness to the world, its people, and God.

In order to begin understanding Maurice's experience of God, I have decided to compose a letter from Maurice to me on this subject. This seems to me especially appropriate since it was in his letters that Maurice was most likely to reflect on his personal experience. Before proceeding, I must state several caveats.

First, the letter is not typically "Maurician." It exhibits a degree of personal intimacy with which I am comfortable in print, but which Maurice probably was not. Not only am I writing in the late twentieth century, I write as a woman. I am not comfortable with theological abstraction, however conceptually brilliant it may be. For me, it is a barrier to realizing the intimacy which the life of prayer involves.

Secondly, while I want to remain honest to Maurice's understanding of God, church, and world, I also want to take the creative step of seeing how he might advise or teach me in my particular social location. I am a white, middle-strata woman who is a single parent from the United States living in the late twentieth century. I am currently an Episcopal seminarian who is hoping to be ordained but having been so far excluded. I am committed to a life of prayer and to justice for all who are excluded from the fullness of life. Maurice is unlikely to have known anyone very much like me. But I do believe that through his commitments to women, to Christian socialism, and the universal love of God, he had spiritual and theoretical bases that would have allowed him to "know" me well. So I extend his insights here to include me.

#1 TO DIANA SCHOLL, SEMINARIAN, CAMBRIDGE, MASSACHUSETTS, USA, ON PRAYER AND WOMEN IN THE CHURCH, FROM OXFORD.

...I am deeply touched and moved in the Spirit by your story and struggles not only for justice and right to prevail in the church and in the world but for that deep, true relation to God your loving Father. Will you have mercy on this poor soul who can only know God as "Father?" I can refer to God only in this way because that is true to who I am even though I have heard and felt sympathetic to the modern concern about this terminology. I have never been one to make words or laws into systems for idolatry. As you know, my constant desire is to see beneath the externals of life and find that foundation of unity which binds us all. I use the term "Father" for God to exemplify, and really to actualize, the immediate, complete, personal relationship between God and ourselves. For me "Father" encompasses all that is good and necessary for us -- perhaps this will become ever clearer as we think together about this primary relationship in our prayer. I, however, do hold to the necessity of the ultimate power of God, and I do see the pitfalls of the possible interpretation of this power from the point of view of women in patriarchal society. But, for me, God is power who never requires slavish submission, but obedience out of the most absolute confidence in the loving kindness that is who-God-is. This too will become clear, I hope.

Nevertheless, I will admit that the feminist perspective on the power dynamic inherent in parental metaphors for God is a significant consideration for me. Being male and living in the time and place that I did, I must confess that this was not brought to my attention. Yet you know of my deep feeling of solidarity with the working men and women of my time who were indeed powerless in so many ways. I believe very strongly that Christianity which does not recognize and act against the confusions and oppression of the children of God is a Christianity bankrupt of its moral foundations. All persons, male and female, Christian and non-Christian, are redeemed by the passion, death, and resurrection of Jesus Christ. Therefore no one, especially a Christian, should erect barriers between God and His people.

As you will recall from my essay on sin, I believe that sin is best known when we find "broken the silken cords which bind (us) to" others resulting in "the sense of solitude, isolation, distinct individual responsibility...painfulness and agony."[1] I understand from our correspondence that many people today, women, the poor, homosexuals, and others, experience this painful separation and isolation from Christianity. I fought my whole life for unity within the Church of England. I know, in the depths of my own soul, the horror of division and hatred and rejection. I will comment on that later. For now, I ask in the name of our all Forgiving and Merciful Father your indulgence and patience in the "old" language of a very "old" man.

With all humility, I would like to honor your sharing of your story and your prayer with a little of my own experience. I speak with reticence because I would never deign to exalt myself as a model for anyone. Yet I choose to speak out of love and concern. My experience is not private or to be guarded jealously. Prayer is understandable only in the web of relationships we are blessed with: relationship with God, with each other, with the universe. Yet I am also a person formed in a certain way and living out my life in a certain historical reality. Therefore, perhaps something of how I have experienced the Spirit does contribute, at least to you who have asked me and who cares!

So, let me speak of the Spirit, the spiritual life. On Sunday you will celebrate Pentecost. How can I emphasize enough the importance of this great celebration of the church?! The gift of the Holy Spirit to the church is the assurance of the constant, abiding presence of God in His people. The Holy Spirit as Counselor, Redeemer, Friend -- the Spirit whose activity in each of us and in the church always works for wholeness, unity, and freedom. The Spirit brings everything to our consciousness: all the good things of our lives, our dear friends, the love of God Himself. It is not emotion which brings us the Spirit, no gust of pious sanctity however dramatic. The Spirit is not dependent on "all the emotions, energies, affections, sympathies in our minds, [but is] the only source and inspirer of them all, this is most necessary for us... To learn that there is a substance for faith to lay hold of, and that faith does not create this substance; that there is a deep ground and source of faith -- deeper of course than all the acts which proceed from it, this is our task."[2] This is the ground and task that I worked toward every moment of my life. Do you see the freedom it offers? The Spirit who prays with and through you, despite your cooperation or even knowledge, always works for your good and the good of the world. Can there be a greater gift from God than this? I think not.

Yet the bringing of this life to consciousness can be painful, I have found. It seems that you have found this also. As I wrote to a priest friend of mine who was considering leaving the church, the very doubts you bring in your prayer to God will be the source of your eventual comfort and enlightenment. I know how hard this is, this moving from the world of the intellect to the world of the Spirit. It is a fearful, haunting, tormenting push to the edge of reason and beyond. The words and ideas seem to arise from the dead and take on a living reality which frightens us. Yet it is good for us to be frightened. It pushes us to ask God to search us and know us. To reveal what is true and to bring us out of the darkness. You see how doubt and faith are so intimately connected. We find ourselves searching back to the faith of the little child; the faith that seeks revelation. But revelation is only accepted by the person of faith, so they must go together. "For we have to find out that God is not in a book, that He is, that He must reveal Himself to us, that He is revealing Himself to us."[3]

Do you also see that this is <u>experience</u>? <u>You</u> must <u>do</u> it! No one else can do it for you, no one else can hand it to you no matter how learned, saintly, or heroic one may be. This is why you must pray to be able to pray. You must pray for the power to be in the relationship with God, to live out your part with mutual integrity. Of course that is frightening! For whom would it not be! Here your faith will overcome fear -- your faith in Jesus and in the Spirit are always within you. "In prayer (you come) to know whether, without a mediator, prayer is not a dream and an impossibility for you, me, everyone. I cannot solve this doubt. I can but show you how to get it solved."[4] I will speak further in a moment about how I understand Jesus in our prayer, but for now I ask that you try to imagine that Jesus is with you, not in a dream, but in reality making your prayer possible.

If this picture seems obscure, I cannot apologize because it is what I am able to see. It may become even less comprehensible when I add, as I must, my recognition of the evil which is in me, as it is in each of us. I think it is a great sin to perceive the evil in others, either individuals or institutions, and not in ourselves. "Evil lies not in some accidents, but in me."[5] Encountering this in prayer teaches me as no theology and no book can teach. This is the most painful part of all -- "anything is better than this dark self."[6] "I cannot bear the darkness. Shall we try if we can grope our way into the light?"[7] This is how I understand our theological efforts at their best -- groping our way out of the darkness and into the light which we <u>know</u> is in us.

Never forget the Spirit! We do this together but also we must go within ourselves. This is the true nature of healing, the intermeshing of self and other so that there is no separation. All of us are held within the loving hands of God. Yet we cannot live a true life of the Spirit without encountering darkness. I would be leading you astray if I told you only the Good News and not also the hard realities. We have both experienced them in our lives of prayer and work. May I assure you that I share the horror of that darkness. I have known it in my emotional life as well as in my spiritual life, and its power and fearfulness are never far from me. Yet I also know it as a place of great blessing because it is the very stage on which the battle of life is played out and God wins His victory.

At this juncture, and really at all subsequent points, it is important to have spiritual companionship. The bishop used to fulfill this role (if he was a sympathetic type of person). However, this may no longer be the case, or not the case for you anyway! But you need someone to talk with so that you are not bereft. Sharing spiritual journeys keeps you always aware of your relationships. You cannot force intimacy with God. Nor can you attain spiritual perfection. God's intimate love is always there for you and for each of us and it is totally a matter of receiving, not of achievement.

To do this you need time for thought and for silence. "Be still and know that I am God" is the text that captures the most profound truth of prayer that I know. We must make time and space for God to speak to us. We must leave off our own speech and sit within the silence and emptiness so that it can be filled with God. "The child sinks in nothingness at its Father's feet, just when He is about to take it to His arms."[8] We come to this contemplative place in our prayer when we know that we cannot answer our spiritual questions with our intellect. We try as hard as we can but it is not possible. All that we can do is discipline ourselves for the contemplation, and the Spirit who brings us all things, whether we want them or resist them, will bring us into "another state of mind altogether."[9] Does this sound very much like the Zen Buddhist meditation we discussed? I think it is very similar, and I am pleased to hear of the spiritual unity you are finding with Zen, which confirms my expectations expressed in my book on the religions of the world.

So you see the truth of my conclusion that there are no works or techniques of prayer which I can lay out for you that will assure for you all you seek with God. That strikes me as a perennial theological aberration which you must avoid assiduously. Consider this: We are in the age of the Spirit; not looking forward to it. You must live all aspects of your life in that truth. The Spirit is in the present, it must be lived now. It is not something to be yearned over as in the past or anxiously awaited as in the future. All of its transfigurative power is currently in the world, in you. You must live it for the glory of God and of your sisters and brothers.

Now, given the obvious complexities of doing this either in the world or in our personal lives of prayer, on what basis can we proceed with any assurance at all? On what do we base our hope? There is not time nor space for a lengthier treatise than this is already becoming, but I must state, as concisely as I can, how I found this assurance in my own search for God. "When I began in earnest to seek God for myself, the feeling that I needed a deliverer from an overwhelming weight of selfishness was the predominant one in my mind."[10] As I described in my letter to Mr. Hort, I came to believe in a God who hated such selfishness and wanted "to raise His creatures out of it."[11] You see now why my understanding of Jesus as Redeemer is of such paramount importance. God was the only one powerful enough to remove this sin (here experienced as selfishness, elsewhere known as division, and as anything that breaks relation with others, including God). I approached relationship with God knowing my separation -- I needed an active, powerful God who bridged the gap in the face of my inability to change myself. I am still considering your point that one can locate oneself from a different starting place, for example one of integrated unity with God taking precedence over the dualistic separation from God. I can understand that, and I certainly believe in unity with God, but my own experience begins from the baseline of separation.

You may also object that I inappropriately give this power to God rather than exercise it for myself. I will consider that objection carefully. My response at the moment is that I do not experience myself or other people as manifesting an ability to remove sin on our own. Yet I would insist that we are never permanently or absolutely separate from God, because of Christ. "Apart from (Christ), I feel that there dwells in me no good thing; but I am sure that I am not apart from (Christ), nor are you, nor is any (person). I have a right to tell you this: if I have any work to do in the world it is to tell you this."[12] I have experienced our separation from God and our unity with God in Christ.

But, you may correctly ask, who do you experience this Christ to be that gives you such assurance, such hope, trust and unity? In the eucharistic prayer of consecration, I find "the great ground of reconciliation"[13] which is, for me, the love of God. Each of us is under this "eternal law of Love"[14] which binds God and people together. It is based in the atoning death of Jesus on the cross: "my Father loves me because I lay down my life."[15] It is the sacrifice of God through the death of Jesus purely for the love of humanity that defines the love of God for all creation. Here is revealed the underlying nature of God as the Holy Trinity: Love is sacrifice, self-sacrifice, a matter of giving up oneself into the primacy of relationship with God, who gives Himself up into His love for us. This is the relationship that must characterize all relationships: mutual self-sacrifice out of love for the other. When we live in this way, we are encircled by the love of God. When we submit ourselves, our wills to the Love that has already Loved us to the end, we are totally and completely safe. Only when we wander away from this relationship are we likely to be in danger of losing our souls.

And yet there is more than this just being a "model" of how right relationship should be. I believe that "he that hath seen me hath seen the Father, so that in the death of Christ all the wisdom and power of God shines forth on all humanity and embodies for me the power that breaks all the bonds of sin and evil asunder. This was and is the ground of my faith."[16] I trust because I know that God prevails over all that is wrong with me and the world. And more: this Sacrifice is in no way just for the few, just for the church; the sins of all humanity over all time are taken up into the Love of God. Humanity is redeemed by Christ's death. The Redemption is free and universal. What remains? To take the cup of thanksgiving, and call upon the name of the Lord.

To enter into God's presence believing that a living way is consecrated for us through the veil, that is, His flesh.

Entering into God's presence in the eucharist is something each of us does together. Though we may be by ourselves, alone, or lonely, we do not celebrate the eucharist alone because we never actually thank God or love God or encounter God alone. The nature of the Trinity assures us of that: the worship of God is always communal, grounded historically and eternally in self-sacrificial love. And that is who we are to be. So, however frightening or confusing your spiritual journey may be, you are never apart from Christ, you are never alone. During my life, I learned that my real sin was in not trusting God. The Christian life is one of trust, and nothing but trust. Trust and total dependence on God in Christ will bring the fruits of the Spirit: sympathy, understanding, the sense of oneness with others, and self-control.

I want to say more to you about the eucharist and especially how important the Lord's Prayer is for all of us. All of our acts of worship are spiritual acts. I have already shared my thoughts on the most powerful part of the eucharist in my understanding of the atoning death of Jesus. All prayer begins and ends with atonement and adoration. What else can there really be? For me, in the depth of the spirituality of the eucharist we "confess a Unity which lies beneath all other Unity; a deep eternal mystery of Reconciliation and Peace which shall overcome the mystery of Division and Evil once and forever."[17] Perhaps I never succeeded in solving the problem of the difference between what was actually in the world and what I envisioned to be the true state of affairs underneath it all. Who can elucidate what is the true reality beneath the forms of the liturgical texts of the eucharistic canon? It is experienced and known by those who are still and listen to the silence of God. You are one of the listeners. And so was I.

You have the "spirit of a learner" which was one of the keystones of my life. Constantly, habitually, look to God, your Divine Teacher. There you will learn all you need to know. Never forget that God teaches everyone -- you are bound to your sisters and brothers by a common Teacher. One way I lived this out was by praying the Daily Office. I will end this long discussion of prayer by reminding you that you are being taught lessons that are not for you alone but are for the welfare of the world. Prayer that is not tied to works of justice for the oppressed, for the suffering people of the world, is not Christian prayer. This is the most prominent manifestation of our self-sacrifice in the Love of God. In Christ, God is forever united to the immediate, bodily suffering and death of humanity as the most perfect embodiment of God's self-sacrificing love. So we must be joined to that same, most painful part of human life in order to bring to it the light of redeeming love. I know how terribly hard this is. It was for me and it is for you and all others who take the exacting demands of Christianity seriously. But I can offer this assurance: God will allow us to see more than we can ask for or imagine as we enter fully into prayer, the eucharist, the suffering of others, and liberating works for all people.

Which brings me to the concluding question you have brought to me related to the sorrows of women's experience in the late twentieth century church. As you know, this was not a major issue in my time (though perhaps it should have been). It is one about which I have little personal understanding. From my own background I can say that I have the greatest respect and sympathy for the knowledge and spiritual insight of the women I knew both in my family and as friends. I recall that one of the last things I told my wife was about the importance of women teaching men about the meaning of the eucharist. It seems that in the twentieth century there has been even more that women have taught men and even more that men need to learn -- about humility, non-violence and compassion. I said once that churches were not built as signs of exclusion but of reconciliation. It appears that much more is known now about the level of reconciliation between men and women necessary in order for the church to live more deeply into its true unity.

Yet I would have you and other women keep very much in mind that the ground of that reconciliation is self-sacrifice in love. Perhaps it is a time for both you and the church to look clearly at what sacrifices of self can be made in order to accomplish the goal of maintaining unity within Christ. I must say, however, that I understand your concern about such a term as "self-sacrifice." Perhaps there is a much better way of speaking of God's love, which men like me need now to learn from women like you.

Once more, I ask your indulgence and mercy as I close using the only language for God and love that I know. You may fault me, as indeed you must if you are able to contribute to the ongoing work of the Spirit. For the future cannot be built on the mistakes of the past, but rather on a recognition that spiritual revelation takes new forms in every generation in order to correct past mistakes, not reinforce them. I encourage you and all women to claim your power as children of God who were baptized into the family of God. This power is to be used to call forth "the heart and conscience of men, so that being first able to see their Father in Heaven truly, (then) themselves in their true relation to (God), (then) to investigate...the conditions under which they themselves and others exist."[18] Do you see how it works? Through our knowledge of God and our right relation to God we are enabled to be in right relation to others and to begin to change the social, economic, and political conditions which are damaging our world. This is all undertaken to speak to the hearts and consciences of people. All Christian prayer and action is only and always for the good of others. That must be your guiding principle even in these difficult days. And you must always have confidence that God is not only your friend but also the one who finally and ultimately loves you and will continue to sacrifice anything, even the divine life itself, in order for you to be free. I will leave you with my blessing: "The knowledge of the love of God -- the blessing of God Almighty, the Father, the Son, and the Holy Ghost be amongst you -- amongst us -- and remain with us for ever."[19] Amen.

NOTES

1.   F.D. Maurice, Theological Essays (London: James Clarke & Co, 1957), p. 37.

2.   Frederick Maurice, Ed.   The Life of F.D. Maurice, Vol. 1, (London: MacMillian, 1884), p. 246.

3.   F.D. Maurice, Toward the Recovery of Unity: The Thought of F.D. Maurice, John F. Porter and William J. Wolf, eds. (New York: Seabury Press, 1964), p. 215.

4.   Ibid., p. 216.

5.   F.D. Maurice, Theological Essays, p. 33.

6.   Ibid.

7.   Ibid., p. 29.

8.   Ibid., p. 59.

9.   F. Maurice, Vol. I, p. 247.

10.   F.D. Maurice, Toward the Recovery of Unity, p. 144.

11.   Ibid.

12.   F.D. Maurice, Theological Essays, p. 67

13.   F.D. Maurice, The Prayer Book (London: James Clarke & Co., 1966), p. 185.

14.   Ibid.

15.   Ibid., p. 186.

16.   F.D. Maurice, Toward the Recovery of Unity, p. 144.

17.   F.D. Maurice, Prayer Book, p. 203.

18.   F.D. Maurice, Theological Essays, p. 36.

19.   F. Maurice, Vol. II, p. 641.

INCARNATION IN RECENT ANGLICAN THEOLOGY

Donald F. Winslow

From the time of Richard Hooker onwards, the doctrine of the incarnation has been the essential core upon which the whole panoply of Anglican doctrinal perceptions depends. No doctrine has been debated more heatedly, no doctrine defended more doggedly, no doctrine more analyzed than the incarnation.

Questioning the centrality of the incarnation invites immediate and critical -- even harsh -- response. The 1921 Girton Conference of the Modern Churchmen's Union, for example, excited considerable popular and scholarly agitation and was the main impetus behind the formation a year later of the Church of England's Commission on Christian Doctrine.[1] The consternation arising from the publication in 1963 of John A.T. Robinson's Honest to God resulted in the Doctrine Commission being called once again to examine the place of doctrine in the Church of England.[2]

More specifically, Robinson's The Human Face of God was perceived as a direct attack upon the "received" doctrine of incarnation,[3] and Maurice Wiles' The Remaking of Christian Doctrine even more so.[4] This typically Anglican view, that if the incarnation, as the very essence of the Christian faith, is called into question then everything else will collapse, reached its high-water mark in 1977 when The Myth of God Incarnate appeared.[5] Before the ink on that volume dried, The Truth of God Incarnate came out, with articles by Stephen Neill and John Macquarrie, among others.[6] Incarnation and Myth: The Debate Continued and The Myth/Truth of God Incarnate followed in 1979, as did Don Cupitt's The Debate About Christ.[7] God Incarnate: Story and Belief [8] added more to the controversy. Finally, a seemingly infinite number of articles and reviews appeared in journals such as Theology, The Anglican Theological Review, and Religious Studies.

Eventually I grew weary of what was becoming, for me, a rather dreary theological "Much Ado About Nothing" -- until publication in 1987, of Brian Hebblethwaite's The Incarnation: Collected Essays in Christology.[9] In several earlier articles, Hebblethwaite had attempted to assert the primacy of the incarnation (and the related doctrine of the Trinity) in opposition to what he believed the authors of The Myth were doing, namely, calling into question the very foundation stone of Christian faith.[10] These articles, along with several others (all but two previously published) are bound in this collection of essays on the incarnation.

Hebblethwaite observes that "popular Christmas carols will ensure that Chalcedonian orthodoxy will be remembered long after The Myth is forgotten."[11] However, Hebblethwaite appears unable to forget The Myth himself: the whole of this volume of his essays is a defense of his understanding of the traditional view of the incarnation. He argues that the authors of The Myth pose, by their non-incarnationalism, an unparalleled threat to a doctrine that stands at "the very heart of Christianity."[12]   He compares them to the "radicals" of the Girton conference who represented an "undeniable break with classical Christian doctrine."[13]He asserts, further, that several of The Myth authors, notably Maurice Wiles and Geoffrey Lampe, typify "a much more extreme form of liberal Protestantism than that of the Girton Conference" -- this resulting from their "undifferentiated monotheism," their "unitarianism," and their obvious affinities with Harnack, Troeltsch, Bethune-Baker and Hasting Rashdall.[14]

Hebblethwaite is not reticent in expressing his displeasure with the "non-incarnationalists" nor is he unwilling to construct an orthodox fence around the doctrinal turf which he insists on defending. He is not sure how to deal with his theological adversaries; certainly he is unsure of how to convince them of the errors of their ways. He admits that the church has not been kind to those it deemed heretical, but asserts that such rigid judgment has not been and is not now the Anglican way. However, to sit back and do nothing in face of so serious a threat would be too passive. Hebblethwaite therefore concludes that although the laity may indeed be allowed a certain flexibility in their views, such flexibility cannot be allowed the clergy who are commissioned to teach the faith. Surely, for them, there are "some views [which] stand way beyond any conceivable limit."[15]

For example, Hebblethwaite urges priests who have given up their belief in an "objective" God to resign their orders and leave the church, but for those who no longer believe in an "objective" incarnation he does not propose sanctions.[16] He says he does not want to "unchurch any of his colleagues and friends." However, he does want strenuously to "repudiate" their views and to answer their "bad" theology with a "better" theology, while still at the same time "tolerating" them since their very errors and mistakes "show up the truth of the matter from another angle, if only by contrast."[17]   Thus he argues the tortured proposition that Christians can learn from The Myth even if it is very much in error and quite incapable of determining the church's doctrinal future.

Less charitably, Hebblethwaite is insistent that the phrase from the Nicene Creed that "Jesus Christ...for us and for our salvation came down from heaven [and] became incarnate from the Virgin Mary and was made man" allows of no other interpretation than what is openly and unambiguously stated there. He contends that it is not to be interpreted mythologically or metaphorically or symbolically, and most surely not as a "fable."[18] Given this presupposition, Hebblethwaite opts for a literal interpretation of the incarnation, asking us to believe that the incarnation was a literal event. There are, he says, a variety of "models" of the incarnation, but the incarnation itself is not a model. God literally became man [sic]; in Jesus we see God in human form. Speaking of a literal incarnation is not only theologically appropriate but also theologically necessary, even though the full meaning of the incarnation ultimately evades our "cognitive grasp."[19] What assistance such literalness provides in our understanding and use of the incarnation doctrine is unclear, and it can be argued that the framers of the Nicene Creed would themselves hesitate to accept so narrow an interpretation.

Further, Hebblethwaite appears to contradict himself in describing what he calls the "relation" of Jesus to the Father. On one side, he speaks of the incarnation as a "model" for all human-divine relation, while on the other he says that "the main point of the Incarnation is not a matter of relation at all. It is a matter of identity. Jesus is God incarnate."[20]

He repeatedly insists that the "moral and religious" significance of the incarnation depends directly upon Christ's being God in person, on his being, literally, God incarnate, but he defines these terms only negatively.[21] He accuses Don Cupitt, for instance, of "sheer perversity in moral judgment," and the authors of The Myth in general of "quite astonishing moral and religious insensitivity to what is under discussion."[22] Unfortunately, for Hebblethwaite the "moral and religious" significance of the incarnation appears to take precedence over the categories of historical evidence, logical coherence or rational comprehension, while at the same time functioning as a ready rhetorical device to attack those with whom he disagrees.

He also describes the "relation" between the incarnate one and the heavenly Father as a relation of "love given and love received within the deity," and that it is an "eternal" and "personal" relation best illustrated by the prayers of Jesus to the Father.[23] "[W]e are struggling," writes Hebblethwaite,

> to speak of the infinite, internally differentiated, being of God, whose own eternal love, given and received within the Trinity, is mirrored in the love of Jesus for the Father.[24]

There is in this formulation a kind of divine narcissism which detracts from Hebblethwaite's other assertions about God's love for all of creation and God's participation in the suffering of the world.

Even though Hebblethwaite tries for consistency of thought through repetition of key phrases, an irritating habit in itself, far more troubling than the exactitude of the repetitions are the many variations on these phrases. He speaks of God in such a variety of modes within the Trinity that there is doubt as to who the subject of the incarnation is: one of the modes (or centers) of the Triune Godhead, or God simpliciter, or Jesus, or the Trinity itself? Wonderment increases at a statement like the following:

> [W]hile the man Jesus in his earthly life was presumably unaware of his divinity, the Blessed Trinity was perfectly aware of what was being done, experienced, and suffered... God, qua God, knew what he was doing; qua man he learned obedience like any other Jewish child... [25]

Despite his appeals to Nicene and Chalcedonian orthodoxy, Hebblethwaite's understanding of the incarnation is highly idiosyncratic and ultimately untraditional.

He demonstrates, for instance, considerable confusion about doctrinal development. He acknowledges the legitimacy of development, but claims that the "rejection of the doctrine of the Incarnation and the Trinity marks a decisive break with the faith of the Church."[26] However, in another place he states:

> I do not wish to tie us down to particular credal formulations; but it is surely not implausible to suggest that while the doctrines of the Incarnation and the Trinity are of the essence of Christianity and thus indispensable, variations of those doctrines are permissible.[27]

What is not clear is where "indispensability" and "permissibility" merge, or if they do. For example, Hebblethwaite appears to afford little room for disagreement and invites little if any dialogue. Arguments are phrased in such ways as to place disagreement outside the bounds of the 'conversation.' There is in this book what might be termed a 'hermeneutic of irrefutable averment,' which is evident in this assertion:

> Theologians must be free to explore and to make suggestions for understandings of the faith, but the Church will not receive their suggestions if the new understanding cannot be related to what has happened before.[28]

Apparently, "what has happened before" (Scripture, ancient creeds, tradition and nearly 2,000 years of Christian history) makes doctrinal development or new understanding hazardous, if not impossible.

*****

In short, Hebblethwaite fails in his attempt to answer the "bad" theology of The Myth with a "better" theology -- and this can be asserted without subscribing to the views of the earlier book. Despite the continuing controversy there is little which is new in The Myth, nor is there any claim to novelty. However, the authors' critique of the doctrine of the incarnation is a critique of a doctrine to which few would subscribe today. The Myth partakes more of the Enlightenment than it does of the Girton Conference, and to that extent it is certainly liberal, often teasingly suggestive, and occasionally theologically provocative. The following observations about incarnational theologizing are offered, therefore, in the spirit of adventure and creativity earlier introduced by the authors of The Myth.

The Myth authors, although not in agreement on several specific issues, do agree that much of what has been taught as the doctrine of the incarnation (e.g., the Formula of Chalcedon or the Athanasian Creed) is inescapably incomprehensible, presenting the believer with a choice between intellectual fideism or patent incredulity. Thomas Erskine opined more than a century ago, "I may understand things which I do not believe, but I cannot believe anything which I do not understand."[29] However, these are not mutually exclusive choices: just as 'myth' contains elements of 'truth,' so too 'truth' can never be grasped as an absolute. As has been said of Richard Hooker, "His was a demand that truth be sought, not a claim that truth had been found."[30]

The point is that Christian doctrine is necessarily fluid by nature; all theological assertions are unavoidably tentative, and historically and culturally conditioned. We do well to remember Charles Raven's perceptive observation:

> The truth of God is changeless: The Nicene Creed is the truth of God; the Nicene Creed is changeless... How easily we slip into such syllogisms. And when once the first step is taken, the process can be extended to include a similar claim for everything that belongs to religion. Salvation becomes conditioned by an iota; faith is transformed into obedience; adventure is a vice not a virtue.[31]

In 1976, the Church of England Doctrine commission concluded that

> Traditional orthodoxy becomes wooden unless it is constantly questioned... Our basic loyalty is to God through Christ, not to any exact doctrinal formulation about him.[32]

Too often sincere Christians, professional theologians among them, are more concerned to defend a specific articulation of a creedal affirmation than they are to discern in such an affirmation something of God. The result is that a creed or doctrine becomes the object of one's belief rather than the God of which it is but an awkward and always provisional expression. Genuine religious experience is thereby excluded as a viable criterion for theological discourse. As Leslie Houlden has written:

> The credal type of statement is...open only to repetition and reaffirmation -- or else to flat denial [whereas] the experiential mode...is in close touch with the springs of religion: it leads us to the place where [one] most deeply responds to God.[33]

Defending a particular interpretation of the incarnation by claiming it as the only correct interpretation is precariously close to idolatry.

Nor can we avoid the hard business of interpretation by resorting only to story-telling. Since we are time-bound creatures, linear thinking is unavoidable when we speak of incarnation. Certainly it is appropriate to articulate our theological awareness through the medium of narrative. As Frances Young says, when we speak of Jesus and the incarnation we are bound to tell more than one story.[34] However, if the emphasis is on events, and if the incarnation is perceived to be the unique appearance of God in human form, then everything before and after 'the event' of the incarnation is left Godless -- deprived of God's animating, creative and redemptive presence.

Telling the Story then is important, but the specific events need to be complemented by the principles to which those events point. Incarnation cannot be -- should not be -- articulated solely in the credal phrase, "Came down from heaven and was incarnate," since that is too narrow a concept. Rather, incarnation speaks of a relationship which exists between God and the Created order. That relationship allows us, for instance, to speak of creation as redemptive or of redemption as creative -- i.e., as principles which are broader and more life-giving than what is said to have happened on a particular day at a particular time in a particular place.

Seeing incarnation, theologically, as more of a principle than an historic event means that God's incarnating presence need no longer be uniquely restricted to Jesus. Stressing the literal uniqueness of God's indwelling of Jesus makes a fiction of the creative/redemptive 'story,' forcing us into a kind of tepid deism in which the 'before' and 'after' of the incarnation place God at an unearthly distance from this world, and an even more unearthly distance from us. Avoiding the literal uniqueness of the God-in-Jesus event allows us to speak boldly of mutual participation, of God-in-me-in-God, a phrase which finds powerful expression in both Hebrew and Christian scriptures.

Further, as Don Cupitt has remarked, the concept of the Word "condescending to men of low estate" is hopelessly inappropriate.[35] In our culture the term "condescension" focuses on humankind's fallen nature rather than on women's and men's innate goodness as created in God's own image. The emphasis on Christ's condescension leads to an anthropological minimalism which traps humankind in the muck and mire of sin, depravity and utter helplessness, thus excluding us from any participation in the work of incarnation and creative redemption. Such a result leads to the conviction that God is a vindictive judge whose justice can be satisfied only if we are punished or if Christ is punished in our stead. The alternative view of the incarnation principle is more affirming of who we are in God's eyes. In this view we are the yearned-for subjects of God's passionate love, a love expressed and bodied forth, incarnated, in self-giving sacrifice. If Jesus is our brother and the apple of God's eye, are we not also?

And if anything said here vexes those concerned to honor the past, an examination of the history of Christian doctrine is suggested. An honest examination reveals the enduring capacity of doctrinal developers to tease and stretch the imaginations of their contemporaries. Comparing the New Testament to the Nicene Creed or the Chalcedonian Formula, for example, shows us how wondrously the "Fathers" wrought new doctrinal positions even as they refused to admit they were doing anything but articulating afresh what was found unambiguously in the Bible. The example sustains Robert Evans' hope

that those who by disposition are inclined towards respect for the past will come to be fully apprised of the degree to which the great fathers of the church were in their own time innovators.[36]

Innovation is inevitable, and an accompanying imaginative faculty is a prerequisite to theological discourse. The vocabulary of such discourse would be greatly enriched by replacing didactic assertions as to what must be believed with such gracious and flexible phrases as "What if," or "I wonder," or "Might it be possible?" Then new discoveries may arise and we can find ourselves moving to wider horizons of understanding. Embracing innovation and imaginative creativity is a promising approach to an understanding of incarnation. Unbending adherence to the past only leads to lackluster obscurantism.

We can learn to treat theology as more an 'adventure' than a contest; winning and losing are categories which render the theological enterprise ultimately meaningless. Pitting 'myth' against 'truth' is no more edifying than pitting 'defenders of the faith' against those who would pose serious questions about the manner in which that faith is articulated. Anglican theology, with its historic emphasis on incarnation, will continue to flourish only as the crippling dualisms of right vs. wrong, old vs. new, orthodox vs. heretical are avoided. In their place we must learn to dance and play, to write poetry, to learn from those with whom we disagree -- and to open ourselves to that creative/redemptive God who is always and forever "doing a new thing."

NOTES

1. The Commission's report, entitled Doctrine in the Church of England, was not published (by SPCK) until 1938. It has been reissued (SPCK, 1982) with a 60-page introduction by Geoffrey Lampe, "The 1938 Report in Retrospect."

2. This report, Christian Believing, was published by SPCK in 1976. Maurice Wiles, one of the contributors to The Myth of God Incarnate, chaired the commission.

3. H.E.W. Turner's review of Robinson's book ended with these words, "C'est magnifique, mais ce n'est pas -- la foi de l'incarnation!" (The Churchman 87 [1973]: 212).

4. Maurice Wiles, The Remaking of Christian Doctrine (London: SCM, 1974). For two diverse responses to this book, compare Colin Gunton, "The Re-making of Christian Doctrine," Theology 72 (1974): 619-74, with my "Maurice Wiles and the Remaking of Christian Doctrine," Anglican Theological Review 59 (1977): 197 - 212.

5. John Hick, ed., The Myth of God Incarnate (London: SCM, 1977). Throughout this essay this work is referred to as simply The Myth.

6. Michael Green, ed., The Truth of God Incarnate (London: Hodder & Stoughton, 1977).

7. Michael Goulder, ed., Incarnation and Myth: The Debate Continued (London: SCM, 1979); Durstan R. McDonald, ed., The Myth/Truth of God Incarnate (Wilton, CT: Morehouse-Barlow, 1979); Don Cupitt, The Debate About Christ (London: SCM, 1979).

8. A.E. Harvey, ed., God Incarnate: Story and Belief (London: SPCK, 1981).

9. Brian Hebblethwaite, The Incarnation: Collected Essays in Christology (Cambridge: Cambridge University Press, 1987).

10. Ibid.

11. Ibid., p. 38.

12. Ibid., p. 1.

13. Ibid., p. 58.

14. Ibid., p. 61.

15. Brian Hebblethwaite, "The Myth and Christian Faith," in Gouldler, op cit, p. 15. This brief essay does not appear in Hebblethwaite's Incarnation.

16. Hebblethwaite, Incarnation, p. 155.

17. Hebblethwaite, "The Myth and Christian Faith," p. 16 and Incarnation, pp. 94 and 163.

18. See Peter Baelz, "A Sermon," in God Incarnate: Story and Belief, pp. 97-102.

19. Hebblethwaite, Incarnation, p. 49.

20. Ibid., p. 52. On the question of identity, see Maurice Wiles, "The Language of Faith: Claims of Identity," in his Faith and the Mystery of God (London: SCM: 1982), pp.31-53.

21. Hebblethwaite, Incarnation, pp. 6, 9. See especially the chapter entitled "The Moral and Religious Value of the Incarnation."

22. Ibid., p. 29.

23. Ibid., pp. 15-16; emphasis added.

24. Ibid., pp. 68ff.

25. Ibid.

26. Ibid., p. 43.

27. Ibid., p. 162.

28. Ibid., p. 109ff.

29. Thomas Erskine, An Essay on Faith (Edinburgh, 1822), p. 25. John Knox' observation is similar: "How incredible that we should be under obligation to believe the incredible!" In his Myth and Truth (Charlottesville, VA: University of Virginia Press, 1964) p. 9.

30.   W.M. Southgate, John Jewel and the Problem of Doctrinal Authority. Quoted by Egil Grislis, "The Hermeneutical Problem in Richard Hooker," in W. Speed Hill, ed., Studies in Richard Hooker (Cleveland: Case Western Reserve University Press, 1972), p. 163.

31.   Charles E. Raven, A Wanderer's Way (New York: Holt, 1929), pp. 184.

32.   Christian Believing, p. 39.

33.   Leslie Houlden, "The Creed of Experience," in The Myth, p. 130.

34.   Frances Young, "A Cloud of Witnesses," in The Myth, p. 37.

35.   Don Cupitt, "The Creed of Christendom," in The Myth, p. 137.

36.   Robert F. Evans, One and Holy (London: SPCK, 1972).

COURAGEOUS INCARNATION: BEING ANGLICAN AND INTIMATE

Fredrica Harris Thompsett

Intimacy is a powerful topic. It informs the identity of individuals, groups and churches -- at once a singular and a social reality. In proper English, "intimacy" does not refer to an abstract, privatized space. Rather, it signifies "pressing into" -- touching and defining -- the heart of a matter, whether that subject is the profound understanding of a person, or the unique characteristics of a relationship between two people, or the corporate identity church members express as they engage one another. Intimacy is about self-affirmation, relationships with others, and our awareness of God.[1]

For me, intimacy is also a matter of living and dying. I remain tender about the death from AIDS of my former husband and lifetime friend, Bruce Thompsett, a man who was both very Anglican and very intimate. Consequently, I want to offer practical theological nurture to those who think Christians today must choose between being intimate and Anglican, spiritual and sexual, repressed and liberating, or any other dangerous dualism that reflects disembodied images of humanity and abstract, distancing visions of God. I am still discovering in concrete, human terms how my theological identity as an Anglican anchors and informs the way I experience intimacy. Therefore I have chosen to "press into" the theological heart of Anglicanism by focusing on what I choose to call "the courageous doctrine of the Incarnation." I believe that in the Incarnation we can witness both remarkable intimacy and the real possibility of overcoming the lingering and still pervasive effects of disembodying and dangerous dualisms.

Like most of our biblical and Reformation ancestors, I believe that theological knowledge can be a source of strength. For many of our early Christian ancestors, knowledge about God -- theology -- was a source of comfort and new life, and an essential element for mission. The apostle Paul knew the practical, persuasive power of the theology of the New Creation. In the earliest New Testament text, he told the Thessalonians, "we would not have you ignorant [about your questions]." The Thessalonians wondered about heaven, who would get there first, and how and when this would happen. These were their local questions. When Paul responded with an image of being drawn up into the arms of God, they were less fearful. He then urged them to "comfort one another" with this knowledge (I Thessalonians 4:13-18). Thessalonian Christians lived in that graceful, liberating period before the Hellenistic world imposed conceptual order on their new religion and before the Constantinian settlement dictated institutional ordering for their church. In early Christian communities, theology often combatted fear.

Church members today are not unlike the Thessalonians. We have our own local questions: questions for example about monogamy, about AIDS, about our own bodies, about self-affirming lifestyles, about whether as Christians we have to make compromises that diminish our fully organic, sensuous selves. I do not believe God wishes us ignorant about our local questions, nor without a theology to combat our fears. We, like our ancestors, are challenged to find in our local Christian communities comfort, strength, encouragement for mission and relief from undue fears. Theology for early Christians shaped group understanding, supported life in a world where people -- including Christians, among others -- held quite disparate beliefs. Theology provided a communication system that opened up choices, suggested innovations, and encouraged movement toward other persons and groups. Theology promoted belonging and community, social dimensions of life essential for persons in all ages.

Our early Christian ancestors found dual dimensions in identity formation: 1) development of values about group boundaries, and 2) articulation of a world view about what needed to be explained to others and how to explain it.[2] This dual theological identity helped them live in a pluralistic world with integrity in mission. Then as now, mature identity is always local and expansive, addressing "Who are we?" and "How do we relate to others who are different from us?" When we reflect for a moment on these two questions we may recognize basic questions that young persons explore in peer groups, inquiries that Commissions on Ministry ask applicants for ordained ministries, dimensions that each of us embody and discover in our sexual identities, questions we whisper to loved ones in our dying. In other words, theology, in earlier eras and now, is about intimate identity -- pressing into, touching and defining, who we are.

In Anglican theology one doctrine, the Incarnation, has been the guiding principle for belief and practice. This central Anglican tenet is built upon the New Testament witness that the potential goodness of humanity is dependent upon the God who came to live among us as God and as human. This fully embodied doctrine -- proclaimed in the Gospel of John, "the Word became flesh and dwelt among us full of grace and truth" (John 1:14) -- offers powerful assurance that God is for us and not against us. It is a theological vehicle that grounds knowledge of God, humanity and the world in which we live.

The Incarnation historically has been a particularly courageous, extra-strength doctrine in the hands of Anglican theologians, including Archbishops of Canterbury who were also constructive theologians -- Thomas Cranmer, William Temple and Michael Ramsey -- and other formative classical and modern theologians, e.g., Richard Hooker, F.D. Maurice, Marianne Micks,

Desmond Tutu, and Carter Heyward.   Following the tradition of that most
famous volume of Anglican theological essays, Lux Mundi, Michael Ramsey has
described the Incarnation as the central principle for thinking about the
inseparability of gospel and sacrament, humanity and God.[3]   A European
theologian once characterized the Anglican Communion as the "Church of
Christmas Day," which is to say, the church of the Incarnation.

The prism of the Incarnation reveals what distinguishes Anglican identity
from other Christian affiliations, illuminating Anglican anthropology in
particular.   Anglican theologians emphasize the goodness of God's direct
relation to the created world.   Even in the Ash Wednesday liturgy, the
contemporary Episcopal Prayer Book affirms a God who "hate[s] nothing you
have made."[4]   Most ancient and modern Anglican theologians do not accept
hardened, conceptual divisions between the so-called moral order and the
natural order, what Max Weber described as a Protestant "disenchantment with
the world."   Instead, Anglicans do not disincarnate God, humanity or nature.
We believe in a God who encourages us, in Prayer Book language, to go forth
"rejoicing in thy whole creation."[5]   This means that God is not indifferent to
this earth or the ways in which we inhabit it.   Whether we wish it or not, God
is in our lives.

Secondly, Anglican theology is notably optimistic about humanity and
about the grace-filled possibilities we are given to amend our lives.   Anglicans
do not have to degrade humanity to elevate God.   As Richard Hooker described
it in the sixteenth century, the purpose of the Incarnation was to alter human
nature toward conformity with God.

"God hath deified our nature, though not by turninge it into him selfe
[God's self], yeat by makinge it his [God's] owne inseparable habita-
tion."[6]

Further, the doctrine of the Incarnation, as described in Lux Mundi,
"must also be taken as necessarily including the Atonement."[7]   On the basis of
the passion, death and resurrection, Christ has already acted for us; together,
the Incarnation and the Atonement express the saving, liberating character of
Christianity.   Richard Hooker described this changing relationship as "an
alternation from death to life."[8]   Thus Episcopalians do not blaspheme God or
humanity in the eucharistic petition that "he [Christ] may dwell in us and we in
him [Christ]."[9]

This relationship implies a third, distinctive aspect of Anglican theology
-- one that is seldom, if at all, affirmed by television evangelists.   The Incarnation presents a radical exercise of mutuality that is for God's sake as well as

ours. In Michael Ramsey's view, "The Incarnation meant not only that God took human flesh, but that human nature was raised up to share into the life of God."[10] What does this mean practically? The doctrine of the Incarnation invites and provides a basis for humanity's co-responsibility with God in Christ. Practically and ethically, Dorothee Soelle and Richard Hooker agree, although Hooker is more radical. Soelle frequently refers to God's needs for us to do God's work in the world, referring to humanity as God's hands.[11] Hooker wrote,

> wee cannot now conceive how God should without man [humanity] either exercise divine power or receive the glorie of divine praise.[12]

It is therefore not only appropriate but necessary, in the ongoing drama of living sacramentally in this world, that we offer God the best we have to give, our fully embodied selves, "our souls and bodies, to be a reasonable, holy and living sacrifice...."[13]

This courageous doctrine of the Incarnation has shaped Anglicanism theologically. Why, when we discuss human sinfulness, do we turn only to the first Adam of Genesis and stop short of the "second Adam" of the synoptic gospels? What if this doctrine -- the event of Jesus: power in flesh -- this doctrine, and not the Fall, shaped our expectations of one another, our relationships and our mission as a church? What if we were to close the gap between our theological heritage and our daily living, so that Anglican theology pressed into and deeply touched the ways we were intimate, and our intimacy pressed into and deeply expressed the ways we were Anglican? What if there were no major crises between being and doing, no seemingly split consciousness between being fully Christian and fully human? What tools, what old ways, would we have to give up? What practical theological tools could help us shape a more humane future? Finally, what would our identity look like if we were courageously incarnational?

Black poet and theologian Audre Lorde reminds us that "the master's tools will never dismantle the master's house."[14] Thus, our first task is to clean out the rusty tool box. Perhaps our most personal work is giving up egocentricity about our own sexual identity. The way we define ourselves can become a barrier to welcoming others. Ethnocentrism is the practice of considering the beliefs, values and customs of other people and cultures only from our own viewpoint (or that of our culture). This scandalous position is represented in Robert Louis Stevenson's A Child's Garden of Verses:

Little Indian, Sioux or Crow
  Little Frosty Eskimo
  Little Turk or Japanee
O! don't you wish that you were me?[15]

In a recent article on intimacy, Robert Cooper wrote, "We are concerned, having such a high view of marriage, that it not usurp other forms of intimacy."[16] The belief that marriage is by nature and divine writ the superior state for everyone is heterosexist. There are other forms of "sexualcentrism." This is a term I have coined to describe the habit of disparaging the sexual relations of others just because they are not our own. We hear hints of "sexualcentrism" in comments like these:

Aren't all single persons lonely? Where do they spend holidays?

Shouldn't marriage be a criteria for ordination? My wife has made my ministry possible, and the priesthood is such a lonely vocation.

Don't all gay men and lesbians have unhappy childhoods? I'm grateful my mother loved me!

I think straights are only straight because society tells them they must be.

My father shouldn't live with her. She's younger and will exhaust him physically.

I don't know what's wrong with you young people! Why would you want to live together before marriage? We didn't!

It's too bad AIDS is spreading to normal persons, like us, who don't deserve to get it.

The most dangerous version of stereotyping an "other" leads to abstracting that person, or groups of persons, into the image of an enemy who therefore becomes a legitimate target of aversion, exclusion, degradation and violence. On such personal roots racism, homophobia, sexism, domestic violence, anti-Semitism and the genocidal "final solution" of the Holocaust were and are nourished.

In addition to throwing out destructive stereotypes we must begin to question and ultimately discard many aspects of traditional Christian history. All historical evidence, especially that about ordinary people, is more or less weak, and what we know about marriage rites and practices in the West, for example, is not good news. Typical biblical and Christian stories about marriage, except for the miracle at Cana, often are steeped in misogyny, the hatred of women. Many biblical stories illustrate the two bases of power which, according to anthropologist Claude Lévi-Strauss, have determined men's cultural dominance: "the exchange of words, the exchange of women."[17] In Western civilization, Catholic and Protestant marriage ceremonies have evolved primarily from practices related to the exchange and inheritance of women, property and other "goods." It is not surprising that there is a larger corpus of church law related to bastardy than to marriage itself. Church officials often became involved in the legal negotiations and oaths of betrothal in order to garner a fee. Wealthy laity took advantage of the church's assistance to guarantee marriage contracts. Common law marriage was the rule not the exception until property was more broadly distributed. Even then, the emphasis was on "giving the bride away," and the new relational covenant remained a contract upheld by law courts.

Traditional Christianity also has shaped a powerful root metaphor for sin: sexuality. This is not a biblical inheritance. As John Snow reminds us in Mortal Fear, the most powerful root metaphor for sin in the New Testament is captivity to the fear of death.[18] The most powerful root metaphor for sin in the Hebrew Scriptures is injustice, refusing to love God and one's neighbor. For most of "modern" history, medieval scholastic thought has dominated theological attitudes about human sexuality. When Thomas Aquinas wrote that a woman was a "misbegotten male," this was the natural conclusion of a culture which loathed women.[19] In Umberto Eco's novel, The Name of the Rose -- which depicts monastic life and learning in the Middle Ages -- women are portrayed as whores, witches, or both. This pathological view became entrenched as institutional Christianity assimilated historical events as divine law, and turned cultural norms into so-called natural law. For example, the church has treated witchcraft and sexuality similarly. In both instances the imaginary, the real and the symbolic have been powerfully and intentionally blurred to instill law and order and to create moral rearmament panics designed to give the appearance church authorities are doing something about sin.[20] We must discard remnants of Thomistic anthropology; the Middle Ages was truly another world!

There is another set of no-longer-useful tools I would like to excise, namely those destructive dualisms, or hierarchical oppositions, which contemporary French feminists Hélène Cixous and Catherine Clément have described as a "double braid" around the necks of all who seek to be fully embodied Christians. These include culture over nature, day over night, head over heart, form over matter, thinking over feeling, and, of course, male over female, master over slave, parent over child, white over black, etc. Without a lesser "other" in a hierarchical relationship there can be no dominance, no submission. If there are no outcasts, those who seek domination have to invent them. According to Cixous and Clément, "that is what masters do: they have their slaves made to order."[21] Cixous and Clément also unmask Freud's reinforcement of patriarchal dominance through his interpretation that it is sexual "inequality that triggers desire."[22]

However, our task requires more than discarding no longer useful tools, vital though that is. We also need to develop and use transformative tools. Fortunately, they are available. I have in mind six -- no doubt there are more -- practical, theological tools that are biblical in their radicality and Anglican in incarnational persuasion.

First, following the practices of those early witnesses chronicled in scripture and the practices of mystics throughout the ages, I suggest we develop our capacities for what Simone Weil once described as a way of looking that is first of all attentive. I do not mean staring, or gazing patronizingly. I do mean the kind of open looking that recognizes tension, ambiguity, difference, wonder and mystery. Such attentiveness allows appreciation of what the anthropologist Clifford Grertz calls the "thickness" of human lives, human cultures.[23] Thankfully the Judean shepherds did not try to explain away, or abstractly philosophize about, the wonder of the star that held their attention.

Secondly, theologians and psychologists alike are recognizing that we need to encourage insights from different and multiple epistemologies. One way of knowing that I believe is essential for members of an incarnational church is described in the recent book, Women's Ways of Knowing, as "connected knowing."[24] This source of wisdom will not be brand new for those of us raised on the educational theory of Jean Piaget or the pastoral theology of Paul Tournier. The French are unusually good at keeping humanity embodied. Connected knowing involves intimacy and understanding between the self and another person or material form. This orientation, Piaget observed, is toward relationship; it encourages ordinary human beings, Tournier believed, to participate in the construction of knowledge about the meaning of persons. Even rationalistic, scientific epistemologies need not be dispassionate or subjected to the unattainable criteria of pure objectivity. Barbara McClintock, whose work on the genetics of a corn plant won a Nobel Prize, said she could write a biography of each of her plants: "I know them intimately, and I find it a great pleasure to know each of them."[25]

Thirdly, since we live in a world of pluralistic cultures, the social sciences, rather than philosophy, need to "play the principle role of dialogue partner" with theology.[26] All sources of knowledge that help us examine the context of human lives should be enlisted, including economics, political science, sociology, psychology and anthropology. The twentieth-century Episcopal bishop, Stephen Bayne, insisted that we must expect to learn from all sources of knowledge.[27] This tradition of apologetics was encouraged by a Reformation bishop, John Jewel, who wrote, "we [Anglicans] lean unto knowledge."[28] The Roman Catholic theologian Robert J. Schreiter, in Constructing Local Theologies, employs the social sciences to reveal the death of monolithic theology and the rich, culturally layered nature of life in all Christian communities. The social sciences can help keep us from disincarnating theology.

Flexibility is a fourth theological tool for courageous incarnationalists. The powerful Brazilian liberation theologian, Leonardo Boff, describes flexibility (kantabasis) as a basic category in biblical theology:

> God was infinitely flexible toward humanity, accepting its reality with its undeniable limitations and onerous ambiguities.... The resulting Church clothed itself in a courageous flexibility toward the Greeks, Romans, and barbarians, accepting their languages, customs, rituals, and religious expressions. It did not demand any more than faith in Jesus Christ.[29]

Indeed Anglican theology has a long history of doctrinal flexibility. Anglicanism was one Reformation religion that consciously avoided becoming a confessional tradition. A 1967 commission led by Bishop Stephen Bayne concluded, "Anglicans do not believe that the Church is inexorably bound to any previous formulation of the church's tradition."[30] The Doctrine Commission of the Church of England recommended in 1981, "doctrine should be authoritatively defined as little and seldom as possible."[31] Our unique Anglican approach understands that the faith continues to be "handed down to us in the context of a living fellowship."[32] Anglicans must not bury incarnational theology like a treasure in the ground producing no profit (cf. the parable in Matthew 25:18). If flexibility ceased to be a basic theological category, Anglicanism would lose part of its intimate identity and become more akin to an evangelical sect.

Theological flexibility requires a complementary mode of exercising authority. A fifth tool for incarnational Anglicans is an ethic of authority more appropriately based on cooperation, rather than subordination, domination or oppressive partnerships (even if these are sanctioned by law). Traditionally, Anglicans have redefined the nature of authority and questioned the way power is exercised in the institutional church. Throughout our denominational history we have reformed both the content of tradition (traditia) and the ways tradition is formed and passed on (traditio). There is no reason to stop now.

Nor is there any real danger of relativism, the opposite error to ethnocentrism. Relativism means accepting all beliefs as equally true. Since Anglicans historically and theologically have lived with both Catholic and Protestant inheritances, we have had to be clear, not blase, about making faithful choices. Like other Reformation traditions, we also have to face the tension of living in the contradiction between maintaining authority and personalizing salvation. An ethic of authority based on cooperation allows us to live with this, and other, creative tensions. This mode of authority is signaled in the very first section of the 1979 Prayer Book "Outline of the Faith" which appropriately begins with a definition of human nature: "we are free to make choices: to love, to create, to reason, and to live in harmony with creation and with God."[33]

There is a sixth theological tool that I find intrinsic to and essential for Anglicans: valuing, not merely tolerating, differences. Our Catholic sacramental heritage implies an "acceptance of heterogeneous elements," an actual and effective integration of concreteness and mystery.[34] Differences do not need to be organized with "an opposition that remains dominant."[35] For example, women and men have suffered from oppressive, culturally derived gender stereotypes of "masculine" men and "feminine" women. If we were to look for gender differences with assistance from the social sciences and with greater theological attentiveness, we would no doubt develop a new appreciation for complexity, a sense of particularity and a good deal of humility. Differences would remain, but there would be a number of new differences, an enriched and not impoverished humanity resulting in the mystic's expanded consciousness for the whole of creation. Our task is to envision God working now as in the days of our ancestors to become better known in our differences. Well might we then proclaim, Vive la différence!

Imagine a concrete, living Christian church in which inclusion, not exclusion, shapes identity; a church in which understanding is valued over assessment, connection is deemed more important than separation, a place with a new immunity to hierarchical "principles," a home where inculcated vileness about human flesh has no warrant and no one has to lie about the embodied testimonies of human experience. My predecessor at the Episcopal Divinity School, John Booty, has written that Episcopalians "need not hide differences and keep peace so much as accept creative tension, assure constant dialogue, and anticipate gain from whatever conflict occurs within the orbit of mutual respect and love."[36]

In an incarnational community that is both Anglican and intimate, there is no such thing as a "no-body." God did not choose to dwell in a nobody! The courageous doctrine of the Incarnation invites, indeed demands, the best we have to offer: our fully embodied, sensuous selves. Whether in the arms of our loved ones or the feeding nurture of the eucharist, Episcopalians are called to be Anglican and intimate.

NOTES

1.   This paper is based on an address to members of the Episcopal Province of New England, gathered November 20, 1987, for a Provincial Convocation on the theme of "Intimacy." I am grateful to the Rev. Gene Robinson and other members of this Province for their support and criticism. A short version of this paper was published as "Courageous Incarnation: A Theology of Intimacy, in the Witness, vol. 72 no. 1 (January 1989), 14-18. Since I am interested in exploring distinctive Anglican approaches to intimacy, I have used the pronoun "we" specifically to refer to Episcopalians. I invite readers from other Christian churches and from other religions to use my paper as an opportunity to reflect on theological warrants about intimacy from the perspective(s) of their own community.

2.   My reflections on theological identity are directly informed by Robert J. Schreiter, Constructing Local Theologies (Maryknoll, New York: Orbis Books, 1985), esp. pp. 44-45 and 105-106.

3.   The complete title of this volume is Lux Mundi: A Series of Studies in the Religion of the Incarnation, edited by Charles Gore (New York: Thomas Whittaker, 1889).

4.   This and other Prayer Book citations are from the 1979 use of the Episcopal Church, The Book of Common Prayer, p. 264.

5.   Ibid., p. 329.

6.   Quotations in the original English are from The Folger Library Edition of the Works of Richard Hooker, Vol. II, Of the Laws of Ecclesiastical Polity, W. Speed Hill, ed., (Cambridge, Massachusetts: Harvard University Press, 1977), V. 54.5.

7.   C.B. Moberly, "The Incarnation as the Basis of Dogma," Lux Mundi, p. 194; in this collection see also the essay on "The Atonement" by Arthur Lyttelton.

8.   The Laws, V.67.11.

9.   The Book of Common Prayer, p. 336.

10.   On the centrality of the Incarnation in Ramsey's theology, see Kenneth Leech, "'The Real Archbishop': A Profile of Michael Ramsey," The Christian Century, March 12, 1986, 266-69.

11.   See Dorothee Soelle, Suffering, trans. by E.R. Kalin (Philadelphia: Fortress Press, 1975).

12.   The Laws, V. 54.5.

13.   The Book of Common Prayer, p. 336.

14.   The title of an essay in Sister Outsider: Essays and Speeches (Trumansburg, New York: The Crossing Press, 1984), pp. 110-113.

15.   Quoted on Christina Larner, Witchcraft and Religion: The Politics of Popular Belief, (New York: Basil Blackwell, 1984), p. 98. I have used Larner's interpretation in discussing both ethnocentrism and relativism; see also pp. 97-100.

16.   Robert M. Cooper, "Intimacy, " St. Luke's Journal of Theology, XXX (March 1987), p.116. Cooper focuses on intimacy as the shalom of God.

17.   Cited in Helene Cixous and Clement, The Newly Born Woman, trans. by Betsy Wing (Minneapolis; University of Minnesota Press, 1986), p. 28. This book was originally published in 1975 in French as La Jeune Née.

18.   The full title is Mortal Fear: Meditations on Death and AIDS (Cambridge: Cowley Publications, 1987), p.35.

19.   For discussion of misogyny in and selections from Thomas Aquinas, see Women and Religion: A Feminist Sourcebook of Christian Thought, ed. by Elizabeth Clark and Herbert Richardson, (New York: Harper and Row, 1977), pp. 78-101; see also Kari Borreson, Subordination and Equivalence: The Nature and Role of Women in Augustine and Thomas Aquinas (Washington, D.C.: University Press of America, 1981).

20.   See Larner on the place of witchcraft in an "Age of Faith", Witchcraft and Religion, especially pp.124-127.

21.   Cixous and Clément, The Newly Born Woman, p. 71; and on the "double braid" of dualisms see pp. 63-65.

22.   Ibid., p. 79.

23. For further elaboration of "thick descriptions" of culture, see Geertz's collected essays in The Interpretation of Cultures (New York: Basic Books, 1973).

24. Mary Field Belenky, Blythe McVicker Clinchy, Nancy Rule Goldberger, and Jill Mattuck Tarule, Women's Ways of Knowing: The Development of Self, Voice, and Mind (New York: Basic Books, Inc., 1986), especially pp. 101 and 112-20.

25. Quoted in Women's Way of Knowing, p. 144.

26. Schreiter, Constructing Local Theologies, p. xii.

27. See, for instance, Theological Freedom and Social Responsibility, a Report of the Advisory Committee of the Episcopal Church, Stephen F. Bayne, Jr., Chairman (New York: The Seabury Press, 1967), for instance, p. 8.

28. An Apology of the Church of England, edited by J.E. Booty (Charlottesville: The University Press of Virginia, 1963), p. 102. This text was first published in 1561.

29. Church: Charism & Power, trans. by J.W. Diercksmeier (New York: Crossroad, 1986), p. 107; this was originally published in 1981 under the title Igreja: Carisma e poder.

30. Theological Freedom and Social Responsibility, p. 19.

31. Believing in the Church: The Corporate Nature of Faith (London: SPCK, 1981), p. 296. For further comments on the flexibility of Anglican theology, see also Owen C. Thomas, "Feminist Theology and Anglican Theology," Anglican Theological Review, LXVII:2 (April 1986), 127-131; and Carter Heyward, "Can Anglicans be Feminist Liberation Theologians and Still be 'Anglican'?" The Trial of Faith: Theology and the Church Today, ed. Peter Eaton (London: Churchman, 1988).

32. A 1922 Church of England report quoted in Sexuality: A Divine Gift (a report prepared by the Episcopal Church, 1987) p. 2.

33. The Book of Common Prayer, p. 845.

34. See Boff, p. 89, "Catholicism implies a courage for Incarnation."

35. Cixous and Clément, The Newly Born Woman, p. 83.

36. John E. Booty, <u>What Makes Us Episcopalians?</u> (Wilton, Connecticut: Morehouse-Barlow, 1982), emphasis added, p. 33.

PART TWO

CHRISTIAN FAITH AND GLOBAL CRISIS:
STRUGGLING TOWARD LIBERATION

TRADITION, TRADITIONS AND THE PRESENT GLOBAL CRISIS

John Booty

Any attempt to construct a theological response to the present global crisis must involve coming to grips with the baggage of the past. Ignoring the past in the name of present dilemmas and future prospects does not eradicate that part but rather tends to perpetuate our bondage to it. Thus bound, we repeat the errors of the past and are inaccessible to much of the motive power for effective thought and action obscured by error. When Mary, the daughter of Henry VIII and Catharine of Aragon, came to the throne of England in 1553, it was with the goodwill of the people and high hopes for a long and prosperous reign. But she ignored recent history, in particular the religious, social and political "revolutions" marking the transition from the medieval to the modern world. She sought to reinstitute an outmoded relationship of church and state and to use repressive and violent means to that end. The results were disastrous for her, but educational for her half sister, Elizabeth, who mounted the throne in 1558 with considerable historical knowledge and sensitivity, capitalizing on the historic energies of her people, an agent for the release of creativity expressed in statesmanship, literature, music, peace, and economic stability. The Elizabethan age was great in large part because, like its most famous playwright, William Shakespeare, it learned important lessons from the study of the past and was able in so doing to differentiate between gross error and potential good.[1]

The ability to study and learn from the past came in large part from the humanists who contrasted the present with the distant past, the present decline and despair with the achievements and vaulting spirits of ancient Greece and Rome. Leonardo Bruni, studying the history of Florence with intent to revive its ancient greatness, together with Flavio Biondo, who dated Europe's decline from the barbarian invasions, established the basic idea of the "Middle" Ages, an intervening period of mediocrity. On the basis of this immensely important concept, reformist and revolutionary activities developed as the humanists and those whom they influenced sought to strip away from the body politic the drab clothes and erroneous thought which was eroding it, and to release from bondage the human spirit with its boundless aspirations.[2]

This humanist regard for the past influenced theologians of the sixteenth century and is in part responsible for the reformation slogan of sola Scriptura and the coordinate emphasis upon the golden past of ancient church Fathers, Creeds and Councils. The Scripture of the Old and New Testaments, together with the ancient church insofar as it did not contradict Scripture, was authoritative, dictating all that is necessary for salvation. But it has been obscured and distorted. Thus it is necessary to strip away from the gospel all accretions, all errors.   Martin Luther and Desiderius Erasmus agreed on this basic principle, although they opposed one another as dangerous heretics.[3]

Beside sola Scriptura, thus, there arose the cry to deny and destroy tradition and traditions which are other than the Word of God written and enshrined in the Bible. And from that time to this, the word "tradition" has had bad press among many people in the West. Growing out of the sixteenth century struggles there has emerged the impression that tradition is suspect, very possibly erroneous, and most likely irrational. Interpreting the word in terms of the popular understanding of "traditionalism" some of us would brand tradition as static, hide-bound, conservative, backward-looking, opposed to change, ignoring the future. Most of us are pragmatic and utilitarian with little, if any, time for the study of the past or concern for tradition and traditions.

It is an irony of history that such fifteenth century Italian humanists as Bruni and Biondo, who were very much interested in the tradition and traditions of ancient Rome, contributed to the struggle against tradition and traditions which has given rise to an anti-tradition tradition. That is seemingly the case and stands behind the problem which we now confront: as we seek to construct a theological response to global crises, what part, we ask, does the tradition of the church play, if any part at all? Built into this question is much suspicion that tradition has contributed to our problem, that we had best wipe the slate clean, and look for ideas and pointers in the present. I would suggest that our question and our suspicion is based in part upon accurate observation, but also upon some misunderstandings, and that we need, before we proceed, to consider the meaning and meanings of tradition for those people who bear the name Christian.

*****

Tradition[4] is, first of all, a process: the verb is active, not static or passive. In Greek it is paradosis, and has to do with transmission, the active handing on of something, or someone. In this sense tradition is not optional, but rather concerns that which we all do, even the antitraditionalists. On this level we are concerned with process or behavior which is true of nature as well as of persons, but it applies to persons in terms of the handing on of ideas and beliefs, customs and mores.[5] The process can go on largely internalized and unexamined, thus the process is itself important and determinative of the future. Or the process can be externalized, examined, and controlled by persons seeking to shape the future in terms of some ideal, their own or some other. An example of the former can be observed in nature within the evolutionary process. The latter was known in Adolf Hitler, his megalomania and the Nordic myth. Tradition as process is inescapable.

Tradition is, secondly, that which is handed on. For Christian folk in history that which is handed on from generation to generation is twofold, although the two parts are always related and always in tension with each other. There is, thus, the Tradition. It is the act of God in history through Christ by the Holy Spirit as encompassed in those various instruments which compose and identify the body of Christ, the Church. Beginning from Jerusalem, the act was transmitted by a chosen few who met together for prayer and the breaking of bread and who ventured out to preach, to teach and to baptize others into their company. Through these means the first Christians remembered God's mighty acts and experienced the presence of the Christ in their midst.[6] As time passed and the expected parousia was postponed indefinitely, the personal and oral memory of Jesus waned and threatening persons and preaching brought confusion concerning the valid memory of the divine acts. Thus the Tradition came to be expressed in terms of rules of faith which sought to locate the essential acts. Tertullian in his De Virginibus Velandis put the Tradition thusly:

> The Rule of Faith is that of believing/ In a single almighty God, Founder of the world/ And in his Son Jesus Christ, who was born of the Virgin Mary, crucified under Pontius Pilate, raised from the dead the third day, received into the heavens, now sits at the right hand of the Father, will come to judge the living and the dead.[7]

This tradition was expressed as well in other, more formal and agreed upon credal statements: baptismal, catechetical and conciliar. We have examples of these in the Apostles' and Nicene Creeds and in various catechisms still in use. Then too, there was the development of liturgies encompassing the Tradition, the mighty acts of God in Christ through the Spirit being re-enacted in the remembrance of them.

The past was thus powerful in the present, the worshipper and the Worshipped meeting in the eternal now. And there were the written records, the written proclamations and explanations, Gospels and epistles which through a long process lasting until 170 A.D. were gathered into a canon, or rule, which authoritatively preserved the experience of the divine acts. The New Testament as we know it took shape through the process of paradosis and became the instrument above all others for measuring and judging expressions of the Tradition. And finally there were persons who came to occupy offices invested with authority for guarding the Tradition, the good news of salvation through God's giving of the Christ. The threefold ministry of bishops, priests (or presbyters) and deacons was an instrument for the preservation and handing on of the Tradition, the bishop in particular being viewed from an early time as the guardian of the truth and the center of unity in that truth.[8]

It must be emphasized at this point that the Tradition is not the rule of faith, nor any credal statement. It is not any liturgy. It is not the New Testament. It is not the three-fold ministry. It is a person: Jesus the Christ, the divine child of God born of Mary, baptized by John, possessed from that moment on of amazing powers of perception and of healing, whose brief ministry was cut short by controversy, as he and his opponents recognized the revolutionary nature of his message and activities. He came to break down the thick wall of tradition which barred the way of children, women and men from the knowledge and presence of Israel's God. He was crucified, he died, he was buried, but on the road to Emmaus and elsewhere his despairing followers encountered him as alive, alive to them in prayer and in the breaking of bread. He was known to them as risen from death, fulfilling the promises of the Old Covenant, conveying those who believed into everlasting life. The instrumentalities exist to facilitate the personal encounter of finite humans with the infinite divine. It is this personal encounter which is at the heart of the Christian faith. It is this out of which all else proceeds and to which all must return. All parts of the Christian phenomenon are inter-related and none can claim to be ultimate. The ultimate is personal, a Person in relationship, related in the Godhead, related in the Church and in the world. The Christian faith is thus dynamic, moving and involving the inclusion of the entire cosmos, of all nations, of all races, of all peoples regardless of sexual identity. It is universalistic not in a dogmatic or abstract sense, but rather in a personal sense. All things, all people are related in and through the personhood of the living God made known in Jesus Christ by the Spirit.[9]

In our age, we know enough of the sociology of institutions not to be surprised that the Church as an institution can and does lose sight of its origin and dedicate its energies to the preservation and expansion of the institution.[10] Forgetting its reason for existence, the parts of the whole compete with one another, absolute claims are made for finite and perishable things, and that which is transmitted seems opposite to that which was meant by the Tradition.

This somber thought brings us to the second way in which we must view that which is handed on. Alongside the Tradition there are traditions, for the Tradition is conveyed through traditions. Here we acknowledge that the Tradition is historical and is constantly qualified by the persons and events of the historical scene. The Tradition transcends and penetrates the particular society to which it is transmitted, but it does so by means of and through persons who arise out of and belong to the particular society. This tradition which is the heart of the Christian faith can only be expressed in limited terms and forms, words and actions wedded to a particular culture. The means in time modify the Tradition, traditions often assuming the authority belonging to the Tradition alone. There is no escaping this, for the only way in which we know the Tradition is through agencies which are encompassed in traditions. Nor is this surprising when we remember how God entered history in human form, identified with the traditions of Israel, qualified by finitude and fear.

This must be firmly grasped. The Tradition involves great risk. Its transmitters are sent into all the world to convey the goodness of salvation through Christ. In order to do so they must speak in terms and act in ways that can be comprehended. But to do so is to commit that Tradition to words and deeds which will qualify it and perhaps even maim it. But the risk is taken. It is commanded by the God who in love reaches out to all creation calling all into relationship with himself and with one another, restoring wholeness and health to the cosmos. The risk was taken in the second and third centuries in Alexandria where in proclaiming the Gospel in the midst of the philosophical schools a Christian gnosticism was developed which, while it affirmed the Incarnation of the Logos, displayed little interest in the historic Jesus. It would be wrong to say that it should not have happened. It happened in obedience to the command of the Lord.[11]

The Tradition as a living, personal entity involves risk and it also involves reformation.[12] That is to say, the Tradition is always conveyed in and through persons who are members of societies possessing their own traditions. The Church in its mission is conditioned not only by the Tradition as its source but also by traditions of the society where it exists. It is sent in obedience and yet it exists as judged by that which sent it out into the world, and being judged it lives as being renewed and reformed by the Tradition. Indeed, the Tradition is constantly working on the Church and in the Church to bring it back to its essential meaning and task, and to condemn all apostasy, all heresy and schism, that it may in and through the traditions which it must not and cannot escape proclaim the Gospel of God in Christ through the Spirit. How does it happen? It happens as individuals and groups rise up in protest and demand reform. The religious orders in the Church began in part as a protest against a Church which had compromised its life, becoming immersed in the worldliness of Roman Empire. The call to poverty, chastity and obedience was a call to reform the Church according to the precepts of the Gospel and the example of Jesus. But in time the monastic establishments themselves stood in need of reform. The great orders, Benedictine, Cistercian, Carthusian and the rest are instruments for the reform of the religious life, as well as for the reform of the Church and ultimately of the world.

Toward the end of the so-called Middle Ages there were those who rose up in protest against the Church, demanding reform. Martin Luther was not alone. He was, in fact, one of a multitude of persons who protested against the ways the Church of Rome, both institutionally and intellectually, had lost sight of its

mission and was condoning the status quo.   Against a Church which sought to
make capital out of the Gospel, Martin Luther proclaimed the utterly free grace
of God who justifies women and men while yet sinful.   And yet that reformist
movement which Luther began soon stood in need of reform itself, the
evangelical message of justification by faith alone without the necessity of any
merit becoming frozen in Confessions which themselves require consent.

But one must add that the Tradition works to reform the Church not only
through individuals and groups within the Church but also through those who
seemingly exist outside of the Church.   The Prophet Jeremiah tells how God
afflicted Israel through Nebuchadnezar, king of Babylon, to bring it back into
the covenantal relationship.   We cannot speak with such assurance of the ways
in which God exercises judgment upon the contemporary Church, nor can we
be as certain as the Old Testament writers often were of the other means which
the Lord of History uses not only to discipline but to lead the people of God on
mission in and to the world.   But we do know that explicitly non-Christian
individuals and groups in the civil rights and peace movements have arisen in
our time to recall the Church to its task and have been means for its reform.

It remains here to consider that reformatio as a characteristic of the
Tradition is not simply backward-looking.   Insofar as the Tradition concerns that
which is Ultimate, it is forward-looking, intentionally directed toward a final
end.   This involves an eschatalogical view of the Church as driving toward the
future and toward the fulfillment of the Tradition in historical and extra-
historical realization of its true being in Christ.   The implication here is that
change is not only for the bene esse of the Church, and, one must add, the
cosmos, but it is also of the esse: without change the Church cannot be what it
claims to be.   Indeed, innovation is expected (in worldly and temporal terms),
if by that word we mean that reformatio which partakes of future fulfillment.
The recovery of the spirit of the originating experience (God in Christ among
us) involves the discovery of that which is for us new.   The Tradition entered
history in the person of Christ as revolutionary, renewing the old law, the old
cult, the old religion for the sake of that which precedes and succeeds the old
in the new.   This is a primary characteristic of the Tradition as it influences us
now.

It must not be forgotten that Christ came as one overthrowing custom
and tradition in terms not only of the covenant made with Israel but also in
relation to the coming Age, symbolized in ultimate terms by the Messianic
Banquet, experienced proleptically at every Eucharist.   Franklin Young puts it
succinctly:

By locating the temple or holy place at the point where God confronts man in the person of the risen Lord (with respect to God's action) or the Church (with respect to response in faith) the possibility of spatially localizing worship in abstraction from the totality of life was impossible.[13]

To attack the Temple at Jerusalem as the holy place was revolutionary. But it was necessary, for Jesus believed that the place and the cult which really matter occur where God encounters the worshipper and the worshipper responds not for a particular time with a particular liturgy but in the entirety of life. Indeed, for the Christian the place and the cult were now a person -- Jesus Christ. And all designated places where particular liturgies were to be performed were intended to serve this goal: response to the "total deed of Christ in one's total existence."[14] From henceforth any separation between worship and work was denied.

In place of the old traditions, Christ in his very self brought a new tradition, that which I have referred to as the Tradition. Taken seriously it is revolutionary in a glorious and saving sense.

*****

When the modern age is studied, the complexities involved in the interaction between the Tradition and traditions becomes apparent. Let us consider late eighteenth and early nineteenth century England. Here we observe how the Tradition is conveyed in a rapidly changing society so that certain traditions emerge and gain independence from the Tradition. The English had for centuries regarded Church and Commonwealth as united in one society. Richard Hooker, writing at the end of the sixteenth century, put it in a way which has been remembered: "There is not any man of the Church of England but the same man is also a member of the commonwealth; nor any man a member of the commonwealth, which is not also of the Church of England."[15] This understanding was a matter of common sense. It could also be viewed in medieval terms with reference to the organic nature of society, possessing both a soul and a body, concerned by necessity for the commonwealth as well as for personal salvation. Furthermore, stressing as it did the wholeness of human beings in society in terms of love and justice, it partook of the Tradition involving the organic unity of all creation.

In eighteenth century England this tradition of the unity of church and state could and did develop into the theory of political obedience propounded by William Paley in his Principles of Moral and Political Philosophy (1785), whereby it was decreed that it is the will of God that the established government, whatever its nature, must be obeyed. This he believed to be the lesson of Scripture.[16] Bishop Horseley made much use of Romans 13 in arguing that whatever the form of civil government, it must be obeyed as an application of that duty which is rightly due to God. As such arguments proceeded, the Tradition receded and apostasy occurred, for the Tradition has never supported blind obedience to the civil powers. The worship of God involves our serving him with the service of a slave. We serve others only insofar as such service coincides with or does not contradict our primary service. To worship in spirit and in truth involves living out our relationship to Christ in all of life.

Along with this conviction concerning the authority of the state there went the conviction that social stratification into classes was according to divine ordinance. Rich and poor there would always be. To speak of the poor rising out of their depressed condition was to incur the charge of Jacobinism and bring to mind the horrors of the French Revolution. Hannah More, a remarkable Evangelical philanthropist and educator, preached social resignation and content, having the character Jack Anvil say:

> I have got the use of my limbs, of my liberty, of the laws, and of my Bible. The first two I take to be my natural rights; the two last my civil and religious rights: these, I take it, are the true Rights of Man, and all the rest is nothing but nonsense, and madness, and wickedness... Instead of indulging in discontent, because another is richer than I in this world (for envy is at the bottom of your equality works), I read my Bible, go to church, and look forward to a treasure in heaven.[17]

In the early nineteenth century the Church came to condone Political Economy and laissez-faire economics, thus giving a particular view of economics the authority of the divine. John Bird Sumner, later Archbishop of Canterbury, defended Malthus' Essay on Population by demonstrating the compatibility of Political Economy with Scripture.[18] Individual initiative and freedom of economic laws seemed to be Christian virtues of the highest order, all understood, of course, within the confines of Hannah More's conviction that the class system was divinely ordained.

Once again the Tradition was distorted and maimed in its transmission. Traditions explainable not in the light of the Gospel but in relation to the cultural context became divinely authorized, if not instituted, laws. Over against such culture-bound traditions was the radical left, but there was also the Anglican theologian, F.D. Maurice, preaching communism. Writing to his friend Ludlow in 1849 he contrasted Church and State, the State by nature being Conservative, concerned with property and individual rights, the Church being Communist:

the Church, I hold, is Communist in principle; Conservative of property and individual rights only by accident; bound to recognize them, but as its own special work; not as the chief object of human society or existence.[19]

Maurice, of course, knew nothing of Marx and Das Capital, he was thinking of Communism as the proper sharing of this world's goods and as:

> a most important principle of the old world, and that every monastic institution - properly so called - was a Communist institution to all intents and purposes. The idea of Christian Communism has been a most vigorous and generative one in all ages, and must be destined to a full development in ours.[20]

Maurice rightly understood that the Christian Tradition could not be enlisted as a means of social control when that control involved not the principle of sacrificial sharing in love, but the perpetuation of social and economic privilege to the detriment, sometimes very severe detriment, of the many.

The trend in all of these matters is for the Church to defend, with the authority of Christian tradition, the status quo, the defense ordinarily identifying the class-boundedness of the defenders. The Tradition stands over against this trend, condemning such views as reflecting that which is traditionally called sin: the self's love of self to the exclusion of all others and all things. Set over against this there is the Incarnation, the going-forth, self-emptying of God, and there is the Cross, the self-sacrifice of the Incarnate One, and there is the coming of the Holy Spirit at Pentecost, the reversal of the Tower of Babel, whereby the various people of this earth become one community of faith, not in some monochromatic sense, but with that variety which is found in the harmonious beauty of the rainbow.

The Christian Tradition in this twentieth century is hampered and distorted by traditions emerging out of our cultures, traditions which support our current status, whatever it may be. In our own time, the Scriptures have been used to support racist and sexist ideologies, social and economic injustice and inequity, international duplicity and cruel war.

The Jewish sculptor, Sir Jacob Epstein, in his first statue of Christ reminded Christians of their leader and shocked the Church so that he was denounced and condemned. Of his work he said:

> I must maintain that my statue of Christ still stands for what I intended it to be. It stands and accuses the world for its grossness, inhumanity,

cruelty, and beastliness, for the First World War and for the later wars in Abyssinia, China, and Spain which culminated in the Second World War. How prophetic a figure! Not the early Evangelical Christ of Byzantium and Rome, nor the condemning Apollonian Christ of Michelangelo, or the sweet rising and blessing Christ of Raphael, but the modern living Christ, compassionate and accusing at the same time. I should like to remodel this 'Christ.' I should like to make it hundreds of feet high, and set it up on some high place where all could see it, and where it would give out its warning, its mighty symbolic warning to all lands. The Jew - the Galilean - condemns our wars, and warns us that 'Shalom, Shalom,' must be still the watchword between man and man. "[21]

This is the Tradition confronting all traditions to bless or condemn them.

Two possibilities confront the people who are the designated bearers of the Tradition. They can hold on to the traditions and die with them, apostate. Or they can seize the opportunity once more to regard the Tradition in the person of Christ, open to its influence, evolving new traditions as the Tradition interacts with the emerging world culture. This is a kairotic moment.

Not only is this a time of reformatio, wherein the Tradition is renewed and new traditions evolve. This is a time when we can look back to discern previous traditions, rooted in the Tradition, which have been the inspiration for good for other peoples. Revolutions concur with a revival of interest in history, a development of historical scholarship that releases the past from its bondage. This is also a time for the most serious consideration of ends or goals, when women and men of faith, rooted in the past, directed by the Spirit, discern the course of the Tradition into the future. Furthermore, paradosis is influenced, rightly I believe, by the Spirit moving in the histories and cultures of the present societies on earth. The exigencies of the present world crisis confront us with the need, as the Second Report to the Club of Rome, Mankind at the Turning Point, puts it, to realize our oneness, our interdependence in the emerging world society. The Tradition and the present situation both call for organic, holistic thinking, planning and working. In meeting such need the Tradition must be proclaimed and the most adequate traditions possible devised for its transmission in word and in action.

*****

The assertion has been made that Christian tradition has reinforced, if not created, the Western exploitation of nature, leading to the present global environmental crisis. In line with the basic argument as presented here, we must regard such an assertion with critical skepticism. The Tradition as found in Scripture, the Old and New Testaments, and thus through the Judeo-Christian tradition of the West, may begin with Genesis 1, but it is not fully comprehended there. I would put it this way:

God created all that is, but in the creation of human beings, God did something which distinguishes humans from other creatures and creations. Women and men as creatures are one with nature, they are creaturely, but they are also creative, that is to say that there is a differentia between human beings and other creatures. The Greeks spoke of this differentia in terms of Reason and traditional Christian theology speaks of spirit, indicating the capacity of humans to regard themselves and the cosmos which they inhabit as differentiated objects and as a result to think and act in ways which create new possibilities. Still subject to the laws of nature, humans exercise some degree of control within the natural order. In Biblical terms we are said to be made in the Image of God and to have dominion over nature. This dominion is put forcefully in Psalm 8:

Yet thou hast made him little less than God,
    and dost crown him with glory and honour.
Thou hast given him dominion over the works of thy hands;
    thou hast put all things under his feet,
all sheep and oxen,
    and also the beasts of the field,
the birds of the air, and the fish of the sea,
    whatever passes along the paths of the sea. (vv. 5-8)

This undeniably is in the Tradition. Furthermore, the knowledge and the power which this dominion involves are affirmed to be in themselves good, a part of the whole creation which is very good.

What is not in the Tradition is any assumption that this dominion provides any warrant for the exploitation or egotistical use and misuse of nature in the service of human ends. The dominion involves heavy responsibility, trust, cooperation with God and with nature, aiming at such harmony as will redound to the praise of all creation. The model here is not that of some arbitrary, coercive, vindictive, domineering dictator God. The model is that of the God of steadfast love, who humbles himself, becomes human, suffers and gives his life in service to humanity and the cosmos. The dominion which the Tradition commends is that which has been exhibited in Christ Jesus and in those women and men who have been Christ's extensions in the world.

That toward which human dominion over nature aims is that paradise envisioned in Isaiah 11:6-9:

> The wolf shall dwell with the lamb,
> and the leopard shall lie down with the kid,
> and the calf and the lion and the fatling together,
> and a little child shall lead them.
> The cow and the bear shall feed;
> their young shall lie down together;
> and the lion shall eat straw like the ox.
> The sucking child shall play over the hole of the asp,
> and the weaned child shall put his hand on the adder's den.
> They shall not hurt or destroy
> in all my holy mountain;
> for the earth shall be full of the knowledge of the Lord
> as the waters cover the sea.

The exploitation of the cosmos for selfish human ends is sin, for it involves disobedience towards God and thus also separation from the Lord who in steadfast love serves the creation rather than exploiting it. Furthermore, our exploitation of the cosmos results in the fracturing and fragmenting of our necessary relationship and inter-relationships with the world. We negate the holistic vision of Isaiah 11, a vision of wholeness and interdependence which arises out of creation and finds fulfillment in the eschaton.

Admittedly, the New Testament writers demonstrate little interest in nature and the earliest Christians minimized humankind's relationship to nature. And yet the idea of the "cosmic Christ" in Colossians (1:15f.), Hebrews (1:3), and the Gospel of John (1:1-4) provides the basis for linkage with the Old Testament understanding of human being and the rest of the natural order. Paul in Colossians, for instance, spoke of Christ in this way:

> He is the image of the invisible God, the first-born of all creation; for in him all things were created, in heaven and on earth, visible and invisible... He is before all things, and in him all things hold together. (vv. 15-17)

Thus Christ is from the beginning; all that is was created in him; and in him all is held in unity. Furthermore, as Charles Gore indicated in his Bampton Lectures:

> While Christ is the consummation of nature, He is also its healer and restorer. The world has been violated and wrecked by the rebellion of

sin, frustrating the Creator's plan and reducing us to helplessness.
Hence, Christus Consummator must needs also be Christus Redemptor,
and it is in the unity of these two aspects that Christ's uniqueness in
nature and history is seen.[22]

The salvation wrought by God through Christ by the Spirit is holistic, extended
toward the whole creation, involving the overcoming of human sin and the
restoration of a right relationship between human beings and the cosmos.

Nevertheless, the distortion of the Tradition in respect to nature began
with the earliest Christians and their presentation of the Gospel. This is a truth
which must be faced. In the history of the Church, the neglect of the issue of
human responsibility toward the cosmos stands as a blot upon the Church's
record. Evidence that the Tradition has continued and cannot finally be
frustrated is to be found in individuals such as St. Francis with his sense of unity
with all creation, and St. Benedict of Nursia with his insistence upon an ordered
relationship with the cycles of nature, and in traditions such as those of the
Western Bestiaries and of Eastern Christianity where noetus and aisthetos, mind
and spirit and senses interpenetrate. How impressive is the lion in this
translation of one medieval bestiary:

> The lion mounts a hill when he hears a man hunting
> Or when by sniffing he perceives someone approaching.
> No matter which way he chooses to descend to the dale below,
> He makes sure to cover over all his footprints,
> Dragging dust with his tail wherever he steps,
> Either dust or mud, so he cannot be tracked.
> He scurries down to his den where he hides himself.[23]

One could learn from this something of the struggle which goes on between
humankind and the rest of nature: medieval women and men viewed nature as
expressive of things divine.

> Very high indeed is the hill which is the kingdom of
>   heaven.
> Our Lord is the lion Who dwells there above.
> When it seemed right to Him to descend here to earth,
> The devil could never comprehend, although he is a
>   cunning hunter,
> Just how it was that He came down,
> Nor how He denned Himself in that gentle maid,
> Mary by name, who bore Him for boon of mankind.

In that which is perhaps the focal chapter of all his work, Richard Hooker, the sixteenth century English theologian, expressed something of that which I can identify as the Tradition concerning women and men and the whole creation in God and under God:

All other things that are of God have God in them and he them in himself likewise. Yet because their substance and his wholly differeth, their coherence and communion either with him or amongst themselves is in no sort like unto that before-mentioned.

God hath his influence into the very essence of all things, without which influence of Deity support them their utter annihilation could not choose but follow. Of him all things have both received their first being and their continuance to be that which they are. All things are therefore partakers of God, they are his offspring, his influence is in them, and the personal wisdom of God is for that very cause said to excel in nimbleness or agility, to pierce into all intellectual, pure, and subtile spirits, to go through all, and to reach unto everything which is.[24]

It is this understanding of the creation extending through time into the eschaton which reveals the falsity of all traditions that fall short of the Tradition, absolutizing some part of the whole to satisfy the lusts of the part which is charged with responsibility to care for the whole. In this is our true and only claim to uniqueness: that we are responsible beings, caring for the wholeness of creation, serving the needs of all as we are in turn served by all.

NOTES

1.   The historical analysis here reveals the bias, and, I trust, the wisdom of a student of Sir John Neale. See especially his Elizabeth I: A Biography (Garden City, New York: Doubleday Anchor Books, 1957); Elizabeth I and Her Parliaments, 2 vols., (London: Jonathan Cape, 1953, 1956); and Essays in Elizabethan History (London: Jonathan Cape, 1958). Concerning the rising interest in past during the Elizabeth Age, see F.J. Levy, Tudor Historical Thought (San Marino, California: The Huntington Library, 1967), espec. Ch. 6.

2.   For a general perspective see Peter Burke, The Renaissance Sense of the Past, Documents of Modern History, (London: Edward Arnold, 1969). For Florence, Bruni and Biondo, see Hans Baron, The Crisis of the Early Italian Renaissance, rev. ed., (Princeton: University Press, 1966).

3.   For Luther's view of the state of things and the need for reform, see especially An Appeal to the Ruling Class of German Nationality as to the Amelioration of the State of Christendom (1520), conveniently found in John Dillenberger, Martin Luther: Selections (Garden City: Doubleday Anchor Books, 1961), pp. 403-485. On Erasmus, with his dictum "Christ requires of us nothing but a pure and sincere life," see C.R. Thompson, Colloquies of Erasmus (Chicago: University Press, 1965), pp. xviii, 549. And see his Enchiridion, in Matthew Spinka, ed., Advocates of Reform, LCC XIV, (Philadelphia: Westminster Press, 1953), espec. p. 338.

4.   For that which follows I have relied heavily upon Albert Cutler's Report of the North American Section of the Fourth World Conference on Faith and Order, Montreal, Canada, 12-26 July, 1963. This is found in the Report on Tradition and Traditions, Faith and Order Paper No. 40, World Council of Churches Commission on Faith and Order, Geneva, 1963, espec. pp. 14-24. See also K.E. Skydsgaard's Report of the European Section, pp. 33ff. For a Roman Catholic viewpoint, see Josef Rupert Geiselmann, The Meaning of Tradition (New York: Herder and Herder, 1966). This latter takes under consideration much of the European discussion of the subject.

5.   For a helpful description of the process of handing on as found in different cultures, see Margaret Mead, Culture and Commitment, (Garden City, New York: Natural History Press, Doubleday and Co., 1970).

6.   For an excellent discussion of <u>anamnesis</u>, see Charles Price, "Remembering and Forgetting in the Old Israel and in the Early Christian Eucharist," Unpublished dissertation, Harvard University, 1964.

7.   R.P.C. Hanson, <u>Tradition in the Early Church.</u> (London: SCM Press, 1962), p. 87. The author provides numerous other examples.

8.   For another view of the process whereby the ecclesiastical institution began and developed, see Joachim Wach, <u>Sociology of Religion</u> (Chicago: University Press, 1944).

9.   For a serious and well-developed statement of the personal element in the Christian faith and theology, see G.F. Woods, <u>Theological Explanation</u>, (Welwyn, Herts., James Niebet, 1958). This is a book which has been grossly neglected and deserves to be widely read and pondered.

10.   This is a major theme in Emil Brunner, <u>The Misunderstanding of the Church.</u> (Philadelphia: Westminster Press, 1953).   See also Wach's <u>Sociology of Religion</u>, op. cit.

11.   See J.N.D. Kelly, <u>Early Christian Doctrines.</u> (New York: Harper and Brothers, 1958), pp. 153-154. He writes: "Soteriologically considered, the humanity of Jesus had little theological importance in his [Clement's] scheme."

12.   On this subject, sec Gerhart B. Ladner, <u>The Idea of Reform: Its Impact on Christian Thought and Action in the Age of the Fathers</u> (Cambridge, Mass.: Harvard University Press, 1959).   See the review by E.R. Hardy in <u>Church History</u>, XXIX, 3, Sept. 1960, p. 358. For an extension of his thought, see Ladner's essay "Reformatio" in Samuel H. Miller and G. Ernest Wright, <u>Ecumenical Dialogue at Harvard: The Roman Catholic-Protestant Colloquium</u> (Cambridge, Mass.: The Belknap Press of Harvard University Press, 1964), pp. 172-190.   And see Giles Constable's report and summary of the seminar discussion of "Reformatio," ibid., pp. 330-343.

13.   Franklin W. Young, "The Theological Context of New Testament Worship," in Massey H. Shepherd, Jr., ed., <u>Worship in Scripture and Tradition</u> (New York: Oxford University Press, 1963), p. 88.

14.   Ibid., p. 90.

15.   Richard Hooker, <u>Of the Laws of Ecclesiastical Polity</u>, VIII. i.2; <u>Works</u>, ed. John Keble, Richard Church, and Francis Paget, 7th ed., (Oxford: Clarendon, 1888), v. III, p. 330. See also, F.J. Shirley, <u>Richard Hooker and</u>

Contemporary Political Ideas, Church Historical Society (London: SPCK Press, 1949), Ch. VI: "Relations of Church and State."

16.   I am relying here upon E.R. Norman's excellent study of Church and Society in England 1770-1970: A Historical Study (Oxford: Clarendon, 1976), p. 29. Norman states that Paley presents the most systematic treatment on political obedience and that his Principles "rejected the idea that the duty to obey civil government rested on contract: 'Wherefore, rejecting the intervention of a compact, as unfounded in its principle, and dangerous in the application, we assign for the only ground of the subject's obligation, the will of God as collected from Expediency.'"

17.   From Hannah More's Village Politics, by Will Chip, quoted in Ford K. Brown, Fathers of the Victorians: The Age of Wilberforce (Cambridge: University Press, 1961), p. 129.

18.   E.R. Norman, Church and Society, pp. 42-44.

19.   Frederick Maurice, ed., The Life of Frederick Denison Maurice: Chiefly Told in His Own Letters (New York: Charles Scribner's Sons, 1884), Vol. II, p. 8.

20.   Ibid., p. 6.

21.   Jacob Epstein, An Autobiography, 2nd ed., (London: Vista Books, 1963), p. 102. For illustrations of the statue, see Richard Buckle, Jacob Epstein Sculptor (Cleveland and New York: World Publishing, 1963), plates 151-155. Epstein labored to portray Christ in different media all of his life. For one of his last and most monumental attempts, one made for the war ravaged Llandaff Cathedral and cast in aluminum, see his Christ in Majesty, ibid., plates 610-612.

22.   As summarized by Michael Ramsey in his An Era in Anglican Theology: From Gore to Temple, Hale Lectures, (New York: Charles Scribner's Sons, 1960), p. 17. Much of the above has been influenced by Hugh Montefiore, ed., Man and Nature, (London: Collins, 1975). This is a report of a working group of the Doctrine Commission of the Church of England. I am especially indebted not only to the report itself but to supplementary essays by John Austin Baker and A.R. Peacocke. Reference should also be made to Ian G. Barbour, ed., Earth Might be Fair: Reflections on Ethics, Religion, and Ecology, (Englewood Cliffs, New Jersey: Prentice-Hall, 1972), and Thomas Sieger Derr, Ecology and Human Liberation: A Theological Critique of the Use and Abuse of our Birthright, WSCF Book, Vol. III, No. 1, 1973, Serial Number 7, Geneva, 1973.

23. The quotations are from T.J. Elliott, A Medieval Bestiary, translated and introduced by Elliott with wood engravings by Gillian Tyler, (Boston: Godine, 1971), no pagination.

24. Richard Hooker, Of the Laws of Ecclesiastical Polity, V.1 vi.5., in Hooker's Works, Keble, Church, Paget eds., Vol. II, p. 247. See also A.M. Allchin, "The Theology of Nature in the Eastern Fathers and among Anglican Theologians, " in Montefiore, Man and Nature, pp. 150ff.

TOWARDS PARTNERSHIP:
RACE, GENDER AND THE CHURCH IN AOTEAROA-NEW ZEALAND

Susan Adams

Mainline, male-dominated, 'European' Christian churches in Aotearoa-New Zealand are facing the challenge of partnership from both Maori people[1] (the indigenous people of this land) and women, especially Pakeha (of European descent) women. Maori people and women are active within these churches, and are pushing towards partnerships which require new structures, new theologies and new relationships. No longer can the churches remain, with integrity, either male-dominated or European in theology and style.

The sharpness of the challenge has its roots in the early days of colonial settlement 150 years ago. The impact of the Pakehas' arrival on the indigenous population and their cultural values is painfully evident, an inescapable fact of daily life. Likewise, the memory of Pakeha women's struggles in an unfamiliar environment -- their dreams and the central part they played in the shaping of Aotearoa-New Zealand -- is still available to us in the stories of our grandmothers and great-grandmothers.

Despite the most persistent efforts of the missionaries and of later Christian church men and women, the flame of Maori peoples' pride in race and culture has not been extinguished. Nor has the determination of the women who left the oppressions of Victorian England to forge a new 'classless' society in the South Pacific expired. This racial pride and egalitarian vision present relentless challenges to church and society today. Both demand a reappraisal of concepts of partnership and a reexamination of the theology and structures which shape the contemporary church, particularly within those churches which came with the missionaries or the early settlers from Britain: Anglican, Roman Catholic, Methodist and Presbyterian. This essay focuses on the Anglican Church in Aotearoa-New Zealand, the church in which I exercise my ministry.

The Missionary Church and the Treaty of Waitangi

The churches arrived in Aotearoa after the first wave of men engaged in whaling and sealing.[2] Initially the churches sought to protect the indigenous people from the licentious behavior of the male communities, and as a consequence the first English Christian missionaries were quick to learn the language of the Maori and to translate the scriptures into Maori. A Maori Christian church, fostered by Anglican, Wesleyan and Roman Catholic missionaries, took root and began to grow. From 1814 to 1841 the Anglican Church was a Maori church, concerned with developing as an indigenous church with local support.

By 1840, with the increasing numbers of new arrivals from Europe, it became evident that a covenant or contract might be required to establish the rights and responsibilities of the two peoples. The British proposed a formal treaty, and the missionary church was persuasive in bringing many of the Maori tribes to the treaty table. British leaders stated that a treaty would safeguard the rights of the Maori people to land, forest, and fishing grounds, as well as protect Maori sovereignty within the British crown. These leaders also promised to ensure Maori rights against the growing influx of English settlers.

Initially, the Treaty of Waitangi[3] -- Waitangi was the place where the first signatures were obtained in February, 1840 -- was understood to be the basis of a relationship of mutual respect and recognition between the two nations inhabiting Aotearoa-New Zealand. "We are now one" became a popular slogan, later leading to policies of assimilation. However, in 1840, the Maori population outnumbered the Pakeha by about 100 to one, and there was no talk of assimilation! In concert with their cultural values, the Maori people continued to extend hospitality to the manuhiri (visitors). More and more settlers arrived, seeking to better themselves by becoming landowners in this new, more egalitarian (for European settlers) society.

Bishop George Augustus Selwyn arrived in 1842, following the treaty signing, and the Anglican church changed its focus to the care of the rapidly growing number of English settlers. In 1857 a constitution for the church in New Zealand was adopted, but, despite an active and flourishing Maori church for 40 years, there was not one Maori signature on what was clearly a settler church document.[4] By the 1860s, with increasing numbers of English colonists arriving to take possession of land sold (sight unseen) in England, the settler church began to flourish. Signs of its vitality included such hallmarks of the church in England as 'civilizing' intentions, strictly defined gender relationships, and the exclusive use of the English language.

In subsequent years, the treaty has been ignored by the Pakeha. Land has been confiscated by the government and sold in individual title, ancestral fishing beds have been polluted with industrial discharge, and the Maori language has been all but lost through the systematic denial of the right to use it.[5] Simply put, the hospitality of the tangata whenua (people of the land) has been abused!

The Settler Church and Women and Maori

The records of the Anglican and Methodist churches show that concurrent with this period of ascendancy for the settler church communities of women from Anglican religious orders, Methodist deaconesses and local mission groups -- plus teachers and nurses -- were working with Maori people. Their work was mainly with women and children, their intention being to support them against the growing tide of Pakeha cultural dominance and disease.[6] And [Pakeha] women organized themselves, as well. The Onehunga Ladies Benevolent Society (founded in 1863) and the Women's Christian Temperance Union (1887) were early organizations of women, responding to refugees from Waikato land wars and the ravages of alcohol, respectively.

Pakeha women also had concern for their own well-being, and groups of women provided support for each other through organizations such as the YWCA (started in New Zealand in 1878) and the women's suffrage movements of the 1870s. The dream of a society different from Victorian England persisted. Women by and large were hardy and outspoken, and churchwomen assumed leading roles in women's organizing. By 1893 women's suffrage was established, New Zealand thus becoming the first place in the world where women and men had equal voting rights. In 1909, the Plunket Society was established to care for the well-being of women and children, and, through the hard work of women, contributed in large measure to New Zealand's leadership in promoting the health of babies and women during the late 19th and early 20th centuries. Of course, it was Pakeha women who benefitted from this progressive program. Further, despite law changes such as the Married Women's Property Act of 1884, Pakeha androcentric society continuously ignored and rolled over women's determination to assume leadership within all spheres of the society, just as that society tried to erase Maori strength and cultural pride.[7]

The Christian church promoted -- in fact, sanctified -- practices and values which elevated the place of white European males.[8] Women were taught their Christian duty to be private, passive, sacrificial, submissive and humble -- in order to earn respect as females in a society stressing the public, aggressive, dominating, go-getter values of maleness -- and to suppress their own desire to contribute responsibly and peaceably to the new society. The church, with its male god and its theology of maleness, pushed women out of the places of actual decision-making, out of effective theological focus, out of the public sphere, and into a private preserve of women's space. Similarly, attempts to develop a Maori response to Christianity (such as that seen in the followers of Ratana)[9] were excluded from the Anglican church.

The Present Church and Feminism

The Anglican Church moved to ordain women to the priesthood in 1978, and the impact of this decision is only now being realized. Feminist women are demanding a clear articulation of the church's androcentric theological system as it exists in mission, liturgy and ministry. As the biases and inadequacies of this system are exposed, women are demanding a new theology which takes their experience and insights seriously. They are also working for increased participation in the structure of the church, in ways which benefit women.[10]

Six years after the approval of women's ordination, in 1984, the Revs. Janet Crawford (Anglican) and Enid Bennett (Methodist) were appointed to the faculty of the Anglican-Methodist Theological College, which is the residential center for ministry training for both churches. Many women expended considerable energy over a number of years to secure these appointments. Similarly, in 1986, those producing an extension unit on theological education yielded to women's pressure and appointed a female colleague to work half-time to assist in developing women's resources. In Auckland, the feminist women's network has finally succeeded in establishing an Anglican Women's Resource Center (funded by the church) which offers workshops, books, and support for women and their issues. Work at the center is beginning to focus on many of the structural issues affecting women in ministry, including maternity leave for ordained women, licensing for team ministry, use of inclusive language, and experiments in spirituality based on women's experience.

An important factor in these movements has been the development of a strong women's network. Aotearoa-New Zealand is small enough to enable good communication and organizing, and therefore small enough for effective pressuring of bishops, committees and other church structures. The women's network is a primary communication and organizational resource and is organized well to achieve significant recognition. For example, in Auckland the bishop has regular meetings with the network, and that consultation has resulted in benefits for women.

Men have joined with women to produce changes on some issues, including the preparation of the new Prayer Book[11] currently in draft stage. The language in this book is inclusive in regard to humanity, and the liturgies incorporate imagery which goes beyond the traditional male images for God, who is referred to at one point as "Father and Mother of us all." There is opposition from some parts of the church to the inclusion of Maori language, as well as to the alteration of texts to be more inclusive of women, but the new material is likely to be accepted. Although many feminists desire further change, this prayer book is clearly a significant step forward.

Women are thus finding ways to participate in policy-making and in shaping the ministry and mission of the church, despite a continuing reluctance of the traditional powers and conservative elements to make room for them. As women grow in clarity and confidence they are becoming satisfied with nothing less than a theology expressing God's demand for justice: the partnership between races and all humanity and creation, in peace.

The challenge to the ecclesiastical "principalities and powers" is a vigorous and discomforting one, calling into question the church's hierarchical leadership, the allocation and use of resources, and the style and emphases of theological education. serious, structural questions are being asked. What is the role and shape of the episcopate if a church is moving towards a non-hierarchical structure? What appropriate style of leadership do women give? How do we enable a woman to become a bishop? Should women buy into the episcopal model? How might the leadership of men be changed?[12]

In a church with a shrinking cash flow but a growing investment portfolio the question of control and distribution of funds is vital. A "user pays" policy is clearly inadequate. The sharpness of such questions is felt keenly by women clergy who most often are placed in poor parishes unable to meet their financial needs. Women traditionally are part of an expendable work force, and many face redundancy in the church today. Thus, women often are forced to compete with other women for the least comfortable positions. A growing number of ordained women are working in non-stipendiary and partially supported positions. Similarly, very often women do not have access to surplus funds -- while constituting a majority of church-going Christians -- and thus face a real struggle for funds to undertake theological education and related training courses.

Traditionally, theology has been shaped by male experience and interpretation -- disguised as universal experience and wisdom. Feminist women believe that the insights and experiences of women constitute equally valid contributions to theology. While it is important that the study of feminist theology, as a distinct enterprise, be available to all who desire it, in the long term it is vital that the critique and insights from women's experience -- brought together in feminist theology -- permeate the entire theological enterprise, in both academic and pastoral settings. Feminists argue that theology must result in actions which promote social justice, and that the church in Aotearoa-New Zealand must re-examine its theology in the light of the history, experience and challenges of this country, its peoples and history.

The Present Church and the Bi-Cultural Movement

Maori people also are offering a vigorous challenge.[13] The Maori challenge includes basic demands: that the terms of the Treaty of Waitangi be upheld; that Maori sovereignty be restored; that land be returned (or at least that appropriate restitution be made for its confiscation); that there be a restoration of forest and fishing rights; that the Maori language be restored to legal usage.   The struggle to achieve these and other demands is a constant one in the courts, on the golf courses and other pieces of contested land, and in the education and health systems.   Maoritanga (culture) is being restored to its rightful place and is demanding recognition.

Several of the mainline churches have responded to this challenge by making a commitment to move towards becoming bi-cultural.[14]   These churches recognize the Treaty of Waitangi as basic to relationships in Aotearoa-New Zealand, and especially in those churches whose missionaries were involved from the beginning of the colonizing period and whose structures subsequently have denied full Maori involvement.   Theirs is a commitment, albeit gradual, to move away from being totally dominated by the English language, British style and structure, and Euro-North American theology.   What is sought is a bi-cultural relationship and church, in which both the tangata whenua (the indigenous people of the land) and the tauiwi (those who came later, the settlers) have equal place, equal power, and equal recognition through language, liturgy and leadership.

The Anglican Church, at its General Synod in 1986, adopted policies promoting a bi-cultural partnership which would recognize the rights of the Maori People.   This commitment required the clergy to learn the Maori language (if they were not already speakers of liturgical Maori).   Further, all dioceses and parishes were directed to examine land holdings and trusts and to consider their return to Maori people, or at least granting full access to them by the Maori section of the church.   Finally, all dioceses were required to establish bi-cultural committees to oversee and support moves towards partnership.

These committees have offered workshops designed to help church members explore their personal responses to these tentative steps toward bi-cultural partnership.   The committees also have planned actions which will enable local parishes, committees, and diocesan organizations to take steps to become bi-cultural in their actual processes and decisions.   Educational materials have been prepared and made widely available.   All these activities have been distressing for some church members, but new understandings are developing as the process unfolds.

The General Synod has appointed a Provincial Bi-Cultural Commission to oversee the entire process.   This commission moves around the country listening and observing the process and offering counsel where necessary.   In 1988 five people were appointed as a Bicultural Education unit for the province. There is also commission examining land issues which will consider appropriate actions of use, return, or compensation for land which was acquired by the church in unjust or illegal ways. Perhaps most importantly, the voice of Maori people in the church is being listened to more and more as the process evolves, while simultaneously there is continuing debate about the extent to which Pakeha people, as the people who currently hold power, need to take responsibility for structural change.

The General Synod, in 1988, was faced with a decision of whether to provide for autonomy for the Bishopric of Aotearoa (the Maori diocese covering all of Aotearoa-New Zealand). This is proceeding, with the development of a new constitution, due to be debated again late 1990. Such action includes a mutually satisfactory agreement outlining specific points of consultation concerning church policy and statute. This new partnership is not based on equality of numbers, but on mutual respect and due recognition for the dreams and history of the Maori people.

Responses in the Church

Inevitably there is a backlash brewing. Pakeha women, feminist women, in the church are feeling the edge of a subtle backlash which plays them off against Maori people: there is a place for either a woman or a Maori, but seldom for both; money for either a Maoari initiative or a feminist initiative, but not for both. Feminism is accused of being only a white women's self-centered, single-focus 'issue,' which must be contained until this phase passes. Nevertheless, amongst Pakeha it is women who, on the whole, continue to work most committedly towards a bi-cultural church and nation.

Clearly, the church, in the present climate, feels it must respond in some ways to the challenge of the Maori -- albeit with structural maneuverings which avoid tackling the theological and spiritual depth of faith and action. However, Pakeha feminist women support a response to Maori claims and challenges which pushes the church to look much deeper, to look to its heart and respond according to God's call for justice and peace. This support for Maori claims often results in accusations, once again, that feminists are single-issue oriented and with little understanding of the complex needs of the entire church. At other times Pakeha feminist support for Maori people results in justice issues around gender -- white male power, language, concepts of competence, male-dominated management and leadership -- being expected to yield to issues of race. Pakeha women are played off against Maori people, in part by a separation of the concerns of race and gender.

The separation of race and gender oppression into opposing concerns fails to account for their common root in an Aristotelian patriarchal system, a system established to ensure control by the right race and by the right men.

This system must be understood clearly, especially within multi-cultural societies which pride themselves on democratic principles. The one man, one vote system does not safeguard or promote cultural equality in a nation of mixed races, especially in a nation where the visitors, the late arrivals, have become more numerous, wealthy, and culturally dominant than the indigenous peoples. Nor does this concept of democracy ensure equality of the sexes while one sex retains the power of ideology creation and information. Further, the separation of race and gender oppression into opposing concerns helps perpetuate the present power structures by preventing those groups with less power from uniting to successfully challenge those with more. What is needed is a new way of distributing power, a new basis of relationship. What is needed is not division, but partnership.

Partnership is of special importance in the Aotearoa-New Zealand context because of the Treaty of Waitangi which is foundational document for all social structures. When it was signed, the treaty was understood to be a document ensuring partnership between the tauiwi and the Maori peoples -- not a partnership between individuals, but one between two sovereign peoples. This relationship does not depend on equality of numbers, nor on shared values and goals, but on respect between peoples who are different, and whose differences are valued and seen as gifts to the other. This partnership is built on justice between peoples, on shared access to information and decision-making mutually valued. Structurally, such partnership enables two groups (Maori and Pakeha, or women and men, e.g.) to have equal decision-making power regardless of the numerical strength in each group.

The bi-cultural movement in the churches is struggling to develop both theology and structures to express and sustain this partnership. The healthy growth and development of this partnership among equals requires a shift in the androcentrism of church theology and structures. Women are leaving the church in Aotearoa-New Zealand and this trend will continue unless there is greater evidence that the efforts of women to share the ministry -- and to participate in incarnating new theological visions -- are valued. Feminist women in the church do not seek a replacement of patriarchy by matriarchy, but rather a transformation of theology and structures which supports mutuality and justice, a sharing of responsibilities, and real peace.

For Christian women and men in New Zealand who are Pakeha, the women's call for partnership is a hopeful sign which indicates a willingness to struggle towards relationships based on mutuality despite years of hurt and disregard. However, establishing such relationships requires of men real efforts to change traditional domineering and power-mongering ways. Not only must individual men change their own ways, but also they must take responsibility to initiate and lead the struggle, among men, to relinquish the privileges inherent in traditional patriarchal institutions.

The Pakeha are being offered a chance for repentance and reconciliation by the Maori people whose hospitality we abused. The hand of partnership being extended to us is a priceless gift. We Pakeha must struggle with our own ingrained superiorities, prejudices and fears -- before Maori patience wears thin -- in order to grasp the historic and gracious opportunity given us. The Maori hand of partnership can be withdrawn, and the loss to the Pakeha -- and to the whole culture -- of the priceless gift of partnership would be tragic.

The coming together of these two challenges -- the feminist and the Maori -- means that church life and structure is considerably shaken. The shaking is inevitable as pressure comes from both church and wider socio-political forces in New Zealand society. Therefore, in Aotearoa-New Zealand, partnership is both a theological and a structural concept. Without change in both these complementary elements, the opportunity to build an egalitarian society first imperfectly envisioned by the earliest settlers will be lost. With change in both these elements -- structural and theological change which incorporates the wisdom of the Maori and the women -- a new and vibrant society and church in which all peoples contribute and thrive will begin to bloom in the land all call home.

NOTES

1.   Aotearoa (translated as "land of the long white cloud") is used in some Maori traditions to describe part of the set of South Pacific islands known as New Zealand. Over recent times, Maori have begun to use the term as a name for the country in order to claim the land for its indigenous people. In days of increased awareness of past history, many now use "Aotearoa-New Zealand" as a way of recognizing the dual histories and present reality of these islands.

2.   Keith Sinclair, A History of New Zealand, Penguin, 1959, provides an overview of the history, interpretation of this history is being revised on recognition that it has been presented dominantly from a European perspective. Elsie Locke, Two Peoples, One Land, (Govt. Print, 1988), provides a simple re-appraisal. The sources in Allan K. Davidson and Peter J. Lineham, Transplanted Christianity, (London: College Communications, 1987), provide an overview of early church history here, while W.P. Morrell, The Anglican Church in New Zealand, (Anglican Church of the Province of N.Z., 1973), relates Anglican history.

3.   Much has been written on this Treaty over recent years. It is now being seen as the "foundation document of the nation", and critical for Maori-Pakeha relations. Claudia Orange, The Treaty of Waitangi, (London: Allen and Unwin, 1987), covers the history and issues in depth.

4.   Te Kaupapa Tikanga Rua: Bi-Cultural Development, The Report of the Bi-Cultural Commission of the Anglican Church on the Treaty of Waitangi, written in 1986, outlines Maori Anglican history and the story of the Constitution.

5.   Much detailed information is now becoming available, such as in Helen Yensen, Kevin Hague and Tim McCreanor (ed), Honouring the Treaty, (London: Penguin, 1989); Te Kaupapa Tikanga Rua, op. cit.; Jane Kelsey, A Question of Honour?, (London: Allen and Unwin, 1990).

6.   See Report of the Ordained Women's Conference 1989, (Anglican Women's Resource Centre, 1990); Ruth Fry, Out of the Silence: Methodist Women of Aotearoa 1822-1985, (Melbourne: Methodist Publishing, 1987).

7.   P. Bunkle and B. Hughes, eds., Women in New Zealand Society, (London: Allen and Unwin, 1980), and C. Bell and V. Adair, Women and Change: A Study of New Zealand Women, (National Council of Women, 1985),

relate the establishment and role of the early groups and the move towards suffrage, as well as more recent issues for women; Christine Dann, Up From Under: Women and Liberation in New Zealand, (London: Allen and Unwin, 1985), focuses on the more recent story; Bev James and Kay Saville-Smith, Gender, Culture, and Power, (Oxford: Oxford University Press, 1989), show the interaction between Maori and Pakeha, women and men.

8. Identified in general by many women writers, such as Rosemary Radford Ruether, Sexism and God-Talk, (New York: SCM, 1983), and Elisabeth Schussler Fiorenza, Bread Not Stone, (Boston: Beacon Press, 1984); and in the New Zealand context by Susan Adams and John Salmon, Women, Culture, and Theology, (Methodist Education and Women's Resource Centre, 1988).

9. Ratana was a Maori leader who sought to re-interpret Biblical material in a Maori context; the Ratana movement still coexists alongside the traditional Christian churches. See James Irwin, "Some Maori Responses to the Western Form of Christianity", in Christopher Nichol and James Veitch, eds., Religion in New Zealand, (Victoria: Victoria University, 1983).

10. Aspects of the role of women in the Anglican church in Aotearoa-New Zealand, the development of the feminist network and Resource Center, and the perspectives of feminist women are related in the Report of the Ordained Women's Conference 1989, op. cit., and Susan Adams, Towards a Reshaped Church: Feminist Projects for Theological Education for Women Within the Context of the Church, Thesis for DMin in Feminist Liberation Theology and Ministry, Episcopal Divinity School, Cambridge, Mass., 1989.

11. A New Zealand Prayer Book: He Karakia Mihinare o Aotearoa, Church of the Province of New Zealand, 1989.

12. In June 1990, the Rev. Dr. Penny Jamieson was ordained as Bishop in the Diocese of Dunedin, the second woman to become bishop in the Anglican Communion, and the first Diocesan bishop. Questions about the style of ministry and leadership offered by women in the church continue.

13. See, for example, Donna Awatere, Maori Sovereignty, (Auckland: Broadsheet, 1984).

14. The Anglican, Methodist, and Roman Catholic Churches have all made this commitment, and the Presbyterian church is moving in a similar direction. See Te Kaupapa Tikanga Rua, op. cit.; John Salmon, ed., Our Methodist Bicultural Journey: Some History, Theology, and Resources, (Methodist Bicultural Committee, 1989).

FAITH AND POLITICS IN LATIN AMERICA

J. Antonio Ramos

The 26 years since I graduated from the Episcopal Theological School, and took with me into a changing world Bill Wolf's lessons in theology, have been a time for shaking the foundations of church and world. My own faith commitments and practice also have been shaken and re-shaped by forces only vaguely perceived in 1962, although even then the winds of change were blowing across the seas from other continents and across this continent from Black freedom fighters. In 1962, in Cambridge, Massachusetts, however, few if any of us could foresee how thoroughly the liberation movements of the Two-Thirds World (including Black, Hispanic and Asian Americans, and women everywhere) would challenge not only the political principalities and powers, but also their brothers in ecclesiastical realms.

I next encountered Bill Wolf at one of those shaking events, this one in Philadelphia on July 29, 1974, where he and I, with hundreds of sisters and brothers, joined our hands in the ordination of the first 11 women priests of the Episcopal Church. The systematic and abstract theology of the classroom suddenly was overtaken by the liberating praxis of a community of faith, willing to disobey the constitutional and canonical order of the church in order to open the Orders of that church to women. It was as if liberation theology had reached the Episcopal Church in the United States of America with the "rush of a mighty wind," throwing into turmoil its ecclesiological structures, and forcing it to a re-definition of those long-standing doctrinal positions which for centuries had denied women priesthood and episcopacy.

In its most popular connotation, liberation theology has to do with the practice of Christians in the transformation of society, liberating it from the powers of death and oppression. However, liberation theology equally has to do with the liberation of the church from its own powers of death and oppression and its transformation into an instrument of God's justice. Therefore, the role of all women, including the priesthood and episcopacy of women called to canonical orders, is a crucial matter which concerns liberation theology and which liberation theologians and movements must address aggressively and creatively. That work for and with women, as the work for and with all the oppressed, calls liberation theologians to witness and struggle for radical change, even at the risk of punishment, banishment or martyrdom. The known and unknown witnesses who have enriched us and our faith remind us that our commitment to stand alongside, and struggle with and for, the poor and oppressed of this world must not grow weaker but ever stronger. Liberation in the structures and life of the church must enable the liberation of God's people, just as the liberation of God's people must enable the liberation of the church to become the sign and instrument of God's just realm "on earth as it is in heaven."

The Emergence of Latin American Liberation Theology

Thus the topic of faith and politics is at the heart of liberation theology. Indeed it is reflection, from the perspective of faith, on the political practice of Christians in Latin America that led to the development of -- and continues to form the foundation of -- liberation theology. This reflection has led to what Puerto Rican church historian Samuel Silva Gotay has called the rise of "Christian revolutionaries" in the witness and role of the church today.

In his analysis of conditions in Latin America at the end of the 1950s and during the 1960s, Gotay states that what came together were

the appropriate conditions, both material and theoretical, for the participation by Christians in a political and social praxis which would lead to a greater radicalization and re-formulation of the theoretical supposition with which they make their entry in the political process.[1]

The events or 'signs of the times' that led to this radicalization of the popular sectors and to a significant revolutionary militancy by parts of the Christian community may be summarized as follows:

1.   The social, economic, political and religious crisis facing Latin America at the end of the 1950s;

2.   The breakthrough in the understanding of 'development' and 'underdevelopment,' i.e., 'the theory of dependence;'

3.   The Cuban Revolution and its impact on Latin America and the United States;

4.   The crisis in Christendom and the birth of new models of church life, i.e., the base ecclesial communities.

Let us look briefly at these four factors.

Pablo Richard, the Chilean priest and theologian who has lived and worked in Central America for some years, dates the development of liberation theology to the colonial period. Latin America, enormously wealthy in natural and human resources, was brought to economic, political, cultural and religious underdevelopment by greedy European powers and local ruling classes functioning as their dependent agents of exploitation.   In Richard's view, it was within this context that Christianity developed in Latin America, confronted with the options of oppression (of Indians and later Black slaves) and liberation. He sees these polar terms, domination/liberation, as standing "at the heart of the Latin American church from the beginning..."[2]

My own experience as a child raised in a rural area of Puerto Rico during the Great Depression, my ministry in Puerto Rico and Costa Rica, and my work during the past seven years in solidarity with the poor and oppressed throughout the region, reminds me of the truth of Richard's words. These historical conditions, prevailing to this day among the masses of people, are themselves a harsh judgment on the church which, generally speaking, has chosen to side not with the poor but with the powers of domination and death. Further, these conditions provide the basis for new understandings in Latin America about the region's relationship with the rest of the world, particularly the colonialists of Europe and North America.

In Latin America, the end of the 1950s signaled the close of yet another decade of social and economic stagnation and increasing repression. Latin America still was trying to recover from the depression of the 1930s. The programs of industrial and social development promoted by populist governments, programs designed to foster nationalist economies throughout the region, had resulted in more general poverty, as well as continuing underdevelopment and greater dependence. In turn, increasing frustration and skepticism greeted development policies offered by the rich nations and their allies among the privileged domestic oligarchies.

The decade of the 1960s, which had been inaugurated with such high expectations by the very popular and charismatic U.S. president John Kennedy, was soon mired in successive frustrations: the failure of the Kennedy-inspired Alliance for Progress, the increasing militarization of the continent, the installation of repressive regimes, and the denationalization of local economies. According to Hugo Assman it is in "this context of accumulated frustrations that the opposition critical of developmentalist models emerges and is brought together in the theory of dependence."[3]   Thus, a new level of political consciousness arose and various sectors came to understand that the underdevelopment of the region is the direct result of the development of the nations of the North which, through their social, economic and political policies, have perpetuated conditions of domination and dependence among the nations of the Two-Thirds World. Throughout Latin America leaders began to realize that the only solution for the region, to deal successfully with the dependent/domination cycle, was to reject the very model which promotes and perpetuates greater dependence -- i.e., the only alternative to oppression and domination is liberation. Only a radical transformation will free Latin America from misery and oppression. The struggle must be more than one against outside imperialism because Latin America is engaged in a class struggle, present inside the region since colonial days. And the Cuban Revolution of 1959 provided new fuel for the struggle.

The success of the Cuban Revolution persuaded increasing numbers of Latin Americans that the only possible response to continuing domination from the North lay not in gradual change but revolutionary action, including armed insurrection, to assume power and achieve social reconstruction. There are at least four ways that the revolution had a significant impact on the whole of Latin America. First, for those seeking radical change from the conditions of colonialism and domination, it represented an act of liberation from an oppressive local regime and the repressive tutelage of the United States, a real declaration of independence by a relatively small island nation. Hope for liberation rose throughout the region.

Second, revolutionary Cuba provided a model of political and economic organization geared to meet the basic needs of the majority of the people, the poor, especially when it adopted, following the stabilization of the new regime, a Marxist orientation and socialist policies. Of course, it was this political decision, not the actual liberation from the Batista dictatorship, which created the excuse in the United States for the policy of punishing Cuba. The adoption of a socialist/Marxist model ran contrary to the economic interests of the local oligarchical interests and their foreign allies which until 1959 had dominated the political and economic life of the country. Since 1959, concerted efforts at the continental level have been made to insure a similar revolutionary outcome is avoided in various countries -- the Dominican Republic, Brazil, Guatemala, Chile, and Grenada, for example. Most recently, Nicaragua has borne the brunt of this imperialist strategy.

Thus, throughout the 1960s and 1970s two opposite but interrelated developments were visible throughout Latin America: on the one hand, a growing radicalization of the popular sectors, leading in some instances to armed insurrection, and, on the other, the implementation of counter-insurgency measures and the installation throughout the region of repressive regimes subservient to a 'national security' ideology. More recently, these repressive military regimes (in Argentina, Brazil, Uruguay, Guatemala, and El Salvador, e.g.) have been replaced by so-called "restricted democracies" -- civilian governments propped up by the powerful elements within the armed forces.

Finally, we must consider the position of the church in regard to the revolution. In 1959, the church and the majority of the Christian community either absented itself or opposed the Cuban revolution and its socialist model. Such was not the case in Chile during the Allende government (1970-73), nor has it been true in Nicaragua (despite the United States' preoccupation with the split between Cardinal Obando y Bravo and the Sandinistas). The Cuban Revolution occurred prior to the rising of political consciousness of Christians and the growth of liberation theology, and of course, the revolution contributed directly to both.

However, another event in January, 1959 (the Cuban revolutionaries emerged victorious on the first day of the new year) signalled change within the church. On the 25th, Pope John XXIII announced the convening of the Second Vatican Council. According to Pablo Richard, these seemingly disparate events

> announced to us in Latin America in a remarkable way the direction of our future Christian and theological evolution: from revolution to council. We experienced a Latin American revolution before the council. Throughout this whole period the experience of events continually preceded the reading of official texts.[4]

The Second Vatican Council (1962-65) met at a time when Latin American Christians were already facing the problems and opportunities of simultaneous faith and revolution. The militant political practice of Christians on behalf of the poor was already finding expression in different forms and at different levels in Latin American society. Both the Second Vatican Council and the more significant meeting for Latin Americans, the Latin American Conference of Bishops of 1968 at Medellín, Colombia, were important because they provided "official expression and an ecclesial dimension to historical processes already underway." Christians, both Roman Catholics and Protestants, were already engaged in a "revolutionary and social practice and had elaborated a theology of liberation" arising out of their specific political practices. Camilo Torres and Ernesto 'Ché' Guevara, and many others who suffered persecution and torture, became heroes.

The Medellín conference legitimated use of the already well developed concept of 'liberation.' In fact, prior to Medellín, the concept of 'liberation' became a vigorous challenge to the church and its traditional theology -- participated in popular movements, leftist parties and actual violent insurrections. During the 1970s and 1980s the process of liberation theology, originally popularized in pamphlets and seminars, became a full body of theological thinking which to this time nurtures the political practice of base ecclesial communities and other popular movements working with the poor and exploited as agents of liberation. Today the church continues to be challenged to reorient its pastoral and institutional life with a "preferential option for the poor" as God's agents and instruments for the liberation of humanity.

The Significance of the Political Practice of Christians in Latin America

The disappearance, torture, imprisonment, exile and death of thousands of women and men, many of them militant Christians, in Argentina, Brazil, Paraguay, Uruguay, Chile, Guatemala and El Salvador, constitute the clearest evidence of the militant political practice of those who have been, and continue to be, willing to follow the 'way of the Cross' for their people. The triumph of the Sandinista Revolution in 1979 and the subsequent participation of Christians in the reconstruction of Nicaraguan society in line with "the logic of the majority" (the poor and dispossessed), continued (until the United States engineered the electoral defeat of the Sandinistas in 1990) as a visible witness to the option which substantial communities of Christians have chosen in the practice of their faith. The emergence and growth of the base ecclesial communities in Brazil, Paraguay and Central America, a church of the poor experiencing a renewed evangelical, pastoral and eucharistic praxis and serving as leaven in their societies, is a strong testimony to the dynamic power of life of the crucified and risen Christ.

The development of liberation theology as a theological process emerging from the praxis of an option for the poor -- from the very womb of the growing base ecclesial communities -- testifies to the revolutionary changes in Christian practice in Latin America. Liberation theology represents a radical transformation of religious thinking in Latin America -- root changes in the 'doing' of theology, in hermeneutics, in the "ways of conceiving evangelization, pastoral activity, the building of the church, and the task of theology." Pablo Richard describes the change this way:

> Theologians moved out of theology departments and seminaries and went to the grassroots movements: a theological renewal began in a direct and ongoing dialogue with Christians who were well on their way to being politically radicalized.[5]

The point of departure for Latin American liberation theology is not revealed truth, established doctrine, or dogma, but the social, economic, political, and religious situation of the continent -- colonized, exploited, dominated, oppressed, suffering Latin America. Its primary foci are the poor majorities of the continent who are deprived of the basic human requirements: food, drinking water, shelter, education, participation in their own self-fulfillment and in the construction of their society and personal destiny.

Therefore, the practice of faith must be based in a solid understanding of the historical reality of the continent. Moreover, this understanding encompasses a critical component which enables action to transform the society. Radicalizing the 'theory of dependency,' liberation theologians and social analysts conclude that the fundamental problem in the history of Latin America is not only one of domination/dependence, but also a question of class struggle inherent in the capitalistic colonial system. In this situation, the tools of Marxist analysis most accurately explain reality and appropriately assist in developing the necessary strategies for a radical transformation of society through socialism -- rather than through the developmental model which serves the interest of the minority ruling classes in Latin America and abroad.

Liberation theology is a reflection on the political practice of Christians as they join the poor in their struggle for liberation and the construction of a new society built on the principles of equality and justice. The re-reading of the Bible and of the church's teachings from the perspective of the poor becomes a primary fact of knowing God, not in abstraction but in the very lives and struggles of the poor and oppressed. God is rediscovered as the God of the Exodus -- indignant and not indifferent to oppression -- who acts to liberate; a God who assumes our humanity in Jesus of Nazareth to make the cause of the least ones a godly cause and inaugurate the realm of God "on earth as it is in heaven."

Liberation theology affirms that the practice of our faith in Jesus Christ is not an apolitical act, but always a political one which involves the church, Christian community, and the individual person in an option -- a class option. We are confronted with the option of God or Mammon, life or death, poor or rich, the human person or the sabbath, liberation or oppression. Our faith engages us in the praxis of the politics of God's realm, of which the church is sign and instrument.

The poor in Latin America, just as the oppressed in South Africa, are evangelizing the church, calling Christians to their true vocation as servants of a liberating God. Standing in solidarity with those who suffer injustice is a pastoral act, a spiritual practice deeply rooted in faith in a just and loving God. As God is just and loving, so, too, is that our call. Reading the homilies of Archbishop Arnulfo Romero of San Salvador, for example, brings us in touch with the deep spirituality present in the struggle for liberation. This man, before his own martyrdom in 1980, was himself converted and transformed by the death and suffering of his own people. In El Salvador, Nicaragua, Brazil, and other parts of the continent, we experience today the emergence of the Church of the Poor. Their very presence is both an announcement and a judgment, for the crucified and risen one is in their midst.[6]

Conclusion

During the past 30 years, we in Latin America have experienced the consolidation of the Cuban Revolution which, despite its setback in 1990, will continue to flourish in ways yet to be discovered. Both revolutionary struggles were applauded when they served to undermine established dictatorships, just as more recently the efforts to overthrow Marcos in the Philippines and Duvalier in Haiti were supported. The central controversy in these instances has not been the practice of Christians and non-Christians to bring down the mighty: in some cases such actions are resisted; in others, supported.

Rather, the process of liberation becomes an issue when those who assume power engage in a conscious political, economic and social project to lift the meek and lowly from their misery and exploitation -- thus fulfilling the prophetic words of the Magnificat. Strongest opposition to liberation movements arises at just that moment when true liberation begins: when popular movements begin to re-organize society, not on the logic of the minority which has exploited the majority, but on the logic of the poor and outcast, the majority, historically deprived of the benefits of their labor and basic human dignity. The reason there has been such violent struggle in Nicaragua is that the liberating forces, the Sandinistas and the Church of the Poor, have been engaged in democratizing the economy and social structures, by actively participating, on the side of the poor, in the class struggle which has marked Latin America ever since the European colonizers first reached our shores. The United States government, recognizing that this struggle has ultimate consequences for the entire hemisphere, has resisted the democratization process and sustained those within Nicaragua whose self-interest lies with maintaining political and economic exploitation. The U.S.-financed victory in 1990 of the United Nicaraguan Opposition was, temporarily, a vindication of the U.S. policy of resistance to the democratization of Nicaragua.

The conscious and massive participation of Christians in the revolutionary process of Nicaragua threatened the principalities and powers -- civil and ecclesiastical -- because people of faith struggled not only to put down "the mighty from their seats, but also to lift up the humble and meek." Such participation was threatening to the institutional church because it denied the historical privileges resulting from the church's alliance with the ruling classes, and because it created the conditions for the birth of new models of ecclesia, the Church of the Poor in the hands of those to whom God has promised the keys of God's realm.

Despite the 1990 election in Nicaragua, the implications of the radical process of social transformation are rich with possibility for the life of the church throughout the Two-Thirds World, liberating it to be the servant church of God in Christ. Moreover, the conscious and massive participation of Christians with others in the popular sectors in Nicaragua represented, throughout Latin America, a liberating force which promises to transform the continent and the wider world into a "new heaven and a new earth," not of the afterlife, but of our times, however long the struggle may be.

Once again, as the history of God's people continues to unfold, faith and politics merge to confront us with the central question: do we stand for God's justice, do we march on the path of liberation, or do we deny our God and perpetuate injustice? This question challenges our Anglican thinking, as well as the Anglican presence and structures in Latin America, and certainly in the United States and elsewhere -- everywhere the struggle between oppression and liberation, death and life, is being engaged, not only academically but also within the daily lives of people.

The Anglican community in Latin America is not only a witness to the confrontation between demonic powers of death and the godly powers of life, but also a participant in the midst of the struggle. No faith community, including the Anglican, can adopt a position of non-involvement, neutrality, or silence. To pretend to be uninvolved or neutral is to take the side of those whose historical dominance has created incredible suffering and death; to be silent is to speak loudly in support of this suffering and death.[7]

Anglican history, worldwide, is tainted with the burden of colonialism, slavery, racism, exploitation, and oppression. Today, Anglicanism, in its Episcopal expression in the U.S., is part and parcel of a society which organizes, supports and funds the powers of death and destruction in Central America. In Central America, Anglicanism is being challenged to overcome its foreignness and elitism, and its traditional catering to expatriate minority compounds -- symbols of the colonial age. The challenge to Anglicanism today is to become rooted in Latin American soil, incarnating the face and destiny of the poor and oppressed, their struggles and hopes. In the United States, Anglicanism is being challenged to become a prophetic witnessing community, freeing an oppressive society from its own demonic powers which so disastrously affect the lives of people at home and abroad.

The profound message arising out of the struggle of men and women of faith throughout the hemisphere is that prior to the survival of the church stands the redemption, liberation and salvation of society and the entire human race from the demonic forces of death. "God so loved the world... " (not the church). Maintaining the status quo is a denial of the principle of solidarity inherent to the life of the church as a Body of Christ. The unity of the church cannot be achieved while structures and conditions of injustice exist both in society and in the church. Neither church nor society can escape the purifying and liberating love of the God who desires justice, whose realm has indeed come.

NOTES

1.   Samuel Silva Gotay, El pensamiento cristiano revolucionario en América Latina y el Caribe (Salamanca, España: Ediciones Sígueme, 1981), p. 29. The quotations from this book are my English translation. The title in English would be Christian Revolutionary Thinking in Latin America and the Caribbean. An excellent book which analyzes the birth and development of liberation theology and its implications for the sociology of religion.

2.   Pablo Richard, Death of Christendom, Birth of the Church (Maryknoll, NY: Orbis, 1987), p. 24. Also an excellent work which focuses on an economic, sociological and political analysis of the church in Latin America, its birth and development, describing how the church functions as an obstacle to or an instrument of liberation.

3.   Hugo Assman, Opresión-Liberación, Desafío a los Cristianos (Montevideo, Uruguay: Tierra Nueva, 1971), p. 43. These quotations are also my translation. In English the book would be entitled Oppression-Liberation, A Challenge to Christians.

4.   Richard, p. 143.

5.   Ibid., p. 147.

6.   Pablo Richard, La Fuerza Espiritual de la Iglesia de los Pobres (San Jose, Costa Rica: Editorial DEI, 1987). This book (in my English translation, The Spiritual Force of the Poor) analyzes the birth and development of the base communities and of the Popular Church or "Church of the Poor," with a focus on Nicaragua and El Salvador.

7.   In ecclesiastical realms, as in secular ones, the 'principalities and powers' often use the tactic of 'divide and conquer' to maintain the status quo. Setting the stage so that proponents of women priests and bishops and anti-apartheid activists must fight against one another rather than join forces against the structures of domination choking both women and racial 'minorities' is a well-worn tactic which often divides liberation forces. So are delaying tactics aimed at soothing the 'feelings' of those in power. However, the Holy Spirit brings hope in spite of the best efforts of oppressors. The election and consecration of Barbara Harris as the Suffragan Bishop of Massachusetts is a sign of hope for these times. The struggle continues.

THE BROKEN FEET

Joanna Kadi

No one ever heard Aunt Rose's dreams about life or hopes for the future. Did she want to finish high school, perhaps earn a university degree? Did she want to travel? To build things, write down ideas, study her beloved music? I don't know and neither does anyone else, but there is a good chance she didn't dream much at all. Class defines dreams as surely as it defines the part of town you live in. The stunting and killing of desires and dreams happen at a young age; it is a necessary condition for working-class exploitation. There are many ways this happens, one of the most important being that dreams are a luxury when survival is at stake. Working-class women of colour have no time for dreams when day-to-day existence demands careful, detailed planning and action.[1]

Dreams or no dreams, the future didn't hold much for Aunt Rose. She left high school before graduation because her father died, and as the oldest of five children she had to help her mother provide food and rent money. After many jobs, she worked her way up to a secure position as secretary at the Canadian post office, an institution known for management mistreatment of labour. In the manager's office, Aunt Rose was somewhat removed from the workers but never forgot where she came from or where her loyalties lay. Through every strike (and there were many) she was adamant in her support of the union and her condemnation of management. "Those people," she would say emphatically, "they don't care one bit about the rest of us."

In many ways she had her class analysis down pat, as we all did. I am still surprised today when someone involved in a movement for social change suddenly discovers the systematic evils of capitalism, something I knew viscerally before I could talk. Aunt Rose understood the politics of the post office. She understood the politics of the General Motors factory where my father and uncle worked, and often condemned the corrupt people in power there. Her class analysis was such that when I told her of my arrest for trespassing at a plant manufacturing guidances systems for the Cruise missile, she snorted and said sarcastically, "They're arresting you?" She knew who the real criminals were.

Aunt Rose was a tiny woman who wore unbelievably high-heeled shoes all her life. I see those heels as a metaphor for her hope that she might be noticed in spite of the three strikes against her (race, sex, class) that made her invisible to so many people. When we would sit and talk at her house, she always had her shoes off. Her feet were grotesque, mangled parodies of feet. The Broken Feet, I mentally titled them. If the heels were a metaphor for attempted visibility, The Broken Feet were a metaphor for what life-long oppression did to her.

It was near the end of Aunt Rose's life that I realized she was an alcoholic. For decades she had been swallowing alcohol, often openly, often when no one was around. The working-class bars are mostly for men. Women drink at home, but the result is the same. The oppressor gains. It is, I think, no accident that all oppressed groups abuse one substance or another and that our oppressors do whatever is necessary to keep us supplied. Drugs work to keep the oppressors in power because drugged-out victims are easy to control and do not revolt, and because drugs help keep us silent. Alcohol was one of the things that kept Aunt Rose silent. Swallow some alcohol, swallow some words. Swallow some alcohol, swallow some stories. Swallow some alcohol, swallow some history. Take the words, the stories, the history -- which this society has no use for -- to the grave. And Aunt Rose did.

By the time I realized this, she was dying of cancer. When I came out to her she was in a coma from which she never recovered. She was a sack of bones, the size of a child. She was the second matriarch of our family to die in this way, my grandmother having died years before. After Gram's death, Aunt Rose had named herself matriarch and was indeed one of the key purveyors of our Lebanese culture and heritage.

No one ever heard Aunt Rose's story except those of us in her family (and even we don't know the whole story). Why? No one wanted to. No one assumed she had anything to say. No one cared. One reason no one cared was because she was working-class. That is one of the big things about being working-class in a classist society. No one cares about your broken feet, your secret drinking, your illiterate relatives, your class analysis, your stunted dreams, your sense of humour. No one cares how or when you die, as long as you have reproduced enough children to take your place on the line.

*****

Like many of us, I thought I had come home when I came out as a radical lesbian feminist.[2] I thought I had reached nirvana. Wrong. Racism, classism, groups working to legalize child sexual abuse (or intergenerational sex, as it is euphemistically called in some circles), and a preponderance of privileged white men in leadership positions were some of the things I discovered in gay and lesbian communities.

Classism operates in a variety of ways in gay and lesbian communities, as it does in other segments of society. There is denial that class differences exist among us and a refusal to take seriously what this means. There is silencing of working-class gays and lesbians; sometimes this happens by informing those of us who are working-class that we aren't REALLY working-class because we're in graduate school, or we're writers, or we own a house, or whatever; sometimes this is done by massive outpourings of guilt by middle and upper-class people who, by doing so, manage to continue dominating the conversation. There is the assumption that the only issue around class is money, and if your group or service is one of the very few in the gay community which has sliding scale payment for dues or events then you're exempt from the discussion.

There is a surprising amount of ignorance among progressive folk concerning class oppression. People with detailed analyses of racism and sexism often know little about this brutal form of oppression. I see two reasons for this. One, as philosopher Marilyn Frye points out, becomes obvious upon hearing the active verb 'to ignore' in the word 'ignorance.'[3] I have come to believe middle-class political activists choose to ignore class oppression; they do not want to examine their personal privileges and oppressive practices. A second reason is the lies, some old and some new, circulated by the ruling class. Some of these destructive and contradictory pieces of disinformation include; class stratification does not exist anymore, class is not an important category, certain types of people are better suited for manual labour (class is a biological construct), class is not one of the major constructs/constraints in a person's life, movement out of a "lower" class to a "higher" class happens easily, class is about income level and nothing else.[4]

Well, class oppression thrives today as it has for centuries. And it seems to me the place to start dealing with classism is by listening to and honouring stories about working-class people like my Aunt Rose. These are several reasons for this. It will lay the foundation for the kind of class analysis necessary for liberation movements. It will allow for a deeper awareness of racism, because so many of us who are working-class are also people of colour. It will also allow for the kind of global and historical understanding crucial for a coherent political analysis; for example, beneath Aunt Rose's experiences of oppression in Canada is France's imperialist takeover of Lebanon that sent many people scrambling for a new country. But, putting all those reasons aside, we must remember these stories are necessary for our survival. Aunt Rose's feet were broken, her dreams were killed before they could take shape. If we don't honour her memory and understand what happened to her, it will keep happening to us.

NOTES

1.   I explore this point and others in relation to the killing of working-class dreams in my Master's thesis, <u>Searching for Words, Searching for Knowledge</u>, Episcopal Divinity School, Cambridge, Mass., April 1990.

2.   For more on the concept of "Coming Home," see S. Hogland's <u>The Coming Out Stories</u>.

3.   Marilyn Frye, "On Being White," <u>The Politics of Reality</u> (Trumansburg, NY: The Crossing Press, 1983), pp. 118-121.

4.   Dr. Katie Cannon, Associate Professor of Ethics at the Episcopal Divinity School, has named 13 factors which determine a person's class location.   These are: ancestry, economic income, style of life, education, interpersonal relations, manners, social distance, values, ideology, religious affiliation, motivations, expectations and language. Dr. Cannon discussed these points in her class, Ethics 180: Genealogy of Race, Sex and Class Oppression, Spring 1990.

PART THREE

WOMEN, SEX, AND POWER:
SHIFTING FOUNDATIONS IN AN UNEASY CHURCH

JULY 29, 1974, PHILADELPHIA: KAIROS AS PARADIGM SHIFT

Suzanne R. Hiatt

One of the legends that persists at the Episcopal Divinity School concerns an annual contest between Bill Wolf and Massey Shepherd, professor of Church History at Episcopal Theological School from 1940 to 1954. It is said that every year Bill Wolf would preach a sermon calling for the immediate ordination of women to the priesthood and that every year Massey Shepherd would storm out of the service in disgust.

The contest was already legend by the time I arrived at ETS in 1961, even though Dr. Shepherd had moved on to the Church Divinity School of the Pacific. Bill's interest in women's ordination had not flagged, however. Largely at his urging, ETS began accepting women (and other non-postulants) into the B.D. degree program in the fall of 1958 and graduated three women in June 1961. I wrote a paper for Bill on the ordination of women in 1964.

His encouragement of and delight in the women students was widely appreciated. He once told me in hushed tones that he had actually met the legendary Florence Li Tim Oi, the Chinese woman ordained priest in China in 1944 and that despite all the raging of Lambeth 1948, she continued her priestly ministry. (Indeed, she was one of the con-celebrants of the eucharist at the ordination of Barbara C. Harris to the episcopate in February, 1989. By that time retired and living in Canada, the first woman priest in the Anglican communion took part in the consecration of the first woman bishop 45 years later.)

In the years between 1964 and 1974 when 11 women deacons were irregularly ordained to the priesthood in Philadelphia, Bill was one of two Episcopal seminary professors who consistently and doggedly encouraged women in our effort to seek this particular sign of justice from the church. (The other was the Rev. Henry H. Rightor of Virginia Theological Seminary.) Bill preached at my ordination to the diaconate in 1971 and on that occasion called for the immediate ordination of women to the priesthood and episcopate as well. Bill's sermon put the theologian's imprimatur on the growing movement in American church circles to do just that.

In 1981 I wrote, in the form of a letter to an English deaconess, the description that follows of the 1974 and 1975 ordinations and their aftermath. Bill had urged me to write about those events and this is what came of his urging. The letter never was sent as I recall, nor was the material published, so it is altogether fitting that it should appear in slightly revised and updated form 10 years later in a _festschrift_ for Bill.

*****

October, 1981

Dear Anne,

You have asked me to tell you in some detail about the irregular ordination of women priests of which I was part in July, 1974. I thought perhaps writing out some of my reflections would be helpful to the movement for the ordination of women in England as you ponder strategies.

As I go over the material in my files in an attempt to pull together how women's ordination happened here, I am struck by what a solid groundswell of effort and commitment preceded any thought of irregular ordination. What I had not realized was how many "false starts" were made along the road to our ordination in July, 1974. The other thing I had not realized was the depth of commitment of the ordaining bishops, the women deacons, and countless others and how long and hard most of them had been working towards this end.

Let me deal first with the false starts. When I first approached the Rt. Rev. Robert L. DeWitt, Bishop of Pennsylvania, about ordaining me (in the summer of 1970), he and I were both excited about the prospect of simply processing me like any male postulant or candidate. Canon law did not expressly state that such persons were to be male and we both thought a good case could be made for interpreting "he" in the relevant canons generically. Since the issue had never come up in General Convention (like the English Synod except it only meets every three years) and there was no great agitation about it, he thought it likely that the Standing Committee (the clerical and lay advisory group in each diocese which must approve all ordinations) could be convinced that it was perfectly legal and proper to proceed with my ordination. Indeed, they did take the first steps and I was officially accepted as a postulant for Holy Orders in September, 1970. You'll notice I did not say for the diaconate -- it was clear to all concerned that I was called to priesthood.

There are two reasons why this procedure did not result in my priesting in due course in 1972. First, General Convention did take up the matter of ordaining women in October, 1970, and the resolution to admit women to all Holy Orders failed by a narrow margin in the clergy order. (I was involved in making sure it did come up, so cannot feel too cheated by that turn of events.) Even after that, Bishop DeWitt still intended to proceed with my candidacy and ordination. He remarked to me at the convention that such a move would be anomalous, but that the church needed a few anomalies (i.e., me) wandering around in its ranks.

However, the convention did vote to admit women to the diaconate in accordance with the recommendation of The Lambeth Conference of Bishops, in 1968. This was an entirely separate move from the earlier defeat for women priests and bishops -- the diaconate as booby prize, as it were. Furthermore, the defeat of priesthood for women was so close -- in fact a majority had voted for it -- that we decided we probably could work hard and get it accepted at the next convention in 1973. It was worth a year's delay to have the ordination of women irrefutably legal and for me to be one of a number of women priests in different dioceses rather than a lone anomaly. So I remained a postulant and met all the requirements for both diaconal and priestly ordination. I was ordained deacon with six men right on schedule in June, 1971.

We had, of course, underestimated the opposition and despite great efforts by many people, the 1973 convention defeated women's ordination by a more substantial margin than the 1970 convention. So we come to false start number two. After the defeat in Convention, Bishop DeWitt assembled a number of "friendly" bishops and women deacons and candidates in their dioceses to talk about going ahead with diocesan ordinations of women priests before the next convention. Again he argued that the canons did not forbid the ordination of women, and though two conventions had failed to approve it, they had not forbidden it. Furthermore, ordinations are diocesan and in our system dioceses have great autonomy.

Most of the bishops and some of the women were shocked and horrified. It was an acrimonious and stormy meeting. Indeed, when word of the meeting leaked to the House of Bishops they quickly passed a resolution condemning any such possible unilateral action before the next convention in 1976. A dissenting group of about 60 bishops issued a statement deploring the convention's failure to act on women's ordination, but did not suggest any specific remedies.

Between October, 1973, and July, 1974, there were two more false starts. Bishop DeWitt, who had resigned his diocesan office as of January, 1974, proposed to ordain me at Episcopal Theological School where I was teaching in December, 1973. Despite the support of the Dean, the Very Rev. Harvey Guthrie, and most of the students and faculty, a few trustees and faculty members were able to dissuade them on the grounds it would mean the demise of the seminary. (They were probably correct in that.) In January, 1974, the Rt. Rev. William Mead, diocesan bishop of Delaware who had become increasingly upset at the injustice of not ordaining women, resolved to do so and I prepared to transfer to his diocese. However, he died suddenly in February.

All of these false starts increased the resolve of various bishops, most especially Bishop DeWitt, to proceed out of the impasse. That resolve was helped by the increasing militancy of the women deacons. After the defeat at the 1973 convention there was a growing number of women who were not prepared to wait patiently and play by the rules any longer. My own decision not to lobby and persuade any longer was forged by two specific events.

First, at the convention, after the defeat, I ran into Mrs. Alice Emery, widow of a bishop and devoted church worker and old friend of my godmother. She remarked to me that she guessed the ordination of women would become the perennial issue at future conventions, as allowing laywomen to be voting delegates had been a perennial issue at every convention from 1946 to 1970 when women delegates were finally seated. I realized instantly that Alice was right and that my vocation was not to eternally ask permission to be a priest but to be a priest.

The second event, a few weeks later, was a meeting of women deacons and seminarians held at Virginia Theological Seminary to evaluate what had happened and where to go from there. It was another acrimonious and frustrating meeting, with the women blaming each other for the defeat (e.g. if So and So had not worn a mini-skirt; if someone else had not nursed her baby; if yet another would only cut her hair or lose weight or shut up, etc.). The moment of decision came for me at an afternoon session where the younger women, mostly seminarians, who had not been involved in the convention planning or lobbying, asked a group of men (old convention warhorses) what had been done wrong and what the women could do to be sure ordination passed at the next convention in 1976. The men of course advised patience, charm, and letting them plan the strategy "for you girls." While the young women hung on their every word, the women who had worked for the change at two conventions quietly died inside. I decided I would not be part of such a humiliation only to see it repeated by new women every three years for the foreseeable future.

A number of us felt that way (at least five of those who were to become the "Philadelphia Eleven" were in that room that day), and it quickly became clear that some other route had to be found. In November, 1973, again at Bishop DeWitt's initiative, a number of women deacons met with a number of bishops in New York City to discuss going ahead with an ordination in 1974. The bishops' caution and hesitance to commit themselves was infuriating and finally the women demanded ordination by a certain date. When the bishops' response was to say they would ask the House of Bishops for permission to ordain us, we walked out on them and met by ourselves across the street at Union Seminary.

Out of that walkout came both the offers to ordain us at ETS and later in Delaware. Out of it also came an action by five of the six women deacons from New York (their bishop, the Rt. Rev. Paul Moore, had been particularly intransigent at the November meeting.) At the diocesan ordination to the priesthood on December 15, 1973, the Reverends Carol Anderson, Carter Heyward, Emily Hewitt, Barbara Schlachter and Julia Sibley, presented themselves alongside the men for ordination. They vested, processed, were presented by priests and laypeople, took their vows and knelt before the bishop for the laying on of hands. Carter Heyward also read a statement of protest on behalf of all five at the point in the service where objections or impediments are called for. When the bishop would not lay hands on them, they, their presenters, other clergy including the bishop's chaplain, the Rev. Canon Walter Dennis (himself later elected Suffragan Bishop of New York) and about a third of the congregation walked out of the service.

About a month later a number of women, again led by the New York deacons, maintained a silent vigil at a service in New York where the Archbishop of Canterbury, Michael Ramsey, was present. Again the protest was quiet and dignified, but again the prelates were appalled. (You are no doubt familiar with this phase of the action.) It was at this service that The Rt. Rev. Edward R. Welles, retired Bishop of West Missouri, was convinced that he must proceed.

In February, 1974, the Presiding Bishop, the Most Rev. John M. Allin, was finally prevailed upon to meet with some of the women deacons. He was insensitive and insulting and once again the women came away with heightened conviction that something must be done soon. Bishop DeWitt has given me his files, and it is clear from them that as the women grew more insistent and the church more deaf, his own resolve grew. His correspondence with Bishop Welles (who had tried to calm the Archbishop of Canterbury at the New York service) and the Rt. Rev. Daniel Corrigan, retired Bishop of Colorado (who wrote in April that "I have crossed the Rubicon or the Jabbock or whatever"), indicates that they too were ever more willing to risk episcopal displeasure and act.

The catalyst for all this came in June, 1974, in the form of three sermons within 10 days. On June 6, Dean Harvey Guthrie of Episcopal Theological School in Cambridge announced in his Commencement Day sermon that he would resign unless the trustees came up with the money to hire an ordained Anglican woman for the faculty immediately. He spoke of the number of women who were being trained for ordained ministry and the scandal of denying priestly ordination to them. On June 9, one of those trustees, Dr. Charles V. Willie, a Black educator and the highest ranking layperson in the Episcopal

Church, in a sermon in Syracuse, New York, called for the immediate ordination of women to the priesthood by whatever bishops would do it. On June 15, the Very Rev. Edward Harris, dean of the Philadelphia Divinity School, preaching at the diaconal ordinations of the diocese of Pennsylvania, also called forcefully for the immediate ordination of women deacons called to priesthood.

I was at that service (two women were among the new deacons), as was Bishop DeWitt. Since he had resigned as diocesan bishop, he was seated in the congregation in the pew ahead of me. Next to me was Ms. Ruth Fiesel, the senior warden of the most anti-women priests parish in the diocese. As the dean finished his powerful sermon Ruth leaned over to me and whispered, "What a brave man!" As we stood for the creed I leaned forward to Bishop DeWitt and asked, "Do you feel the swish of a gauntlet across your face?"

After the service Dean Harris, Bishop DeWitt and I made arrangements to meet the next afternoon to plan an ordination. We decided to call a meeting of bishops, priests, deacons and laypeople who would commit themselves to planning the when, where and how of an ordination. Each of the three of us contacted trusted people -- impressing upon them that the meeting was not to discuss whether but when.

So I return to my first point. It wasn't just a few disgruntled souls getting together in June 1974 to make mischief for the church. There was a large number of people, women and men, who had been in the ordination struggle for at least four years and who had arrived by different routes at the same conclusion that summer. When we began to contact our trusted friends we found that out. There were some who were not themselves ready to proceed, but nobody among those we contacted at that point was adamant that it was a bad idea. Some of our friends were frightened badly after the news broke by the reaction of the church, but only a few had advised us beforehand not to go ahead.

In any case a meeting to plan an ordination was held July 10, 1974, in suburban Philadelphia. I had prepared an agenda with alternative whens, wheres, and hows for the group to consider. There were five bishops, seven priests, six deacons and four laypeople (including two friendly journalists) present. It was decided to proceed with an ordination on July 29 at a local church (it was my parish and the rector, the Rev. Paul M. Washington, was present and offered to host it. The congregation was also eager to have us.) The deacons were to try to recruit others. At one point, one of the bishops suggested we go ahead then and there, but since Dr. Jeannette Piccard, our senior (79) and most respected deacon was not at the meeting we decided to wait. The bishops were also to try to recruit others to be present if not to participate in the ordaining.

Four of the bishops were ready to proceed. The fifth, the Rt. Rev. Lyman Ogilby, the Bishop of Pennsylvania, was the only person present who had come to try to dissuade us. He insisted that as an individual he was all in favor of the plan, but as bishop of the diocese where it was to take place in one of his churches and involve one of his deacons he could not approve it. He was pained but immoveable -- ultimately he was the person who revealed to the public that the ordination was to take place.

Bishop Ogilby alone voted against a resolution to proceed on July 29 at the Church of the Advocate in Philadelphia. Bishop Welles insisted that we use the 1928 prayerbook ordination service rather than the new liturgy then authorized for trial use. He did so out of a preference for traditional liturgy, but as it turned out it proved a good plan on several counts. First, unlike the trial service the prayerbook made no mention of the ordinands being qualified "in accordance with the canons". It is also clear that ordination is conferred by "the imposition of our hands" and not any legislative process apart from the ceremony. But mainly, using the traditional service spared us any additional criticism for being "trendy" and not serious about what we were doing.

July 29 was chosen from an array of women saints' days within the next six weeks. Others considered were Mary Magdalene (July 22), The Virgin Mary (August 15), the nativity of the Virgin (September 7). We also considered the Transfiguration (August 6). July 29 seemed best in terms of timing (not too soon to get ready but not a long wait for word to leak out) and the saints honored (Mary and Martha of Bethany).

We left that meeting with barely three weeks to wait and to prepare. The deacons and bishops were to try to enlist more of both. A small group of Philadelphians were to actually plan the service. Two deacons were to plan a retreat for the group on July 28.

Our plan was to proceed in secret and not to announce our intentions until just before the service. At that time the bishops would release an open letter to the church explaining their action. The women would release a similar statement. Both these documents would have been mailed to all bishops, standing committees, women deacons, supportive priests and laypeople, timed to arrive in the July 29 mail. Our press contact, Betty Medsger, one of the journalists at the meeting, took charge of the preparation and distribution of a press release to go out at the time of the ordination. We agreed that should word leak out prior to the event we would offer no comment and refer all questions to her. It was a good thing we had laid these careful plans as word did get out on July 20. More of that shortly.

The night of July 10 and the next morning the deacons began contacting other deacons by phone. We contacted every women deacon we knew who had been a deacon at least six months and who we felt would not be unalterably opposed to such a plan. Five more joined us almost without hesitation, several others thought seriously about it but decided for a variety of reasons they could not risk losing their jobs at that time. No one to whom we spoke tried to dissuade us, nor did any of the women deacons break the confidentiality in which we spoke with them. Several were thrilled and many made plans to be present. The bishops had less success, though several bishops said they would be present and join in the laying on of hands (in the end only one of these men turned up). I was reluctant to pressure anybody, but Emily Hewitt, one of the other deacons and a politically acute person, felt strongly that we should get as many women as we could, preferably an even dozen. In the end there were 11 of us: Alla Bozarth-Campbell, Merrill Bittner, Alison Cheek, Carter Heyward, Emily Hewitt, Suzanne Hiatt, Marie Moorefield, Jeannette Piccard, Betty Schiess, Katrina Swanson and Nancy Wittig. We were canonically resident as deacons in eight different dioceses.

In retrospect, I am grateful Emily insisted on numbers -- we could have used at least twice as many, both deacons and bishops. When the reaction came it made all the difference that there were so many of us. I sometimes wonder what would have happened had one bishop ordained one woman in any of our false starts. The more participants, the more diversity -- in terms not only of personality but of churchmanship, diocesan affiliation, political affiliation, friends and church connections.

The bishops, while all lacking jurisdiction (except the Rt. Rev. Antonio Ramos, the Bishop of Costa Rica who came only to support and lay on hands) ranged in churchmanship from Anglo-Catholic (honorary president of the American Church Union -- our ultra-catholic organization) to evangelical, and in age from 36 to 74. Politically they also covered a wide spectrum (though more left than right of center). The church was a Black mission congregation in the Philadelphia ghetto and Bishop Ramos was Hispanic.

The women, too, covered a wide range of churchmanship, political views and age (27 - 79). At one point we had considered asking Bishop Corrigan to ordain Jeannette Piccard and forgo the other ordinations. Both Daniel and Jeannette were highly respected and widely beloved in the church. He had also been her rector many years earlier. Her presenter, the Rev. Denzil Carty, was an elderly Black priest also well-known and widely respected. We thought such an ordination would avoid charges of uppity young women and ambitious, self-aggrandizing bishops. In the end we decided on safety in numbers and it proved a wise decision. The venerable trio were, however, the principals in the first of the 11 ordinations that occurred on July 29.

On July 19, plans were proceeding on schedule when Bishop Ogilby called Bishop DeWitt to inform him that he was sending out a mailing to all his clergy announcing there would be an ordination. He said that he'd heard so many rumors that he felt his only course was to tell the clergy what he knew and to tell them he did not approve of such a plan. Earlier that same day one of the four bishops who had been present on July 10 had called Bishop DeWitt to withdraw. Betty Medsger had the press releases ready so, deleting the name of the bishop who withdrew, she began contacting the media. She felt it was important they have the first word from us rather than from the Bishop of Pennsylvania.

We spent the day on July 20 duplicating the bishops' and women's statements and getting them mailed. The story had broken in the press on July 19.

The next 10 days saw enormous pressures put on the three bishops not to proceed. The women were pretty much left alone by church leaders (apart from one telegram from the Presiding Bishop). We had all informed our own bishops in confidence of our intentions. In two cases the diocesan bishops attempted to get the approval of their own standing committees to proceed to ordain their women deacons themselves within their own dioceses. In both cases the standing committees withheld consent by the narrowest of margins -- one vote in the Diocese of Virginia and a tie vote in the Diocese of Rochester.

The press was clamoring to interview us, but we refused comment as we had agreed prior to the ordination. The bishops were bombarded with pleas not to proceed and threats in case they did anyway. Most of the pressure was from other bishops and clergy. They were accused of personal pride, massive self-delusion, breaking "collegiality" and canons, deceiving and insulting the church, being wolves not shepherds, etc. Most often they were accused of using and exploiting the women deacons (no hints, so far as I know, that any of us had seduced any of them, though there were rumors to that effect later on. By and large the rumor mill had us all lesbians).

The bishops were threatened with ostracism and deposition. Above all, they were urged to reconsider, often being told by "friends" that they'd made their point and everyone was sufficiently alarmed to redouble their efforts to get ordination approved at the next convention in 1976. That being the case, there was no need to really take this drastic step.

The women were spared both the pleas and the threats, the assumption being that we were pawns and would acquiesce quietly if the bishops decided not to proceed. Or perhaps our reaction was considered irrelevant since the bishops had the power. Once the ordination had occurred we were subject to more abuse and censure. Interesting, I think, because then we were seen as having the power that goes with indelible ordination, however irregular. We then became loose cannons on the deck; if not more respected, certainly more dangerous.

Meanwhile, we deacons and bishops and our small band of priests and laypeople were supporting and consoling each other. Our resolve was strengthened by the virulence of the opposition. One bishop very nearly withdrew, deciding only in the wee hours of July 29 to go ahead. He and I had several intense conversations during those very long 10 days.

The retreat was held as planned on July 28. The bishops confronted us with all the reasons for not proceeding. We firmly told them that we had already gone too far. Should we go to the brink and not take this step our careers would surely be ruined, but more important we would be disobedient to the call of God. The meeting ended very late with Bishop Corrigan instructing us in the rights and duties of a deposed priest.

With quiet help from many friends in Philadelphia, we had planned and rehearsed the service to the last detail. A male deacon, the Rev. Stanley Dull, who worked part-time for the Diocese of Pennsylvania, had secured and reproduced ordination certificates. Bishop Welles' grandson, William Swanson, who was skilled in calligraphy, filled in the blanks on July 28. Ms. Ann R. Smith, my lay presenter, bought Bibles for us to receive. The women of the parish of the Advocate made a frontal for the altar which proclaimed "there is neither Jew nor Greek, Black nor White, male nor female; we are one in Christ."

We had been worried about security, some of our opponents being fairly crazy. A local priest, the Rev. David M. Gracie, a scarred veteran of the civil rights and peace movements, recruited and organized marshals from among our supporters and a local radical lesbian group. (David's remark to me after the service was to the effect that a policeman's lot is not a happy one and he preferred the mob's side of the barricades.)

A small group of us had been meeting every few days since July 10 to plan the details. We had argued over what to do about bomb scares. Father Washington, another civil rights veteran, took the attitude that God would protect us, while I was of the mind that "in this world God's work must truly be our own." Since he was my presenter and parish priest, we found our division painful -- he called me at 3:00 A.M. one morning to talk about the spiritual dimensions of trusting God and doing the right thing. I do not know to this day if a bomb scare was phoned to Paul before the service; if it was, he ignored it. Unknown to all of us, the father of one of the ordinands, a retired military officer, was also fearful about security. He envisioned a crowd of agitated whites at a much respected black community church in the heart of the ghetto and took it upon himself to alert the Philadelphia police. They came in bus loads but, uncharacteristically, were cool enough to stay out of sight several blocks away.

Also unknown to those of us at the center of the storm was the fact that Episcopalians all over the nation (bishops excepted) were making plans to attend the ordination. We knew from various groups in Philadelphia who had offered hospitality that people were coming from far away. We also knew the opponents were organizing local groups to come to protest. (They had also tried to bring a court injunction to prevent our using the church, but as our lawyer, John Ballard, explained, the court refused to hear the arguments and the judge advised us that such matters should be settled within the church in the usual manner -- at the stake.) We also expected a sizable crowd from the media.

When we arrived at the church at 9:00 A.M., on Monday, July 29 (the service was scheduled for 11:00 A.M.), it was already two-thirds full. The church is a barn of a building -- an exact copy of Amiens Cathedral -- that a wealthy Philadelphian, George W. South, had built and named for himself in the late 19th century. It holds in excess of 2000 people. We had contingency plans in case of riot or interruption of the service. There was a basement room where we met to vest and to take the oath of conformity and where we planned to reassemble (bishops and deacons) in case of emergency to finish the ordination. By that time I was focused on the idea we must go through with it and be ordained no matter what. Because the opposition was so shrill and violent, I was sure we had chosen the right course. I think we all felt the same steely determination that morning.

By 11:00, the church was packed -- standing room only -- and the press and TV cameras were adding to the general bedlam, heat, and excitement. As we lined up to process (from a side aisle -- we didn't want to risk the opponents on a procession the length of the church), head usher Donald Belcher came back to tell us the church was jammed with supporters. A local group from

Rochester, New York, had brought orange lapel ribbons for supporters of the action to wear and two-thirds of the crowd were wearing them. A small group of protesters was wearing blue ribbons, and an even smaller group who were pro women's ordination but opposed to this action were wearing white ribbons. The press and some of the congregation and the vested clergy weren't wearing ribbons at all.

Paul Washington, rector of the church and master of ceremonies, quieted the crowd and began the proceeding with an eloquent welcome on behalf of the parish. He compared our situation to that of a pregnant woman -- the church says it's an inconvenient time to have a birth, but the baby comes when its time is here. This analogy was followed by the opening strains of the processional hymn, "Come, Labor On." The accident of juxtaposition produced a roar of laughter in the congregation and on that note the procession entered the church, led by crucifer Barbara C. Harris, Senior Warden of the parish (and 15 years later the first woman bishop in the Anglican Communion).

The service itself lasted three hours due to all the cheering and protesting and general hoopla. The procession was slowed by people pressing in to embrace us and general and sustained applause and cheering when the bishops emerged. Bishop Welles -- the tallest -- wore an antique red mitre. When the crowd saw that they really began to cheer. I remember my lay presenter, Ann Smith, a woman experienced in the ways of the church, shouting to me over the din, "They're going to do it, Sue. They're really going to do it. The Holy Spirit has grabbed them by whatever hair they have left and they're actually going to do it!"

The sermon came first -- another sermon by Charles Willie, the same black layman who had preached in Syracuse in June. He spoke of justice delayed as justice denied and made the obvious parallels with Martin Luther King and the civil rights movement. He was repeatedly interrupted by applause and cheers.

When the time came for objections there was a line of black-suited clergymen. By pre-arrangement the objectors had agreed to limit their remarks and only have one speaker for each group. A few also insisted on objecting as individuals. Also by pre-arrangement, Bishop DeWitt retired to a side-chapel to hear objections to the fitness of any specific ordinand, while objections to women or methodology or legality were made before the whole congregation. Bishop DeWitt knew all our secrets and was prepared to counter them if necessary but in the relative privacy of the side chapel. No one ventured there to speak with him. One of the objectors in the church raised the question of Jeannette Piccard's advanced age and declared she'd unfairly take money from the Church Pension Fund. Her three sons were infuriated and the man was roundly booed.

The other objections were what you would expect. One young priest, the Rev. George Rutler, was eloquent if insulting, and his remarks were prominently featured on national TV that evening. He told the bishops he could no longer call them bishops and that they were "raising the sight and sound and smell of perversion" in their action. Others objected to our timing and the illegality of our action. When all had had their say, Bishop Corrigan, who was presiding, read a simple statement to the effect that we had weighed our action carefully in the light of Gospel imperatives and were not dissuaded.

The service continued with the epistle being read by Katherine Lloyd Mead, Bishop Mead's widow. The Gospel was read by the Rev. Patricia Merchant Park, a newly ordained deacon and the co-chair of the group that had organized to plan strategy for the next General Convention in 1976.

Then the ordaining began. We all took our vows together, then Bishop Corrigan ordained Jeannette Piccard, Betty Schiess, Alla Bozarth-Campbell and Merrill Bittner. Bishop DeWitt ordained Carter Heyward, Emily Hewitt and Marie Moorefield. Bishop Welles ordained Katrina Swanson, Alison Cheek, Nancy Wittig and me. The fourth and youngest bishop, Bishop Antonio Ramos of Costa Rica, had come to offer support and lay hands and that is all he did.

I would remark in passing that each of the four bishops had a long-standing and close relationship with at least one of the ordinands. Bishop Corrigan had been Jeannette Piccard's parish rector years before. He was also acting dean at Bexley Hall Seminary at the time Betty Schiess and Merrill Bittner were educated there. Bishop DeWitt had been deeply engaged in the ordination struggle and knew a number of us well. He had been my diocesan bishop and employer for several years. Bishop Welles was the father of Katrina Swanson, and he and I had grown close in the course of his decision to proceed. Bishop Ramos had been a seminary classmate of mine and we had spoken together on a panel on the ordination of women at the 1970 General Convention.

About a hundred priests joined in for the laying on of hands -- the line stretching to the back of the huge church. The press contributed much pushing and shoving and flashing of cameras. The spirit of the day was high excitement and delirious joy. The recessional hymn was lustily sung and followed once more by cheering and applause. The opponents had left after making their objections. We had been prepared for just about anything, but the outpouring of love and support from so many people was astonishing. It was a sign to us that the kairos was right -- a truth we'd sensed but now knew beyond doubt.

I don't know how much more to say. The ordination was only the beginning of 18 months of intense struggle for us and our friends. It was followed by a special meeting of the bishops in mid-August that declared the ordinations so irregular as to be invalid. That was a blunder on the bishops' part as it was theologically indefensible and many churchpeople were drawn into the argument on our side because they were so appalled by the bishops' reaction.

The media, especially TV, turned out to be our best friends. Americans love to see the establishment challenged and women defying bishops became a favorite topic for cartoons, editorials and general "light" news items. Keep in mind that all this happened as the country was facing up to the need to impeach our president -- a course that had been seriously contemplated only once before in American history. Richard Nixon resigned his office in early August after months of cat and mouse games as Congress looked for and finally found "the smoking gun." Our ordination and the subsequent uproar in the church provided some relief from that painful national disgrace.

After the bishops declared us invalid we began functioning as priests whenever and wherever we could. Prior to that August meeting we had refrained from priestly ministry to give them a chance to decide how to deal with us. When they refused to deal with us at all we felt we had no choice.

At that same August meeting, procedures were initiated to try the ordaining bishops for violating canon law. In time, a Board of Inquiry ruled they should be tried for heresy or not at all, since it was a matter of doctrine (ordination of women) rather than discipline (ordaining deacons without their bishops' permission) at issue. The bishops declined to proceed with a heresy trial -- they looked foolish enough in the media already -- and the ordaining bishops were censured but never tried or deposed.

In the course of the next 18 months we celebrated the Eucharist in many parishes and dioceses and were on the TV and lecture circuit every chance we had. The debate on whether ordination would be approved at the 1976 General Convention was hot and unceasing. Had it been possible, the bishops would have "put us away quietly," as Joseph was minded to do with the pregnant Mary, but the media and our friends would not let that happen.

Eventually, two male priests, the Rev. William Wendt and the Rev. Peter Beebe, were brought to ecclesiastical trial for permitting us to celebrate the

Eucharist in their parish churches. Though both were convicted, the media made mincemeat of their bishops, William Creighton of Washington and John Burt of Ohio, both good "liberals" on all causes but the obedience of clergy and women. In the Diocese of Rochester, the Rt. Rev. Robert Spears appointed a "blue ribbon" commission to investigate the validity of our ordinations. When that group of theologians found the ordinations clearly valid but irregular, Bishop Spears asked his Standing Committee to advise him on whether he should recognize and accept the priesthood of Merrill Bittner, the Philadelphia ordinand in his jurisdiction. They recommended that he should accept and license her. When the decision was finally and solely his, however, Bishop Spears stepped back and refused to recognize her -- a truly heartbreaking disappointment.

In September, 1975, four more women deacons, Lee McGee, Alison Palmer, Betty Rosenberg and Diane Tickell were ordained priests in Washington by a fifth resigned bishop, the Rt. Rev. George Barrett. They were canonically resident in two more dioceses. While that ordination didn't get the media play of the earlier one, it was crucially important because it said to the church that women and bishops would keep doing this until the General Convention authorized the ordination of women. A number of other deacons and a few bishops had also made it plain that if women's ordination were defeated in 1976, they too would go ahead irregularly. Thus the 1976 convention had 15 embarrassing ordinations behind it and the prospect of more ahead if it failed to allow women's ordination.

Whereas in 1973 most deputies had seen it would be more trouble to ordain women than not to (due to the noisy opposition within the church), by 1976 it was clear it would be more trouble not to ordain women that to do so (due to the embarrassing play all these women get in the secular media). I am convinced that is why they voted for it in 1976 -- no great change in hearts and minds, but the only possible response to the roar of Philadelphia and Washington.

How much of this applies to England I don't know. We are not an established church, hence were never involved in breaking civil law. We have no king in this Israel as Bishop DeWitt points out, hence we never had to give a thought to how the crown would react. We were fortunate in our timing, hitting the crest of the wave of feminist sympathy in this country. As it happened, all things worked together for good. Yet our prime motivation and the defense we always fell back on was unreasonable and uncalculated -- the will of God in calling all of us to what we did.

Philadelphia was founded by English Quakers in the late 17th Century, and the influence of the Society of Friends still permeates the city. The Quakers have a motto when confused about what to do next -- "way will open" they reassure each other. For us, way did open in directions and forms impossible to calculate. I'm sure it is opening for you too. If there's any way we can help prop the door ajar, let us know.

Love in the struggle,

Sue

A CLOUD OF WITNESSES:
BLACK WOMEN IN THE ANGLICAN COMMUNION*

Barbara C. Harris

"The Lord gave the Word; great was the company of women who bore the tidings." (Psalm 68:11)

The Psalmist's assertion, according to at least one translation, provides an interesting backdrop for reflection on the role of Black women -- lay and ordained -- in the life of the Anglican Communion and particularly the Episcopal Church in the United States.

The latter half of the stanza cited above was appropriated some years ago by Dr. J. Carleton Hayden, Associate Dean at the School of Theology of the University of the South, Sewanee, as the title of a two-part series on Black women that appeared in LINKAGE, the newsletter of the national Episcopal Church's Commission on Black Ministries. Thus, I am not alone in making the connection. Incidentally, the Psalmist goes on to state that "Kings with their armies are fleeing away; the women at home are dividing the spoils" (Psalm 68:12).

Proscriptions and limitations notwithstanding, history offers considerable hard evidence that attests to the determination, the perseverance and the creativity exhibited by many Black women who have sought to serve the church over the last century. Like much of the Black community's history, an appreciable amount of information available concerning women of color in the church has been passed down through its extensive oral tradition. Only a few definitive books have been written. The entire church is indebted to Dr. Hayden, a priest who formerly chaired the Department of History and Geography at Morgan State University in Baltimore, Maryland. The Black Episcopal Church in particular leans very heavily on his scholarly research and writing in this area, as I do for purposes of this reflection.

As might be imagined, most of the women about whom we know anything were engaged in educational and missionary work, primarily in the Southern part of the United States. Following the Civil War, Dr. Hayden points out, Northern churches and abolitionist societies sent teachers to the South to educate freed men and women. In 1865, the General Convention of the Church

---

* This reflection is based upon a paper which was presented to the Conference on Afro-Anglicanism, held in Barbados in June, 1985.

established the Protestant Episcopal Freemen's Commission to undertake such work in that region. It recruited and supported lay and clergy teachers. The Commission, Dr. Hayden writes, especially sought Black teachers because they were paid less than white teachers and could secure free room and board with local Black families. It was estimated that five Black teachers could be sustained at the same cost as one white teacher. Moreover, they were felt to be just as efficient as white teachers and to have a greater "moral effect" on their Black students. Even then, the importance of role models was recognized.

About one third of the Episcopal missionary teachers, Dr. Hayden notes, were Black women. Noteworthy among them were Cordelia Atwell and Mary E. Miles, both of whom were well trained and dedicated to their calling. It is interesting to note that much of the work and the affiliations of these two women, undertaken in the late 1800s lives on in new forms today.

Native Virginian Cordelia Jennings, for example, was educated at what is now Cheney State University near Philadelphia; she attended the still-active Church of the Cruxifiction in that city; and the private school she founded and headed was later incorporated into Philadelphia's public school system. Following her marriage to the Rev. Joseph S. Atwell in Louisville, Kentucky, where she headed a parochial school at St. Mark's Church, she became the principal of St. Stephen's School in Petersburg, Virginia. When her husband was called as rector of St. Philip's Church in New York City, she headed St. Philip's Home for the Aged and, after his death, taught at what was then St. Paul's Normal and Industrial School in Lawrenceville, Virginia. The name of Cordelia Jennings Atwell is etched in the history of institutions we know today as St. Paul's College (Lawrenceville), Virginia State University, and the old Bishop Payne Divinity School, which was absorbed into Virginia Theological Seminary.

Mary Miles began her ministry as a Presbyterian missionary in Africa. There she married an English missionary, became an Anglican, and taught in mission schools in Sierra Leone and Liberia. While new incarnations of her work cannot be readily identified, she is credited with developing one of the most extensive educational ventures of the Episcopal Church in rural Virginia. Returning to this country from Africa, she founded four mission schools with 11 teachers and 600 students. Out of this work in Halifax Country, Virginia, emerged a Black Episcopal mission.

No early historical reference to the work of Black women in the Episcopal Church would be complete without mention of and tribute to distinguished educator and stalwart churchwoman Artemisia Bowden, who lived from 1879 until 1969. Born in Albany, Georgia, Miss Bowden was appointed by the Bishop of Western Texas to assume administrative and teaching duties at St. Philip's School in San Antonio in 1902. She has been referred to as the "savior" of that institution, which is today not only an accredited Junior College, but a unit of the San Antonio Junior College District.

Miss Bowden gave 52 years of dedicated service to St. Philip's and was personally responsible for its survival through the depression of the 1930s. Her persistence and personal determination is credited for the school's development -- its expansion of land area, curricula, faculty and other personnel, its student body, its increase in buildings, and its emergence and acceptance into the San Antonio public education system in 1942.

There is no way to record or convey the tenacious leadership of Artemisia Bowden as she entered into and brought to successful fruition long and sometimes painful negotiations to win recognition and public support for a faith venture in Black education. The venture began in a brick schoolhouse consisting of two classrooms, a kitchen, a closet, two halls and a gallery, built behind a church. From Saturday evening sewing classes and an enrollment of 21, to more than 8000 students today, St. Philip's stands as a living monument to a daughter of the faith.

Joyce M. Howard of Washington, D.C., in a paper developed for the Episcopal Church Women's History Project in 1982, writes of a cadre of Black women who in later years trained and worked under the auspices of the Woman's Auxiliary of the National Council of the Protestant Episcopal Church. Graduates of Windham House and the all-Black Tuttle School, these women held degrees or certificates in Religious Education. Many, whose surnames would be recognizable in the Black Episcopal community because their fathers or other male relatives were priests of the Church, functioned as social workers and teachers of Christian education as well as nurses, recreational directors and day care and nursery workers.

Attached to parishes and missions, they filled these roles while also organizing women to be effective in their local congregations through the work of the Altar Guild, choir, Church School and branches of the Girls' Friendly Society and the Daughters of the King. Their modest salaries were paid not by the Church, but by grants from the United Thank Offering -- the contributions of yet other women.

Two "Negro" Field Secretaries, Este Virginia Brown and Fannie P. Gross (later Jeffrey), roamed the country during the early 1930s and 1940s, serving as liaisons between work that was distinctly Black and that which was distinctly white. Attached to the national staff of the Woman's Auxiliary, the

Field Secretaries interpreted the Woman's Auxiliary program and recruited yet more missionaries, nurses, teachers and social workers. These women, as Howard reports, "did much in the way of quietly and persistently working to break down the wall of brazen racism within the Church that exhibited itself in such ways as segregated seating patterns in conferences and meetings held in churches, and the proposing of commendable works without the accompanying funds to implement them credibly."

One further note on the Field Secretaries: they went to a diocese, according to Joyce Howard, on the invitation of a bishop and could work there from one to six months. The Secretary would meet with the bishop to work out a plan of action that could consist of visiting institutions of all kinds, including correctional facilities, leading groups in mission study and setting up summer conferences. She might also preach. Mrs. Gross-Jeffrey recalled, in a personal conversation with Mrs. Howard, preaching at five different missions on a single Sunday.

If seeming to dwell overlong on history, it is because of the importance of noting that Black women have been in the vanguard of those who have served the Church since its antebellum days in the United States, when this branch of the Catholic faith had an even lesser appeal to masses of Afro-Americans than it does today. While they were not accorded the status, recognition, or support they merited, as we are reminded in the letter to the church at Ephesus: to them "his gifts were that some should be apostles, some prophets, some evangelists, some pastors and teachers, to equip the saints for the work of ministry" (Ephesians 4:11).

Perseverance, determination, creativity and a sense of vocation do not, however, belong to history alone. Black Anglican women continue their struggle to witness effectively in the Church and in the society to which the Church increasingly is called to minister. What needs to develop is a keener appreciation and utilization of the gifts Black women bring and the gifts they have to offer. They come from a variety of backgrounds with an abundance of skills ranging from administrative to pastoral, and their spiritual formation has been forged in the crucible of rejection and shaped and molded in a thrice jeopardized community of oppression -- Black, female and often poor.

Some few hold paid posts on diocesan staffs and at the national church level; however, a recent survey shows no Black women in positions of power in the U.S. Church or in the Church of England.** In that respect, Black women are not unlike Black men -- clergy and laity.

Increasing numbers of Black women are seen on parish vestries, Commissions on Ministry, on other diocesan and national boards, commissions and committees, and as deputies to synods and General Conventions. Most, however, continue to find their greatest opportunities for service in the traditional areas of Altar Guilds and sacristans, churchwomen's groups, Mothers' Unions, Church Schools and choirs. And let us not forget the beleaguered parish secretary, especially in small congregations, who often keeps the whole parish machinery moving.

It is important to remember, particularly for women themselves, that Black women's agendas in the church, as in society, are different in many respects from those of white women struggling to claim some prominence in the Episcopal Church and in the Anglican Communion. Black women's agendas are largely focused on developing and strengthening the Black community so that the total community benefits. Black women and other women of color cannot be seduced by the personal power games so often blatantly operative in some sectors of the feminist movement.

The Union of Black Episcopalians, the church's 20-year-old Black caucus, has increasingly become a forum in which women -- particularly laywomen -- are finding expression and are able to fashion their own agendas. Given the rapidly changing complexion of the Anglican Communion, the Union is well advised to continue forging international connections. Spreading in some relevant form to other cultures, it might well provide a vehicle for expression for Anglican women of color around the globe who, too often, are victimized by the remaining negative vestiges of colonialism practiced by the Church.

Another significant development in the Episcopal Church has been the formation in recent years of the Conference of Black Clergy Wives and Widows. This organization has become an important support network for women who, with their husbands, frequently find themselves serving in isolated situations. It is also a vehicle for sharing an understanding of ways in which women can better support their spouses' ministry. Continued growth of this conference is essential to the life of the Black church.

---

* EDS. Note: Barbara Harris was consecrated Suffragan Bishop in the Diocese of Massachusetts on February 11, 1989.

The numbers of ordained Black women remain small and there is no foreseeable glut of Black women clergy. In the United States, there are (in 1985) about 21 Black women priests, about 12 deacons -- almost half of whom will remain in the Order perpetually -- and some 15 or more in the "pipeline" at seminaries or in alternative programs of study. The numbers in other countries that we know of such as Kenya, Uganda, and Canada, are smaller yet. That they are present at all is encouraging. Again, most have come with an abundance of gifts for ministry and skills honed in other fields of endeavor. And their late vocations, for the most part, bespeak a maturity often lacking in younger males.

Women in Orders remains a thorny problem for many in the Black church as it does in the larger Church. Acceptance is hard won from the early stages of aspirant and postulancy through ordination and deployment. Once deployed, some suffer the isolation and loneliness of the missionary in the field without ever leaving home. Even some Black men who sit on Commissions on Ministry find it difficult to imagine their own sisters (or mothers) as pastors, proclaimers of the Word, pronouncers of absolution or channels of benediction. I have found the matter frequently more of a problem for Black clergy than laity, many of the former being bound by some aspects of traditional Anglicanism that enslave the mind and stifle the spirit.

I have preached the ordinations of two Black women: one a 65-year-old to the diaconate, the other, considerably younger, to the priesthood. In charging them, I reminded both of them of their marginality as Black women in a male dominated and racist church. Yet I encouraged both to remember, as I had been charged, that while their Anglican heritage has given them the melody of their song, their Black religious experience, which cuts across denominational lines, has given them the lyrics and the courage to sing it. And their role models must, indeed, come from other denominations, some non-liturgical, where Black women have long been evangelists and ministers.

What of the future? Just as the past informs the present, the present can provide direction and guidance for the future. Women comprise better than 60 percent of the communicant strength of most congregations and are likely to remain in dominant numbers in Black churches. So great a cloud of witnesses should be utilized to the fullest potential of their human as well as their traditional resources for the building up of the kingdom.

Sensitive to the cultural differences that pervade and permeate various countries, particularly in Africa and the Caribbean, I refrain from proposing any absolute model for enabling the full ministry of Black women -- ordained and lay -- in the loosely bound communion called Anglicanism. More women in

Orders in the United States, for example, would greatly alleviate the dearth of Black clergy vocations here. The U. S. has no glut of Black clergy. This may not be the case in other places. Even if it is, the ordination of women might not be the full solution.

The whole church must develop models relevant to its corner of the vineyard. It is to be hoped that the words of the Psalmist with which this essay began will become recognized throughout the church for the living reality they bespeak. And like Esther, the beautiful queen, who knows whether we -- Black Episcopal and Anglican women -- "have not come to the kingdom for such a time as this?"

FEMINIST THEOLOGY AND ANGLICAN THEOLOGY*
Owen C. Thomas

The relation between feminist theology and Anglican theology is beginning to emerge as a crucial issue in the Episcopal Church.[1] The immediate reason is of course the rapidly increasing presence of women in the priesthood of the Episcopal Church and in the student bodies and faculties of the Episcopal seminaries. In 1988, there were 1,409 women clergy, and 958 women priests, of whom over 300 are in charge of Episcopal parishes. The percentage of women degree candidates in the accredited Episcopal seminaries has tripled in the past decade. The number of women teaching full time in these seminaries has increased five-fold in the same period.

The contemporary women's movement has affected deeply all areas of American life in the past 20 years, including our religious life. Feminist scholarship has grown rapidly in all fields of the humanities and the social sciences.[2] As a part of this development, feminist theology has become one of the most important and challenging forms of theology today.

Feminist theology can be defined as theology which is written from the point of view of women's experience and which sees sexism, defined as gender privilege of males over females, as a fundamental form of sin. Feminist theology takes a variety of forms today. Some feminist theologians, such as Mary Daly and Carol Christ, have decided that the Christian tradition is essentially sexist in character and oppressive to women, and therefore that it is irreformable. They believe that they must go beyond Christianity and look into other religious traditions to find resources that are illuminative and supportive of feminist commitments. Other feminist theologians, on the other hand, such as Sallie McFague, Rosemary Radfdord Ruether, and Letty Russell, are persuaded that Christianity is not essentially and irredeemably sexist in nature and that it therefore can be reformed and purged of its sexism. They argue that the sexism of the Christian tradition is in fact a corruption of its essential character as a religion of equality and liberation.

The vast increase in feminist writing in all areas of theological scholarship over the past 15 years has made available to women (and men) in the Episcopal Church the resources for understanding, criticizing, and reforming the patriarchal bias of the Christian tradition in general and of Anglicanism in particular, and for envisioning new ways of interpreting the Christian tradition which are liberating for all people.

---

* This essay was originally published in the Anglican Theological Review, LXIII:2, 1987.

In this essay I want to explore the relation between Anglican theology and feminist theology. These are obviously quite different phenomena. One is a rather amorphous centuries-old ecclesial tradition, and the other is a diverse, largely twentieth-century, theological movement that flourishes in most western ecclesial traditions, including Anglicanism. In effect we are exploring the relation between Anglican theology and one theological movement that exists within it and beyond it. Our inquiry is more like the relation of Anglican theology to process theology than investigating its relation to Lutheran theology, for example. Since both feminist theology and Anglican theology are quite various in character, such an exploration will have to be carried out by means of typical examples.

Since no comprehensive statements of feminist theology have been written from an Anglican point of view, I will use the writings of Rosemary Radford Ruether as an example of feminist theology, and especially her recent Sexism and God-Talk: Toward a Feminist Theology[3]. I choose Ruether because she is one of the leading feminist theologians in the world today. She is a member of the Roman Catholic Church and was trained as a historian.[4] In regard to Anglican theology, I will be taking a historical perspective based on my own point of view in this tradition.[5]

A useful place to begin this exploration is with Ruether's address at the annual meeting of the American Academy of Religion in Chicago in December 1984, entitled "Feminist Theology in the Academy."[6] She states at the beginning of this essay that "feminist theology arises as a critique of the patriarchal bias of traditional theology." In Sexism and God-Talk she defines patriarchy as "not only the subordination of females to males, but the whole structure of Father-ruled society: aristocracy over serf, masters over slaves, king over subjects, racial overlords over colonized people."[7] A key point in Ruether's essay is her statement that "feminist theology is engaged in a critique of the androcentrism and misogyny of patriarchal theology," with androcentrism defined as the view in which "the male is taken to be the normative representation of the human species, the norm for imaging God, and for defining anthropology, sin, redemption, and ministry." Misogyny is defined as "male dominance engaged in self-defense of its right to define and control women and all other reality."[8] Ruether poses sharply the issue we are addressing.

To ask about the future of feminist theology..., therefore, is not to ask whether the patriarchal tradition and feminist theology have a future together. Of course they don't. It is to ask whether feminist theology will sufficiently transform theology as it is taught in the seminaries and preached in the churches, so that we no longer have patriarchal theology but an inclusive theology that affirms the full humanity and interrelationship of women and men.[9]

I believe that Anglican theology can and should be so transformed and that therefore feminist theology and Anglican theology are potentially reconcilable and coherent. I want to make a formal point and note some material points. The formal point is that historically and in principle Anglican theology is flexible enough to undergo the transformation mentioned. The material points are that Anglican theology historically and at present is as patriarchal as any other tradition and probably more so than some, that therefore the transformation will be slow, and that there are many points on which Christian feminist theology and Anglican theology are in tension. I will explore one of these.

I believe that the key to the formal point is that, of all the traditions that were deeply influenced by the Reformation of the sixteenth century, Anglicanism is the only one which avoided becoming a thoroughly confessional tradition.[10] To be sure, there are the Articles of Religion, but it has often been noted (see the essay by N.T. Wright referred to below) that they do not function in Anglicanism at all in the way that the Augsburg, Westminster, Tridentine, and other confessions function in their traditions.[11]

What I mean by this historical point is that Anglicanism has always (or almost always) avoided requiring or enforcing adherence to a detailed statement of doctrine and has always (or almost always) proceeded very cautiously and slowly in dealing with what appeared to be novel teaching. There are many examples of this in Anglican history. This tradition of doctrinal flexibility has been exemplified especially in the liberal, broad, and modernist traditions in the Church of England, in the person of F.D. Maurice, in the nineteenth-century volumes Essays and Reviews and Lux Mundi, and in this century in Foundations and the three reports of the Doctrine Commission of the Church of England. This tradition is also exemplified in the response to such radical Anglican authors as Barnes, Pike, Robinson, Wiles, and Cupitt, namely, discussion and debate rather than trial and removal.

To be sure, most of this data is English, but the name of Bishop James Pike reminds us of what is perhaps the finest statement of theological freedom to appear in this century. I refer to the volume entitled Theological Freedom and Social Responsibility,[12] which is the report of the committee chaired by Bishop Stephen Bayne which was appointed to advise the Episcopal Church on the issues arising out of the censure of and request for a trial by Bishop Pike. It deals with the questions raised for the church by the allegedly radical social, political, and theological activity of Bishop Pike, including the ordination of a woman to the diaconate five years before such action was approved by the General Convention. Moreover, in the Episcopal Church much of the concern of those influenced by feminist theology has been focused on the patriarchal and sexist character of the Book of Common Prayer and especially its lack of inclusive language in regard to humanity and God.[13] The report treats this issue indirectly and proleptically. I shall quote it at length.

> The Church's obligation to minister in Christ's name to men and women requires that it enter fully into the world's always new, always agonizing search for truth and justice.... Where it is clear, as in the life and ministry of a sensitive teacher, that Christians share in the world's pain and uncertainties and mean to join the world's search for honest answers, fruitful engagement in theological and social inquiry becomes a reality.

> Therefore, the first requirement for the Church, in meeting its obligations, is that it sincerely mean to share the world's pain, and face with the world the frightening enigmas of its life. Along with this, a second characteristic is required, that of devotion to freedom of conscience.... To espouse freedom as a ruling principle entails the risk which the Church of all human associations must be the first to be willing to run. Why do we say this? Because the Church realizes that a faith which does not liberate cannot claim to be the authentic saving faith of Christ.

> That the Church be truly one with humanity and at humanity's side, and that it be seen fully to respect [human] freedom, are the two indispensable characteristics of any responsible engagement on the theological and social frontiers. Those characteristics grow out of the church's nature. In turn, they must control the Church's response...

> Anglicans do not believe that the Church is inexorably bound to any previous formulation of the Church's tradition. There is no infallible propositional statement of the Christian faith, as we understand it.... The community, no doubt, is ultimately responsible for determining what constitutes the marks of "recognizable continuity" at any given time. But to say that requires that it also be stressed that the community -- to assure its own authenticity -- must be prepared to learn even from its severest critics to discern new marks and adopt them, leaving with the critics, as long as is humanly possible, the decision to maintain or sever the relationship...

> When Episcopalians are questioned about the supposed orthodoxy or heterodoxy of one of their number, their most likely response is to ask whether or not he [or she] wishes -- sincerely and responsibly -- to join

them in the celebration of God's being and goodness in the prayers and worship of the Prayer Book. Assuming his [or her] integrity, they would not be likely to press the question beyond that point.

No doubt this attitude is often an excuse for sentimentality and vaporous thinking, even for the postponement of fundamental spiritual decisions. No doubt it opens Anglican practice to the risk of mere conformism. Nevertheless, we would still say that the willingness of a person to share in the worship of the Prayer Book with a consenting mind is, for most purposes, an adequate test of his [or her] right to claim the privileges of the community.

Such a test implies two responsibilities. One is that of the individual.... The other responsibility is that of the Church, to recognize and provide for the constant review of its liturgies as central instruments of its renewal. In our Anglican tradition, the Prayer Book is far more than a manual of worship. It is a principal agent and effective means of maintaining our corporate identity, of our continuity with the whole Body, of our ministry of the tradition of the Church. Therefore it must be a principal frontier of the Church's constant encounter and dialogue with the world. Liturgies are rightly conservative, in that they play so central a part as guardians and transmitters of the tradition. But for exactly those reasons, liturgies are inescapably in the forefront of reformation and renewal. In them the continuing reinterpretation of the tradition is best found; in them is expressed the passionate partisanship of the Church with the world's pain; in them the Christian is confronted by the wholeness of the Faith and its glorious gifts and radical demands, spelled out in terms of his [or her] daily concerns. There can be no escape, then, from the Church's corporate obligation to liturgical experiment and change, if it is to keep faith with its Lord...

God makes [people] free. It does not behoove [the] Church to try to hobble their minds or inhibit their search for new insights into truth. The Church not only should tolerate but should actively encourage free and vigorous theological debate, application of the Gospel to social wrongs, restatement of Christian doctrines to make them more intelligible to contemporary minds, and experimentation with new forms of worship and service. Any risks the Church may run by fostering a climate of genuine freedom are minor compared to the dangers it surely will encounter from any attempts at suppression, censorship or thought control...[14]

The formal point is made in a similar way in another official Anglican statement, Christian Believing, a report by the Doctrine Commission of the Church of England.[15] This report stresses the diversity of theological views within the Bible and the Anglican tradition. "Right from the very beginning of Christianity there is pluriformity in the faith." And this is "no merely superficial feature" but is "ingrained, ineradicable, generated by the essential nature of biblical religion."[16] The pluralism in the theology of the New Testament can be "a genuine pointer to the character of the Christian message."[17] Therefore the heterogeneous character of the Bible, the diversity and tension, is not a defect but is the way in which God is best communicated to a variety of people.[18] The report also refers to the variety of attitudes toward the creeds in Anglicanism, all the way from being considered the norm of Christian belief to being considered provisional and not central. None of these attitudes should be ruled out, but all must remain in creative tension and dialogue.[19]

This same general theme is explored in yet a different way in the most recent report of the Doctrine Commission, entitled Believing in the Church: The Corporate Nature of Faith.[20] It emphasizes the necessity for the freedom of those investigating new and more adequate ways of interpreting the tradition. It affirms that "doctrine should be authoritatively defined as little and as seldom as possible."[21]

N.T. Wright argues in this volume that the Anglican approach to doctrine derives from the peculiar circumstances of the church in sixteenth-century England. These led to a common commitment to maintain unity in diversity through avoiding the over-definition of doctrine. This was related to the principle that some matters are secondary and others primary; "this principle is close to the heart of the Anglican approach to doctrine."[22] It was in this milieu that the Articles of Religion were produced and that their role and function in the church developed, which was quite different from that of other sixteenth-century confessions. Their comparative brevity and latitude state "by implication, that there are several widely debated theological issues on which a loyal Anglican is not enjoined to take up a particular stance."[23]

John Taylor in the same volume argues that "it is in fact, more typical of Anglicanism to rely upon custom, ceremony, and, above all, its forms of public prayer to reveal its doctrine by implication" than to rely on explicit doctrinal formulations.[24] He claims that the more basic doctrine is more likely to be preserved in myth, symbol, ritual, and behavior patterns than in explicit formulations. Such implicit doctrine is more effective and enduring in the life of the church. John McManners claims that "the Anglican Church has a genius for...forbearance.... The cement that holds our church together" is an attitude of "compromise, tolerance and agreement to differ...a respect for the individual conscience, a love of freedom, a distrust of authority."[25] Anthony Harvey summarizes some of the themes of this report when he states that individuals and groups of theologians have the right and duty to explore and experiment with radically new formulations of doctrine. The church should support them, but it must also assess their proposals in public discussion. Both the integrity of the church and the freedom of conscience must be respected.[26]

So my first and formal point is that Anglicanism has a flexibility in regard to doctrine which should make it in principle more open than some other traditions to the presence and critique of feminist theology. As we have noted, however, Ruether states that feminist theology is not interested in coexistence. She states that feminist theology and patriarchal theology have no future together, and she calls for the replacement of patriarchal theology by an inclusive theology. Feminist theology is calling for the condemnation of the sexism of traditional theology and for the purging of its patriarchal bias. The problem is that coexistence is the middle name of Anglican theology. Given its history and commitment to maintaining diversity in dialogue, there is not much chance of Anglican theology's becoming confessional even on so fundamental a point as patriarchal bias. History suggests that feminist theology will become a stronger movement within Anglican theology but in varying degrees in different provinces. I am suggesting that the relatively non-confessional and diverse character of Anglican theology will make it more open to the presence and critique of feminist theology but it will also make it more difficult for feminist theology to transform Anglican theology.

The discussion of this formal point may have given the impression that the situation is one in which Anglican theology sits in judgment upon feminist theology rather than the other way round. This impression, however, derives from the way in which a particular ecclesial tradition goes about assessing any critique of itself. It has to consider the validity of the criticism made by the reformers. As the Bayne Committee report puts it, "the community -- to assure its own authenticity -- must be prepared to learn from its severest critics." So my way of presenting this formal point should not suggest that I am unaware of the radical character of the challenge of feminist theology.

This leads to the material question of the actual and possible relation between feminist theology and Anglican theology. In this connection it must be admitted that Anglican theology is as patriarchal as any other Christian tradition and probably more so than some. This is symbolized by the fact that all members of the Bayne Committee and the three Doctrine Commissions of the Church of England are (white) males. The issue of the ordination of women appears only in the 1981 report and only in passing as an example of the complexity of the exercise of authority and of the interconnections of doctrine, and no position is taken on it.

So are feminist theology and Anglican theology potentially reconcilable and coherent or not? It obviously depends on how they are defined. Given some definitions, the answer is No; given others, the answer is Yes. There is a rough liberal-conservative spectrum in feminist theology as there is an Anglican theology. Of course these spectra are not coextensive, but there is probably some overlap. Therefore, one can argue either way. It depends on what is considered to be essential in Anglican theology and in feminist theology. I believe that patriarchy, sexism, androcentrism, and misogyny are not essential in Anglican theology, although it has always been characterized by them in varying degrees. But, again, all depends on what is included in these terms.

What are the probable points of tension or disagreement between feminist and Anglican theology? They are of two types. One comprises those aspects of patriarchy which may be considered essential to Anglican theology and anathema to feminist theology. These might include the limitation of the criteria of theology to the Bible and the tradition in the form of creeds and councils, exclusive male imagery for God and the Trinity, the universal significance and validity of male experience, the limitation of Christology to the strict interpretation of the Chalcedonian definition, the limitation of salvation to reconciliation within God, the limitation of the mission of the church to evangelism, and the exclusion of women from the ordained ministry of the church on the basis of Scripture and tradition.

The other type comprises those affirmations which are considered to be essential to feminist theology and which may be considered to be outside the bounds of Anglican theology. Using Ruether's Sexism and God-Talk as an example, these might include women's experience as the criterion of theology, the absence of a doctrine of creation as origination, the equivalence of humanity and nature, the limitation of Christology to prophecy, the tendency to limit salvation to liberation from social, economic, and political oppression, and the limitation of eschatology to hope for historical progress.

These are all very complex issues. I will comment briefly on the first one of each type, which deals with the criterion of theology and is thus decisive for the other issues.

Ruether states that "feminist theology draws on women's experience as a basic source of content as well as criterion of truth."[27] She argues that this is not a novel claim, since all theological reflection is based on experience. Scripture and tradition are "codified collective human experience." A religious tradition begins with the revelatory experience of an individual, which is then appropriated by a group. The received tradition is always tested by the experience of the community. Thus "human experience is the starting point and the ending point of the hermeneutical circle.... Received symbols, formulas, and laws are either authenticated or not through their ability to illuminate and interpret experience."[28] The uniqueness of feminist theology is its use of women's experience, which has been almost entirely excluded from theological reflection in the past.

Ruether supplements this appeal to women's experience with the assertion that "the critical principle of feminist theology is the promotion of the full humanity of women.... Theologically speaking, whatever diminishes or denies the full humanity of women must be presumed not to reflect the divine or an authentic relation to the divine.... This negative principle also implies the positive principle: what does promote the full humanity of women is of the Holy, it does reflect true relation to the divine."[29]

According to Ruether this also is not a novel claim. "The uniqueness of feminist theology is not the critical principle, full humanity, but the fact that women claim this principle for themselves."[30] This cannot become a reverse form of sexism, however; full humanity must include both genders as well as all social groups and races. Finally, Ruether states that she is able to find usable foundations for feminist theology in five areas of cultural tradition: Scripture; marginalized or heretical Christian traditions, such as Gnosticism, Montanism, Quakerism, and Shakerism; classical Christian theology; non-Christian Near Eastern and Greco-Roman religion and philosophy; and critical post-Christian world views such as liberalism, romanticism, and Marxism.[31] She declares that all these traditions are sexist, but that all provide intimations of alternative concepts of God, humanity, and the world not entirely distorted by sexism.

How is Ruether's theological criterion related to the traditional Anglican norms of scripture and tradition as stated in Articles 6, 8, 20, and 21 of the Articles of Religion? Ruether makes no explicit acceptance or rejection of the Scripture principle, but she states that the origin of the Christian tradition is in the revelatory experiences recorded in Scripture, and she explores the biblical basis of each of the theological topics she treats. She also argues that feminist theology claims the "prophetic liberating tradition of Biblical faith as a norm through which to criticize the Bible." This is "a tradition that can be fairly claimed, on the basis of general Biblical scholarship, to be the central tradition, the tradition by which biblical faith constantly criticizes and renews itself and its own vision."[32] She offers a careful description of the formation of the canon of Scripture on the basis of revelatory experience,[33] and she warns against the encapsulation of Jesus in the remote past as a once-for-all disclosure of God now closed and separated from the ongoing presence of the Spirit. Given the patriarchal bias of the whole Bible, Ruether would be uneasy about the traditional Anglican Scripture principle. But, on the basis of her practice in theology, it is possible to argue that her implied view of Scripture is coherent with a liberal interpretation of the Scripture principle.

Ruether also offers an illuminating description of the formation of tradition, of the necessity of tradition, of the ways in which a tradition becomes corrupted, and of the crises of tradition. These crises occur when the received tradition is seen to contradict contemporary experience in significant ways. These crises can occur through exegetical criticism, through the discovery of the corruption of the institutional structures that transmit the tradition (as in the Reformation of the sixteenth century), and when the total religious heritage appears to be corrupt (as in the view of the Enlightenment and Marxism). Even in the case of this latter ideological criticism, a residue of genuine insight can be allowed to the prophets and Jesus, because no interpretation of contemporary experience can be made apart from some tradition. Ruether implies, although she does not state, that the feminist critique is a case of this third and most radical crisis of the tradition.

Ruether's criticism of the sexism and patriarchal bias of the tradition does not include detailed criticism of the creeds and conciliar definitions. She is highly critical of Chalcedonian Christology, not of its specific formulations, but rather of the central role it played in the culmination of patriarchal imperial Christianity. Ruether states that she has made use of what she calls the "basic paradigm of classical (Christian) theology." She describes this as affirming

> an original good human nature, united to the cosmos and the divine, contrasted with an alienated, fallen historical condition of humanity (sin, evil). Revelatory, transformative experiences (conversion) disclose the original humanity and allow one to liberate oneself from the sinful distortion of existence. This new humanity is then related to a redemptive community that gathers together and announces a prophetic, critical, transformative mission against sinful society.[34]

Thus in summary it can be said that Ruether affirms the necessity of tradition, is highly critical of its patriarchal distortions, and calls for a radical reformation of it. This is similar to many criticisms of tradition by contemporary Anglican theologians,[35] and it is, I believe, coherent with a liberal interpretation of the Anglican view of tradition.

Finally, what shall we make of Ruether's thesis, which she shares with most feminist theologians, that women's experience is the basic source as well as criterion of truth for feminist theology and that the promotion of the full humanity of women is the critical principle of feminist theology? Since a criterion of truth and a critical principle are probably the same thing here, I assume that these are the formal and material aspects of the criterion of feminist theology. That is, a theological proposal is assessed by whether or not it is verified in women's experience (perhaps in Tillich's sense of "experiential verification"[36]), and a proposal is assessed positively if in their experience it promotes the full humanity of women and negatively if it does not. Ruether asserts that this criterion is not novel since all theology is based on experience. The novelty is that it refers to women's experience, which has been excluded heretofore.

It is certainly true that all theology is based on experience, for all human knowledge is so based. It is also true that a theological proposal is confirmed or disconfirmed in an obscure and complex manner over the long term in the experience of the individual and the community. This is more the case with a cluster of doctrines or a whole theology, however, and it occurs over a period of years, a lifetime, or a century. Thus it is not a process that an individual theologian can observe or investigate in a period of, say, a year while assessing a particular theological proposal. This process, however, is perhaps the cause of the fact that a theologian affirms or denies a particular theological proposal. That is, a theologian can be aware of such a tidal movement in his or her own convictions, and it can be the basis of testimony to the meaningfulness and validity of a proposal for the individual.

Thus it may be that most theology is done backwards in the sense that it is the exploration of the possible grounds in Scripture, tradition, and other criteria for a theological conviction arrived at in some other way.[37] It is clear, however, that the experience of one theologian, even if confirmed by some colleagues and friends, can hardly function as a warrant in a theological argument, no matter how representative and universal it is believed to be.

Another way to put this difficulty in the appeal to women's experience is to note that it is not clear which women are being referred to and how the information about their experience is to be gathered on a wide enough scale. It is not clear whether Ruether is referring to all women, Christian women, or liberated Christian women, nor how these will be defined and on what grounds. Also, how is the testimony of these women to be gained? If by means of social science research, then is it from a scientific sample in one denomination in one area of one country, or in all denominations in some areas of all countries? What is the minimum scope that could be considered significant in assessing a particular theological proposal? It seems that the difficulties in a truly empirical approach are formidable.

Another approach to this question is proposed by Judith Plaskow. She defines women's experience by means of the figure of Martha Quest in Doris Lessing's five-volume series of novels entitled The Children of Violence.[38] With some help from Simone de Beauvoir and Margaret Drabble, Plaskow offers a picture of women's experience that is quite different from the image of naturalness and passivity presented in much modern psychology. This is a very creative depiction of the experience of white middle-class women, but to claim universality for it would be to fall into the error for which feminists criticize traditional male-centered theology. In any case, she is able to use it very effectively to criticize the doctrines of sin and grace in the theologies of Niebuhr and Tillich.

These problems (and there are others) are not unique to feminist theology but apply to all theologies that appeal to experience as a criterion of theology.[39] In any case, Ruether's appeal to women's experience is coherent with Anglican theology, which has almost always appealed to experience in some form.[40]

So I conclude that on this particular issue of the criterion feminist theology as exemplified by Rosemary Ruether is not incoherent with Anglican theology in my interpretation. On a strict construction of the Articles of Religion it could probably be argued the other way around. But my point has been that Anglican theology has only rarely and atypically affirmed a strict construction of cither Scripture or tradition.

We have considered only one of the many issues which have emerged between Anglican and feminist theology, and it is clear that the more difficult material issues lie ahead. Much exploration remains to be carried out. At this stage I believe that Anglican theology needs and should welcome the critique being made by feminist theology, and it may well have a vocation to function as a bridge of communication between feminist theology and traditional theologies.

NOTES

1.   This will also be the case in other provinces of the Anglican Communion as they begin or continue to ordain women to the priesthood. Of the 27 provinces of the Anglican Communion, nine now ordain women to the priesthood. Other churches are debating these issues as well. See the discussion of the relation of feminist theology and Lutheranism in Dialog 24 (Winter 1985).

2.   See The Women's Annual, ed. Barbara Haber, 1980-82, and Sara M. Pritchard, 1983 (Boston: G.K. Hall).

3.   Rosemary Radford Ruether, Sexism and God-Talk: Toward a Feminist Theology (Boston: Beacon, 1983). For an introduction to this work, see the Study Notes on it by Margaret R. Miles and Owen C. Thomas published by Trinity Institute, New York in 1984. Although two extended theological essays have recently been published by Anglican women priests, they are not comprehensive enough for my purposes. I refer to Carter Heyward, The Redemption of God: A Theology of Mutual Relation (Lanham, MD: University Press of America, 1982), and Patricia Wilson-Kastner, Faith Feminism, and the Christ (Philadelphia: Fortress, 1983).

4.   Her first book is entitled Gregory of Nazianzus: Rhetor and Philosopher (New York: Oxford University Press, 1969). She has written 10 other books on historical, feminist, and liberation theologies.

5.   See my Introduction to Theology, rev. ed. (Wilton, Conn.: Morehouse-Barlow, 1983); and my essay on William Temple in The Spirit of Anglicanism, ed. William J. Wolf (Wilton, Conn.: Morehouse-Barlow, 1979).

6.   Christianity and Crisis 45 (1985): 57-62. This is an adaptation of the address; the original is published in JAAR 53 (December 1985): 703-13 ("The Future of Feminist Theology in the Academy").

7.   Ruether, Sexism and God-Talk, p. 61.

8.   Ibid., p. 58.

9.   Ibid., p. 57.

10.   Since I am not a historian of the sixteenth century, I rush in foolishly. Obviously some traditions which developed later, such as Separatism and Methodism, are even more nonconfessional.

11.   A recent example of the latter is the Observations of the Sacred Congregation for the Doctrine of the Faith in The Final Report of the Anglican-Roman Catholic International Commission (1982).

12.   (New York: Seabury, 1967).

13.   It should be noted in this connection that the 1985 General Convention voted to request the Standing Liturgical Commission to develop trial services with inclusive language.

14.   Theological Freedom and Social Responsibility, pp. 8, 10, 19-22, 31f. Gender inclusive brackets added.

15.   Doctrine Commission of the Church of England, Christian Believing (London: SPCK, 1976).

16.   Ibid., p. 28.

17.   Ibid., p. 50.

18.   Ibid., p. 29f.

19.   Ibid., pp. 35-39.

20.   Doctrine Commission of the Church of England, Believing in the Church: The Corporate Nature of Faith (London, SPCK, 1981).

21.   Ibid., p. 296.

22.   Ibid., p. 118.

23.   Ibid., p. 125.

24.   Ibid., p. 141f.

25.   Ibid., p. 234.

26.   Ibid., p. 296.

27.   Ruether, Sexism and God-Talk, p. 12.

28.   Ibid.

29.   Ibid., p. 18f.

30.   Ibid., p. 19.

31.   This can be compared to Paul Tillich's list of the sources of systematic theology: Bible, church history, and the history of religion and culture. See his Systematic Theology, 3 Vols. (Chicago: University of Chicago Press, 1951-63), 1:34-40.

32.   Ruether, Sexism and God-Talk, p. 23f.

33.   Ibid., pp. 13-16.

34.   Ibid., p. 38.

35.   See, for example, the essays by the five Anglican authors in The Myth of God Incarnate, ed. John Hick (London: SCM, 1977).

36.   See Systematic Theology, 1:44, 102-5.

37.   See my essay "Where Are We in Theology?" in New Theology No. 9, ed. Martin E. Marty and Dean G. Peerman (New York: Macmillan, 1972).

38.   See Plaskow's Sex, Sin and Grace: Women's Experience and the Theologies of Reinhold Niebuhr and Paul Tillich (Lanham, Md.; University Press of America, 1980).

39.   See my essay "Theology and Experience," Harvard Theological Review 78 (1985) 179-201.

40.   See Wolf, ed., The Spirit of Anglicanism, pp. 146-51; and John E. Booty, What Makes Us Episcopalians? (Wilton, Conn.: Morehouse-Barlow, 1982), ch. 5.

KEEPING SEX IN ORDER:
Heterosexism in Episcopal Church Policy[*]

Anne E. Gilson

There should be an urgency among progressive Christians these days surrounding the discussion of sexual ethics. Unfortunately, there is no such urgency. This lack of concern suggests the extent to which the liberal church may be resting on its laurels. Furthermore, among Episcopalians, it is a sign of a peculiarly "Anglican" reluctance to do anything that might threaten the "unity" of the church. Concern over sexual ethics is expressed only when "unity" among churchmen who hold ecclesiastical authority is threatened. Even then, such men tend primarily to establish committees to "study" sexuality or make the occasional pronouncement in times of public agitation. This situation reflects an attitude which is unrealistic and irresponsible given the day-to-day lives of many church people.

The institutional church upholds heterosexual, monogamous marriage as normative. Marriage, marital fidelity, and sexual chastity are the standards of Christian sexual morality.[1] This is the ideal toward which all good Christians are encouraged to strive. However, this standard does not take into account the growing numbers of church people whose lives do not reflect it. The result is that a lot of pretending goes on while the realities are ignored.

What are the realities? The realities consist of much more than the traditional nuclear family. Many heterosexual never-married people find the traditional notion of sexual chastity outside of marriage to be inadequate. Framers of church policy must not assume that never-married people refrain from having sexual relationships. The standard of sexual chastity is further challenged by the growing number of coupled heterosexual never-married people who choose to live together without "the sacrament of marriage." In the mainline Protestant denominations, divorce is usually tolerated.[2] But divorced people, like people who have never married, often do not refrain from sexual relationships.

The idealization of marriage has closed many peoples' eyes to the problems faced by battered women or incested children. Too often, this

---

[*] This essay is the revision of an extended research project begun in 1988. Tom F. Driver's wise guidance made the research of this essay possible. Conversations with Beverly Wildung Harrison have influenced the shape this essay took. Kathleen Greider offered advice on an earlier draft. And, Allison Moore read and commented on a later draft. To the four of them, I am especially grateful.

idealization generates a silence on the part of the church in the face of domestic violence and sexual abuse. This silence serves to isolate and trivialize women and children. It often happens that the church's silence leads to an increase of violence because it is "heard" as consent to the subordination of women and children. After all, marriage is to be the ideal male-female partnership. Violence is not supposed to happen in the lives of nice people.[3] Nor are nice people supposed to be the perpetrators of such violence.

If the situation is difficult for heterosexual people, it is even more difficult for lesbians and gay men. Within the church family, lesbians and gay men are the biggest scandals of all. The standards of marriage, marital fidelity, and sexual chastity do not even begin to address the realities of the lives of lesbians and gay men. Lesbians and gay men are prohibited from entering into the sacrament of marriage,[4] are accused of promiscuity simply by being lesbian or gay, and are urged not to "practice" homosexuality. Lesbians and gay men are often encouraged either to convert to heterosexuality or take vows of celibacy. Such responses attempt to silence lesbian and gay voices.[5] Thus it is that the biggest challenge to ecclesiastical authority on the subject of sexuality these days comes from lesbians and gay men.

In reflecting on the failure of much of liberal church policy to adequately address the concerns of church people in relation to sexuality, it occurred to me that not only are such policies inadequate for many people today, but they were not created ex nihilo. We do not operate in an historical vacuum. Certainly many centuries of theological rumination have influenced current sexual ethics. Examining a recent part of that history -- namely, the sexual ethic defended against the burgeoning sexual revolution and pronounced anew in the late 1950s and early 1960s -- I was struck by the similarities between what was pronounced then and the recent statements emanating from Episcopal church authorities. This similarity seemed to have important implications for understanding what is at stake in the current debate on sexual ethics in Episcopalian circles.

To that end, I will explore the work of two theologians from the earlier period -- Lutheran ethicist Helmut Thielicke, whose work on sexuality is highly regarded among many mainline Christian theologians, and Anglican theologian, D.S. Bailey, whose work on sexuality would be considered "enlightened" still today. In mainline modern Protestantism, Thielicke and Bailey might be said to represent a "generic" position on sexual ethics: Thielicke, as proposing the agapic redemption of erotic love, and Bailey as posturing a theory of the complementarity of male and female sexuality. Both theories and both theologicans can be cited, fairly, as progressive by traditional Christian standards. My concern here is not with whether these two theologians' work has been cited or used in detail by contemporary Episcopal church policy makers, but with whether their "generic" positions have been, in any way, clarified, challenged, sharpened, or changed by the shapers of sexual ethics (who are also the makers of church policy) for the Episcopal Church today. This essay will conclude with my own suggestive and constructive approach to sexual ethics.

WORKING DEFINITIONS: Sexism, Heterosexism, and Homophobia

Critical to a project such as this is the identification of the perspective from which I approach this study as well as the ways in which certain terms are understood. Part of working as a Feminist Liberation Theo-ethicist[6] entails an ongoing analysis of how the various facets of my identity impact my work. On the one hand, I have power by virtue of the middle class, white, Episcopalian, and well-educated aspects of my identity. This is so because ours is a world-church[7] in which such people dominate. On the other hand, I am on the underside of power by virtue of my female and lesbian identities. This is so because ours is a world-church which is dominated by male, seemingly heterosexual, people. Thus it is that I speak as a white, well-educated, lesbian, middle class, decidedly feminist, Episcopalian woman with a great deal invested in the topic at hand. It must also be kept in mind that those responsible for the policy in the first place also have a great deal invested in the topic.

In order to unmask, debunk, and disentangle[8] the normativity of sexism, heterosexism, and homophobia, these terms must be concisely defined. This is a critical task in the work of sexual ethics, as these forces serve to mystify and render invisible their impact on our lives.

A. Sexism

Sexism is rooted in the dualistic negation of that which is female, sexual, eros, flesh and earthy. It is the assumption of female-gender inferiority and the presumption of male-gender superiority. Sexism is the domination of women by men. It is a force which would keep women and men in neatly constrained gender roles. Sexism affects women across age, racial, cultural, sexual, and economic lines.

B. Heterosexism

Heterosexism is inseparable from sexism. Heterosexism is the glue which holds sexism in place. It has to do with male control over female sexuality. Heterosexism encourages the sexual exploitation of women and is held in place by heterosexual privilege. Heterosexual privilege is the security and protection bestowed on women for the price of male control over female bodies.[9] For

example, a woman is much safer at night if she is walking down the street with
a man than if she is alone or with another woman.

Compulsory heterosexuality is the institutionalization of heterosexism.
It is the foundation upon which the control of sexuality is built. It assures that
heterosexuality is perceived as being normative, indeed as being the only option.
It denies the possibility of woman-to-woman bonding. It also denies the
possibility of specifically sexual man-to-man bonding. However, heterosexism
affects women differently than men because men, by the very fact that they are
men, hold more power than women.[10] Indeed, society is structured around the
compulsory nature of heterosexuality so that homosexual possibilities -- the
existence of homosexual images, relationships, and cultures -- are kept hidden.

C. Homophobia

Homophobia is an attitude reinforced by the structures of sexism and
heterosexism. It is a social disease which is out of control. Homophobia
literally means fear of the same. It manifests itself in the fear-filled hatred of
lesbians and gay men. Those who would prefer that lesbians and gay men keep
silent and remain invisible fear who self-affirming lesbians and gay men can
become and fear as well the challenges to the normativity of heterosexuality.
Homophobia reveals the extent to which sexuality is controlled.[11]

With these initial definitions I turn now to an examination of the work
of Helmut Thielicke and D.S. Bailey. It is important to note that while the
current project is based on two time periods -- circa 1959 to 1964 and 1977 to
1990 -- there are deeper historical roots to such pronouncements on sexual
ethics. Nevertheless, the point is that the historical tradition of sexual ethics
was re-examined, adapted, and much of it re-affirmed in the late 1950s and
early 1960s. It continues to influence church policy today.

IN DEFENSE OF SOME SEXUAL ORDER: Helmut Thielicke and D.S.
Bailey

A. Helmut Thielicke and the Redemption of Eros

Helmut Thielicke's book The Ethics of Sex was published in the United
States in 1964. Originally delivered as a series of lectures at the University of
Chicago Divinity School in 1963, those lectures were "so framed...in terms that
would be intelligible to medical men, jurists, and all educated persons who are
concerned with the problems of sex."[12]

Writing from post World War II Germany, Thielicke worked at a time when the concept of homosexuality was hidden, not discussed much, and when it was discussed, it was categorized as a perversion. The late 1950s and early 1960s brought a new age of sexual permissiveness and experimentation to the fore. Thielicke, and others, realized that the theological reflections on sexuality from years past which stressed the procreational function of sex were inadequate for responding to the situation which faced them. They were anxious to provide some moral guidelines for Christians about sex. Thus was The Ethics of Sex born.

As is true with any theologian, how one views the relationship between humanity and God is central to the theology espoused. Thielicke believed that the God-human relationship is foundational for theology and encloses all dimensions of human existence. The God-human relationship is indivisible.[13] Within this theological framework, Thielicke viewed sexuality as God's gift to humanity. One's sexual encounters could not be separated from one's relationship with God, however much one might wish it.

While this view did much to affirm human sexuality and took sexuality out of the realm of mere grin and bear it "function",[14] it also provided a strong basis upon which to build an ethics of sex. If sexuality was to be seen as not just pure biological function, but as interconnected with the spiritual-moral life of human beings, then sexual partners could not be viewed merely as interchangeable players. For if human sexuality was only functional, then, argued Thielicke, there should be no reason why "prostitution should not be legalized and made a social institution." He adamantly opposed a functional interpretation of human sexuality and noted that there was a much deeper criterion for human sexual encounters than the mere "ability to perform the erotic function." To him that deeper criterion was the engagement of the total person in the sexual encounter -- including the spiritual person.[15]

Thielicke moved quickly from his assertion that experiences of one's sexuality cannot be separated from experiences of one's spirituality into a detailed exposition of "the theological phenomenology of the human sex relationship" -- namely, that there were two types of love: eros and agape. All aspects of the person were involved in the "sex community."[16] That being the case, it was not sufficient -- nor desirable -- to view eros as being the only dynamic that established a relationship between two people. Going further, Thielicke noted that eros itself not only expressed itself in erotic situations, but by definition involved the other person's being as well.[17] Illustrating this, Thielicke wrote:

The only question is whether I can see the whole person if I do not see him in his relationship to God and therefore as the bearer of an 'alien dignity.' If I am blind to this dimension, then I can give the other person only a partial dignity insofar as I estimate his importance 'for me' -- even if this includes far more than his mere functional importance for me! -- but not insofar as I see in him his importance 'for God.'[18]

Thielicke was trying to place eros in a context which reached beyond its connotation of having to do with the purely erotic, the fleshly, the explicitly carnal nature of sex. He wanted to bring to eros the consideration of the entire person including that person's relationship to both God and a lover. He was attempting to correct the long-held notion that the erotic was something that good Christian people should not experience.

If Thielicke had been satisfied enough to let his broadening of the definition of eros suffice with a more wholistic and integrative approach, he might have done better in improving the reputation of eros. Although the question must be asked if the cost of improving the reputation of eros would have been to desexualize eros. As it was, Thielicke brought in agape to supplement eros. The more highly valued agapic part of a relationship became, for Thielicke, that which ultimately permitted the other to appear "not merely in [her/his] 'being as [s/he] is,' but rather in [her/his] 'being before God.'"[19]

Thielicke played heavily on the distinction between eros and agape. In eros it was the worth of the other person as a sexual being that was the object, whereas in agape the object was the authentic being (Eigentlichkeit) of the other person. According to Thielicke, agape produced "loveworthiness" and supplied the "neighbor" characteristic to one's perception of one's erotic partner. These two types of love intersected in the "sexual community."[20]

In an effort to incorporate agape even further into Christian ethical thinking on sexuality, Thielicke grounded it in scripture and placed it above eros in importance. He is worth quoting at length here:

(Agape's) characteristic is that it does not 'seek its own' (1 Cor. 13:5) and yet receives all things 'as well.' Agape takes hold of a tendency which is built into the creaturely sex nature of [human beings] in the form of a sign, a challenge, and transforms it into a motive. It gives meaning and purpose to what instinct may do ignorantly and relates it to the whole of human existence and community for which [human beings were] created. In this way sex has its effect upon the physical elements of the relationship... Agape should be seen as that which helps and liberates and fulfills <u>even in the realm of the libido</u>.[21] (emphasis mine)

Thielicke started out fine by bringing in a relational, more wholistic interpretation of eros. But, in making such a distinction between eros and agape, Thielicke contradicted his earlier, more positive statements on eros. What appeared to start out as an affirmation of the erotic nature of intimate relationship, turned into a theo-ethical statement that eros could not stand alone in relationships but instead must be supplemented by agape in order to make eros even remotely acceptable. Agape all but eclipsed the presence of eros in intimate relationships. This served to underscore the aspersions that Christian theology historically had cast on the erotic.

In looking at this material from a perspective of analyzing heterosexism, several questions must be raised. How has such a categorization of love contributed to heterosexism? By diminishing the power of eros for creating strong, mutual relationships, has Thielicke undermined his earlier intention to affirm the erotic nature in human relationships? Is Thielicke communicating that eros needs redemption? Concomitantly, does agape not need redemption?

Thielicke backed out of affirming eros, I suspect, because the power of eros, the power of the flesh and, by implication, the power of the female, threatened his need, as a Christian ethicist, to bestow and maintain order. If agape does not chasten and shape eros, how does God participate in all aspects of human relationships? If God participates in human relationships, does God participate in eros and in the flesh? And if God participates in eros and in the flesh, is God involved in femaleness? Thielicke brought agapic love to the rescue. It was, I suggest, a way of keeping eros under the control of that which patriarchal Christianity has named "God," a disembodied spiritual principle. Thielicke's alternative was to risk losing control -- not only of eros but of the flesh, women, and perhaps even God.

Such use of eros and agape underscores a false split in the Christian understanding of love. Eros and agape are used against each other in order to control human sexuality. Thielicke was concerned that, without such control, people might feel that premarital and extramarital sex were permissible. Pushing the scenario even further, the institution of marriage might be challenged. The structure of compulsory heterosexuality might crack. In short, by setting eros and agape in two such distinct positions, Thielicke laid the groundwork for an ethics of sex which served to sublimate eros and bring agapic love to the fore.

The following examples bear this out. According to Thielicke, men's sexuality is wide awake. Woman's sexuality -- Thielicke qualifies this by adding, parenthetically, "the untouched woman,"-- must be awakened.

...She requires a process of awakening, which takes place in stages over a longer or shorter time. This awakening naturally cannot simply be an unconcerned pursuit of the male sex, but rather requires self-denial, self-control, and 'selfless' compliance. Thus what we have called agape, namely, self-giving, serving love, which therefore also serves to awaken the other person, manifests itself again as an integrating force in the sex community, which breaks down when it is completely absent.[22]

The way that Thielicke has used the distinctions between eros and agape sets up the continued infantilization of female sexuality. Female sexuality must be awakened by male sexuality. The wheels of compulsory heterosexuality are set in motion: the man must play the role of the concerned, agapic aggressor and woman must play the role of the innocent, sleeping beauty -- sleeping eros.

Once awakened, it is the female who desires to cultivate what Thielicke termed the "erotic atmosphere." He noted:

...The human being -- especially the female -- yearns for a continuing erotic atmosphere, for personal intimacy, and for many small proofs of solidarity which give tone to the atmosphere and do not merely flash through it like a stroke of ecstasy... The institutional form which is designed to maintain this atmosphere is found in marriage.[23]

According to Thielicke, because the female yearns so for an erotic atmosphere, only the male is able to take appropriate responsibility. He is to make certain that eros does not get out of hand while the female yearns for eros. In short, the male must control eros. The only way to insure such control is by participating in the institutionalization of the relationship; namely, marriage, the ultimate agapic relationship.

The final components of compulsory heterosexuality are snapped into place in Thielicke's discussion of monogamy.

...Out of the center of her nature the woman strives to make the totality of her experience correspond to her total submission to the man. Her goal is to make not only the physical side of the man her own...but rather to own the man's very self. The motive of monogamy lies essentially in the very nature of female sexuality.[24]

Not only is woman portrayed as the one who desires a continuing eroticism, but woman must possessively devour the male. Since woman is the one whose hunger for eroticism is unquenchable and thus demands ownership of the male, she must pay the price of total submission. Thus, the groundwork is laid for the institutionalization of monogamy as well as misogyny.

Thielicke's view of heterosexual relationships foreshadowed his view of homosexuality. To him, homosexuality was a perversion. The homosexual had to be willing to seek treatment of healing for his (sic) condition.[25] The role of the pastor in such cases should be to encourage sublimation of unnatural desires. Thielicke thus branded homosexuality outside the realm of possible human relationships.

All this he did in the name of the agapic love of God who participates in all the various aspects of human relationships. The end result of his interpretation was that eros was controlled by subordinating female sexuality to male sexuality and by upholding the institution of marriage.

B. Derrick Sherwin Bailey and the Complementarity of Male and Female Sexuality

Anglican theologian D.S. Bailey worked in the late 1950s and early 1960s in England. He wrote during the period in which the Quaker Report on Sexuality affirmed homosexual relationships and The Wolfended Report recommended the decriminalization of homosexuality to the British Parliament. Like Thielicke, Bailey wrote at a time of changing sexual mores and was anxious to respond within a Christian moral framework.

To Bailey's credit, he was quick to admit that his work took place in the Christian culture of the West. Much of his historical analysis focused on debunking the cult of virginity. In history, Bailey noted, virginity had been held as being a higher state than marriage. This was indicative of an aversion to things of the flesh; indeed, a spirit/flesh dualism in which things of the flesh were evils to be avoided. In setting a context for the work which followed, Bailey stated that part of his work would be to challenge that age-old dualism so that virginity and marriage would cease being set against each other and things of the spirit and things of the flesh could be brought together.

Bailey worked to construct a Christian sexual ethics. He defined sexual ethics as "moral principles which govern the mutual relations of men and women."[26] Bailey asserted that, in beginning, it was crucial to ask two questions: "what is sex?" and "what is (humanity)?" These two questions were inseparable since each informed the other. He wrote:

> Human sex is...nothing less than the expression in personal terms of a distinction existing essentially in [humanity] -- a distinction which is bound up with the very nature and structure of humanity.[27]

Adament that sex could not be separated from human life, this was the definition upon which Bailey would base his sexual ethics.

This definition also laid the groundwork for an intricate explication of the complementary nature of the sexes. Humanity, according to Bailey, is a dual entity, male and female. Scripture was his authority for this assertion.[28] That humanity was created in imago Dei, affirmed humanity's constitution as a sexual duality. Sexuality was for Bailey, as it was for Thielicke, God-given.

The interconnectedness of humanity and sexuality meant that in a Christian sexual ethics, each person was expected to fulfill two primary duties: 1) to preserve one's sexual integrity (by which was meant to accept one's gender and what that thereby implied about one's sexuality and 2) to accept the duty of sexual partnership.[29] The implications of fulfilling these two duties, for both the lives of individuals and for the life of the community, rested in gender role differentiation.

For Bailey, gender role differentiation was reflected in the question of how to determine what is "truly manly" and "truly womanly." Such a determination would be the criteria by which the sexual mores of a society would be tested. Indeed, the only manner in which one could gain sexual knowledge of oneself -- of what it meant to be a woman or a man -- was through relation with the opposite, or complementary, sex.

> Alone, or among others of the same sex, one is not conscious of sex as a personal quality -- for to recognize that one is male or female conveys no awareness of sexual polarity and no understanding of manhood or womanhood. But to enter into sincere relating (of whatever kind) with a member of the complementary sex is to move into a new dimension of experience through encounter with another who is human, but in a radically different way from oneself -- who is so like one, yet so very unlike. Now, and only now, does sex become meaningful as a personal quality.[30]

Bailey intended to establish that one knows oneself only in relation. True knowledge of oneself is reflected in the other --in particular, the other who is of the complementary gender. This is how one was meant to go about fulfilling the first duty: that of accepting one's gender.

Through this work, Bailey set out to renounce his earlier position which had supported the subordination of women. He hoped, instead, to portray a picture of sexuality in which woman was the equal of man. The theory of complementarity was the way in which Bailey saw women as equals. Unfortunately, the result was not the equality of women but rather the enforcement of compulsory heterosexuality. If, as Bailey maintained, sexual knowledge only came about through relationship with the opposite sex, one could only know one's true womanhood or manhood within that situation. Self-knowledge or self-questioning was contained within a necessarily heterosexual framework.

In explicating the second duty of accepting sexual partnership, Bailey further built the case for compulsory heterosexuality. He wrote:

> Sexual partnership means nothing less than the free and equal association of man and woman in all the manifold interest and enterprises of social, political, and ecclesiastical life, hence liberating the creative dynamic of sex for the furtherance of the common good and the enrichment and elevation of human life as a whole.[31]

While some would argue that Bailey had set the stage for the equal participation of women in all the various aspects of society, I would suggest that a closer look reveals something different. As sexual self-knowledge was limited to a relation (of whatever kind) with the complementary sex, so too was knowledge of oneself in every other sphere of life. Compulsory heterosexuality was set up in this statement by confining the sexual partnership in which human beings were to participate to the heterosexual mode. It was cemented by the assertion that such relationships would further the common good. All aspects of society were cued to support and maintain the compulsory nature of heterosexuality.

In all of this talk about sexual partnership, Bailey had not yet dealt with intimate sexual details. He preferred to use the term "coition" when referring to specific "venereal" activity. Like Thielicke, Bailey sought to set coition in a context in which those involved (especially men) would be moved to accept responsibility for their actions. In encouraging this, Bailey noted that coition could never be seen as only an individual's act (it does take two, after all) but must be seen as changing those involved forever. Concerning premarital sex, he wrote:

> Once done, it can never be undone; its effect, though imperceptible, is indelible, and repetition only serves to deepen the impression made upon the personality, either for good or for ill.[32]

In this statement, Bailey moved closer to his assertion that coition must be kept within the sacred bonds of marriage. Although it is doubtful if Bailey would have admitted it, a threat of coition leaving an indelible mark on those who engaged in it (the implication here is that because it was premarital sex it was engaged in under the "wrong" circumstances) contained a suggestion of a modern scarlet letter.

We who come from a feminist liberation position in regard to sexuality know, without too many leaps of the imagination, that the indelible mark of "illegal" coition is left on the woman. This is even more likely given the socio-historical milieu in which Bailey was writing, as well as his insistence that a role of the "truly manly" man is to bestow respect and protection on the "truly womanly" woman. Sexism is at work here in the double standard of sexual ethics in which men and women play, and women carry the indelible marks. So too is heterosexism at work in Bailey's developing argument against sex outside of marriage.

In the chapter on chastity, Bailey acknowledged that all too often the authors of sexual ethics invoke the fear of pregnancy or diseases as a way to drive home their argument against premarital sex. Bailey preferred to approach it from a different perspective and offer reasons of more substance and relational value than those based on fear and threats. As an alternative, Bailey attempted to convince the reader that premarital sex was unwise by invoking consideration for others and what he saw as the way to be in right relation. He argued that one should not engage in coition outside of marriage because one never knows how the individuals involved, women, will react. After all, coition often sets into gear a maternal instinct in women. What was intended only as a moment's gratification could contain unpredictable emotional implications and could well "cause unexpected suffering or unhappiness."[33]

Ultimately, the bottom line for Bailey was that coition must take place solely within marriage because that was the only possible context in which the pair could be irrevocably committed to each other. If the threat of unhappiness or irrevocable commitment did not move his readers to compliance, Bailey reinstated the threat of pregnancy and the plea to consider the well-being of an unborn child.

What comes across in Bailey's attempt at limiting coition to marriage is the message that despite his efforts to prove the contrary, the basic understanding of coition as evil (as in the work of Augustine, for example) still lurks in the minds of men, albeit with a modern twist. The message is clear: sex outside of marriage is bad. It is only the partnership of marriage which can redeem a fallen sexuality (eros).

When writing of the complementarity of the sexes in all aspects of life -
- the social, political, professional, and ecclesiastical -- Bailey asserted that was
how sexual knowledge is gained. Since, according to Bailey, understanding
one's gender and one's sexuality comes only from interaction with the
complementary sex -- same sex association cannot supply self-knowledge.
Bailey went so far as to urge against single sex schools for children as they may
encourage "false sexual ideas."[34]   This points to another aspect of the
heterosexist order which Bailey constructs. The heterosexist myth of complementarity functions to devalue same sex friendships. In fact, Bailey does not
refer to friendship between members of the same sex. Such an omission is
glaring in a book which deals extensively with interpersonal relationships and
intimacy issues. One can only assume that Bailey is suffering from a case of
severe homophobia in setting up a system of complementarity which seems to
presuppose that one can do without close relationships with same-sex friends.[35]

Throughout his work, Bailey held to the implications of the complementarity theory as he had drawn it. He referred to homosexuality as "one of the
gravest moral problems of our time."[36]   Not surprisingly, Bailey diagnosed
homosexuality as a symptom of the decay of moral standards. He noted:

...The so-called 'problem of homosexuality' which confronts us today is
really a problem arising from...the abandonment of moral responsibility
in the field of heterosexual relation -- both as the result of false or
imperfect conceptions of the nature of sex, and of ignorance or rejection
of the will of God for man and woman.[37]

This clearly underscores the importance to Bailey of compulsory
heterosexuality. The archetypes of the "true man" and the "true woman" are
sanctioned by his appeal to divine will. Homosexuality was anathema.

Not only was Bailey against homosexuality in general, but it annoyed
him that gay men often faced punishment while lesbians got off free. Bailey
only addressed lesbian sexuality as a threat to existing heterosexual marriages
-- not as an entity in itself. He was convinced that, more often than not, it was
the lesbian who interfered with heterosexual marriages by seducing married
women and causing marriages to fail.[38]   Such behavior, according to Bailey,
could not be tolerated. Both male and female homosexuals should have to face
the consequences of their actions.

The remedy to such a moral problem?   Bailey predicted that the
promotion of happy heterosexual marriages would achieve better results than
punitive legislation which targeted the private practices of adults. One must,

after all, pay some pastoral attention to the disease (namely, the lack of interaction with the complementary gender) that had produced homosexuality.

We are left with a sexual ethic which keeps men and women functioning in a tightly constrained manner. According to Bailey, men and women belong together, for it is only through relation with a member of the complementary sex that one can gain any knowledge of oneself. This means that one accepts the duty of sexual partnership and does so within prescribed limits. If one steps outside these limits, one risks damaging relations with oneself, the other, the community, and probably God himself (sic).

CURRENT EPISCOPAL CHURCH STATEMENTS ON SEXUALITY

The assumption that eros must be redeemed by a "higher love" and that this can happen only between a man and a woman is a notion alive and well in the contemporary church. In it, we are handed an ethic that espouses life-long, monogamous, heterosexual marriage as the only arena in which sex is permissible for faithful Christians.[39] This not only affects a large number of heterosexual women and men. It strongly affects lesbian and gay people as well.

Episcopal Church statements on sexuality posit marriage as the expected form of sexual relationship for Christians:

> The Committee is uniformly agreed that life-long, monogamous marriage is the normative, or ideal, context for moral, intimate sexual expression between Christians![40]

The implication of this statement is that those who engage in any other kind of sexual relationship run the risk of being immoral and unchristian. This is a clear illustration of heterosexuality as compulsory in church policy. This manifestation of compulsory heterosexuality conveys the message that alternatives to heterosexual, monogamous marriage should be kept inaccessible, shut behind the proverbial closet door. Nowhere is there any acknowledgement that an increasing number of churchpeople will at some point in their own lives experience premarital, extramarital, or post-marital (after divorce or being widowed) sexual relationships -- or lesbian/gay sexual relationships.

In the same vein, a statement from the House of Bishops the previous year declared:

> While they are urged to offer love, forgiveness and pastoral care to all persons, neither the clergy nor the laity of this church should encourage

any attempt to legitimize any sexual behavior other than that which is appropriate between a man and a woman united in holy matrimony.[41]

The House of Bishops posited that not only is marriage the normative, moral and Christian mode of sexual expression, but it is also the only one that can conceivably be sanctioned. At its best, this is a blatantly "love the sinner, but hate the sin" theology which isolates the growing number of church people who do not conform. At its worst, it psychologically and spiritually traumatizes those who do not conform. It promotes a sexual ethic that tightly constrains women and men, encouraging a growing alienation from our bodies, one another, the world, and God.

The church's stress on heterosexual marriage as the medium of sexual expression is rooted in scripture and reflects the natural order.

Both in the Old Testament and in the New Testament the understanding of sex is rooted in the conviction that the divine image in humanity is incomplete without both man and woman. Hence, the aim of sexuality as understood in Christian terms is not merely satisfaction or procreation but completeness.[42]

The complementarity theory is at work here and is authorized by appeal to scripture, tradition, and divine intent. Man and woman belong together. Explicitly, man plus woman equals completeness. Implicitly, woman plus woman, man plus man, woman alone, or man alone equals incompleteness. Furthermore, the message is not only that homosexuality is incomplete, but also that it is a perversion of the natural order.

The frequently invoked 1979 General Convention statement on the ordination of lesbians and gay men continues the completeness theme by insisting on "wholesome examples."[43] It goes on to state that there should be no obstacle to ordaining either heterosexuals or lesbians and gay men as long as their behavior is considered wholesome by the church. Wholesome in this usage means that if one is heterosexual, one must not have sex outside of marriage. Although, it must be noted that many bishops are so relieved when candidates for ordination are heterosexual that their sexual activity outside of marriage is ignored. For lesbians and gay men it is a different story. Unless one is willing to take a vow of celibacy, then according to both the statement and the practice of most dioceses one cannot be considered for ordination.[44] Perhaps this "wholesomeness" is a manifestation of agape, that which redeems and controls eros. At any rate, in this statement "wholesome" precludes homosexuality.

When this statement is challenged as being oppressive of lesbians and gay men, the reply is often that it is not oppressive because lesbians and gay men are Children of God. The defenders of the statement hasten to add, however, that being a child of God does not guarantee one's consideration for ordained ministry. What they overlook in this caveat is that to deny the vocations of Children of God who are lesbian or gay to ordained ministry denies not only our status as Children of God, but also the wholeness of the church. It excludes a priori the ordained ministries of an entire group of people.

Responding to this statement, 23 dissenting bishops drafted an opposing statement.[45] They expressed appreciation for the ordained ministries of known homosexual persons "formerly and presently engaged in the service of this church." The dissenting bishops noted that the resolution was "a cruel denial of the sexual beings of homosexual persons" and also that it condemned

... countless lay persons of homosexual orientation who are rendered second class citizens, fit to receive all other sacraments but the grace of Holy Orders, unless -- in a sacrifice not asked of heterosexual persons generally, they abandon all hope of finding human fulfillment, under God, in a sexual and supportive relationship... We do not believe that either homosexual orientation as such, nor the responsible and self-giving use of such a mode of sexuality, constitutes a scandal in and of itself.[46]

The authority of this dissenting statement is summarily dismissed -- most recently in a statement coming from the office of the Presiding Bishop -- as not being "the stated and authoritative position of the church at this time."[47]

Appeal to the authority of the church is a major theme these days in response to issues raised by lesbians and gay men. In the aftermath of Bishop Spong's ordination of a self-affirming, practicing gay man,[48] bishops scurried to invoke the theological tradition of the church, orderly process in church life, as well as the traditional Anglican appeal to the unity of the church.

We decry the action by the Bishop of Newark, which...has polarized our community of faith. What is at stake is the discipline of the church in addressing actions that violate the spirit of our common life... Bishops are called to safeguard the unity of the church.[49]

The unity of the church has become a greatly mystified source of authority in Anglican tradition. The curious thing is that those who plead for unity never seem to realize that the church is not unified. It is already split and has been for years. I suspect that what would be closer to the meaning of the authoritative appeal to unity is "don't alienate the good Anglican gentlemen" or the mainstream, the keepers of the status quo. The fact that women, lesbians and gay men, and racial/ethnic people have been alienated, split from the church for years, seems not to register. Appeal to the unity of the church is a somewhat desperate attempt by church policy makers to control sexuality.

These sexual ethics reflect the dualistic assumptions that erotic love must be redeemed by a higher spiritual love, and that this redemption can happen only between male and female. Within the last 10 to 15 years increasing numbers of theologians and ethicists have challenged both of these assumptions. Beverly Wildung Harrison, James Nelson, and Episcopal feminist Carter Heyward, to name only a few, have attempted to show that the profound devaluing of erotic love and the "romantic" notion of sexual complementarity as redemptive reflect the badly broken spirituality of an oppressive religious tradition. Recent policy statements in the Episcopal church, as in most other churches, have all but ignored this critique. Church leaders need to take a more realistic approach to sexual ethics if they wish to take seriously the actual fabric of peoples' lives. To maintain any connection with the realities of the lives of church people in the late twentieth century, church policy makers must begin to approach sexual ethics from a open-minded and justice-seeking standpoint. It is with this possibility in mind that I offer a constructive reflection on sexual ethics from a feminist liberation theo-ethical perspective.

SEXUAL ETHICS AND THEO-ETHICAL ROOTS

In developing a sexual ethics, the methodological assumptions which inform such attempts must be examined. Consideration of my own assumptions led me to realize that, like Frederic Denison Maurice,[50] my metaphor for theologizing is digging -- a grubby, earthy digging for roots. Roots symbolize for me an intensely powerful erotic connecting between human bodies and the earth. They are a metaphor for life-sustaining and life-enhancing connections between and among ourselves, one another, other earth creatures, the earth itself and God. Roots lie under layers of soil. One must dig to find them. Roots center what is planted in the soil. And as they grow, they move inch by inch into the deep, dank, dark and damp soil of justice-making.

In what follows I will describe particular roots and suggest how each might challenge the sexual ethics of the institutional church as reflected in current policy. The reader should not think of these roots in a chronological order. They grow from the same source -- a faith commitment to the love of God, to justice; to relationships which enhance the well-being of oppressed sisters and brothers, earth, sky, and sea creatures, and the earth itself. Each of these roots nourishes and is nourished by others.[51]

1. The theo-ethical root of suspicion. Suspicion is a critical starting point for those doing work from a liberation perspective.[52] We must be suspicious of the patriarchal tradition which has been and is used to maintain oppression. We must ask questions about what has appeared to be unquestionable in order to overturn that which keeps the downtrodden down. It is from our articulated particular and common experiences -- and even our experiences which we have been unable to speak -- that questions emerge.

Who has what to gain by the control of sexuality -- female sexuality in particular? What would happen if we took bodies, lovemaking, and our yearnings seriously? Who defines what "wholeness" is? Why must sexuality be constrained within a heterosexual monogamous model? What would happen if compulsory heterosexuality wasn't compulsory? Would the walls come tumbling down? The theo-ethical root of suspicion can be used in sexual ethics to get at invisible presuppositions, hidden agendas, and historical structures of normativity.

2. The theo-ethical root of particularity. All liberation theologies are based on the particular experiences of the oppressed. Drawing on our particular experiences to engage and raise questions of theology is part of the power of liberation movements because to speak honestly of our lives and to hear others speak of their lives pushes open the question of what is "normal," and of what is "normative," for human beings as we actually live. Particularity grounds us in the everyday reality of our lives and the lives of others. The differences among us -- of race, gender, sexual orientation, age, class, nationality, physical ability -- as well as the commonalities among us, matter deeply. They make us who we are.

In a theo-ethical root of particularity, the details of our "child of God-ness" cannot be based on a goal of "completeness," or "complementarity" within a tightly controlled reality. Nor can they be based on a rigid perception of "the truly womanly woman" or "the truly manly man." Rather, our "child of God-ness" must be based on a shared responsibility for creating justice which honors the particularities of the lives of marginalized people.

Taking our particularities seriously, what is claimed as morally "normative" becomes a question of what enhances or detracts from our well-being and that of others. Battered women who share stories with one another soon find that their problems are not just their imaginations. Lesbian/gay people join together and are enabled to name ourselves affirmatively. Heterosexual couples, living outside the bonds of matrimony, share visions of new relationships. Shared particularities become parts of common experience, common life. Shared particularities become our shared power together.

3. The theo-ethical root of love of neighbor as self.[53] One cannot love God without loving one's neighbor as oneself. And, conversely, one cannot love one's neighbor as oneself without loving God.[54] The point seldom noted concerning women in particular is that we have been socialized into putting everyone else before ourselves. We have not loved ourselves. Without a love of self, we are unable to love our neighbor. And the reverse is also true: without a love of neighbor, we are unable to love ourselves. Such inability to love fosters fear of our neighbor because we are afraid we might see ourselves in this relation with neighbor. We fear our neighbors as ourselves. And ourselves as our neighbors.

For sexual ethics, this theo-ethical root means that those of us who do not fit in with the sexual ethic of the church -- "that which is appropriate between a man and a woman united in holy matrimony" -- must take ourselves seriously. We cannot sit around waiting for the institutional church to take us seriously. We must not let ourselves be rendered invisible by a love, by agape, which would cover up the role of eros in our common lives. Loving our neighbors as ourselves means that we must reclaim the power of the erotic to transform sex-negative policies into a sex-positive affirmation of loving. The erotic does not, under any circumstance, signify sexual power-over or the sexual abuse of women and children. In loving our neighbors as ourselves, the erotic becomes our source of creative power.[55]

4. Coming to love our neighbors as ourselves encompasses the theo-ethical root of re-connecting.[56] We are born into a world/church built and maintained on the theory of categorization, which keeps pieces of our lives separate as well as keeping us separated from intimate knowledge of one another. As in loving our neighbors as ourselves, this root must overcome fear. We remember that it is a fear of re-connecting, of being intimate with one another. Indeed, a fear of our own bodies has ruled our lives. Our fear destroys the earth, the human, the sexual, the flesh. Connections between us are destroyed because we are so afraid. This fear is evident in the responses of many people to AIDS. Fear encourages denial and prevents us from learning about practicing and eroticizing "safer sex." Lives are at stake. We must begin to transform fear before it is too late.

We must re-connect what has been disconnected. The theo-political work of structural analysis enters into this root as re-connections are made between sexism, heterosexism, racism, classism, and other forms of oppression. The knowledge that these are not isolated occurrences but rather are structurally interconnected in the fear of our common-ness has the potential of empowering marginalized people into action.

In sexual ethics, a theo-ethical root of re-connecting must take into account the differences among us regarding our access to power and privilege. The input of racial/ethnic people, women, and lesbians and gays must be sought in the process of formulating church policy. This input must be decisive, not merely token. Re-connecting, the friction between us born of our differences creates a life-giving erotic power which turns over the death-dealing attempts of the powers that be to divide and conquer us.

This root continues the just, mutual, and erotic re-connecting between people begun in the root of loving our neighbors as ourselves. An explicitly sexual theo-ethical root of re-connecting is one in which the intimate details of our lives can be affirmed within our common-ness, within the friction born of our differences, between and among our bodies. Freeing ourselves from fear, we touch and are touched, move and are moved, heal and are healed, earth and are earthed into the loam of each other's and our own bodyselves. Re-connecting, we meet the feelings, the people, and the bodies from which we have been disconnected. Reconnecting, eros is coming -- coming unchastened, coming unshaped, coming unbound, coming unruled/unruly.

5. The theo-ethical root of solidarity. A theo-ethical root of solidarity means that we must not be blinded by either our power or our own oppression to seeing the oppression of others. We must ask: How do we stand together, you and I? How shall we be accountable to one another? Who are my, your, and our people? Who will stand with us when they come to get us? Accountability is critical to this root and it entails a willingness to risk, to confront, and to disagree.

In a theo-ethical root of solidarity, there is no room for those who want to be comfortable, who want to keep other people from being disturbed, who want to keep the status-quo, who want to be liked by everyone, or who want to push a premature reconciliation without justice. Solidarity is about raising a ruckus in the face of injustice.

Solidarity is also concerned with unity. This unity is not that unity which is so frequently invoked in appeals to Anglican authority. Unity doesn't always mean agreement. It doesn't ever mean the same.[57] It means the commitment to keep on struggling together to find a common ground in spite of, indeed because of, our differences.

In the development of a sexual ethic, the root of solidarity requires that we recognize our limits and those of the institution, and at the same time challenge those limits. We must engage in work with all people with AIDS -- whether they be infants, gay or bisexual men, women, blood transfusion recipients, or intravenous drug users.   This work must consist not only of pastoral and physical care, but also <u>sex-positive</u> education about safer sex practices.   Curing "promiscuity" by a compulsory "monogamy" is not the issue.[58]   Education is.

In addition, we must challenge the limits of current church policy on ordaining self-affirming, sexually active lesbians and gay men.   Until open lesbians and gay men can be ordained on the same basis as people who are not lesbian or gay-identified, lesbians and gay men will continue to be on the periphery of the church and will continue to leave it and...be left by it.

Solidarity requires that we walk the boundary together, you and I, coming face to face into difficult places with one another, coming together for sustenance, and coming to draw strength from our shared erotic power.

TOWARDS A GREATER URGENCY

As in the cases of Thielicke and Bailey, the Episcopal Church policy statements on sexuality are responding to a sort of "sexual revolution."   What has changed in the intervening years since Thielicke and Bailey is that men and especially women have grown more in touch with their bodies, integrated their sexuality more fully into their lives, and are unwilling to put up with the message that the only appropriate sex is that which takes place between a man and a woman in marriage.   As Thielicke and Bailey realized that the emphasis on sex as procreation was outdated, so too is it time for the Episcopal Church to realize that the stipulation of sex only within heterosexual, monogamous marriage is outdated.

The hour is drawing nigh.   This is not just another plea to study the issues in committee.   It is past time for that.   No longer are people willing to believe that <u>only</u> male plus female equals the divine image and is, in that sense, redemptive.   Nor, increasingly, are people willing to believe that God wills us to love only those of complementary gender within the context of life-long monogamous marriage.   We can no longer afford the high cost of alienation. Our faith communities, our God, and our sexualities are <u>not</u> separate pieces of our identities to be played off against each other.   Our faith, our church, our loves, and our lives are at stake.   We must approach the task before us with urgency.

NOTES

1.   1979 General Convention statement concerning the ordination of lesbians and gay men.

2.   Divorce is more easily tolerated among the laity than among the clergy.   Some dioceses will not ordain divorced people.

3.   A good theological resource on domestic violence is Joy M.K. Bussert, Battered Women: From a Theology of Suffering to an Ethic of Empowerment, (Division for Mission in North American: Lutheran Church in America, 1986).

4.   Whether or not to have marriage available to lesbians and gay men is not only a current debate in the Episcopal Church, but is also a debate within the lesbian/gay community as well.   Some lesbians and gay men believe that "holy unions" only mimic heterosexual institutions instead of creating a form of relationship which is authentic to lesbian/gay experience.   Other lesbians and gay men are attempting to have "holy unions" approved by the church.   The Diocese of Newark, New Jersey, is one place where this has been examined in depth.   See John Shelby Spong, Living in Sin? A Bishop Rethinks Human Sexuality (San Francisco: Harper and Row, 1988).

5.   Exceptions to such treatment of lesbians and gay men include the organizations within mainstream denominations like the Roman Catholic 'Dignity' and the Episcopalian 'Integrity.'   'The Oasis,' in the Diocese of Newark, NJ, is another place, which is focused on lesbian/gay ministry as is 'The Parsonage' in San Francisco.   In addition, the Metropolitan Community Church is a denomination created to serve the particular needs of the lesbians/gay community.

6.   "Feminist Liberation Theology" is a theology which takes into account the ways that sexism, racism, classism, and heterosexism intersect in the lives of women and so function to oppress women.   It is concerned with the 'hearing to speech' (Nelle Morton) and liberation of all women.   The term "theo-ethics" is intended to convey the way in which the fields of ethics and theology interface with each other.

7.   "World-church" is a term which denotes the ways in which church and world are connected.

8.   These terms are used by womanist ethicist Katie Geneva Cannon in her method of liberation ethics.

9.   See Carter Heyward, Touching Our Strength: The Erotic as Power and the Love of God (San Francisco: Harper and Row, 1989); Andrea Dworkin, Woman Hating (New York: Dutton, 1974); and Zillah R. Eisentein, "Developing a Theory of Capitalist Patriarchy and Socialist Feminism" and "Some Notes on the Relations of Capitalist Patriarchy" in Capitalist Patriarchy and the Case for Socialist Feminism, Eisenstein, ed. (New York: Monthly Review Press, 1979), pp. 5-55.

10.   Bell Hooks, Feminist Theory: From Margin to Center (Boston: South End Press, 1984), p. 155. See also Adrienne Rich, "Compulsory Heterosexuality and Lesbian Existence" in Powers of Desire: The Politics of Sexuality, Ann Snitow, Christine Stansell, and Sharon Thompson, eds. (New York: Monthly Review Press, 1983), pp. 177-205; Carter Heyward, op. cit.; and Carter Heyward and Mary Hunt, "Lesbianism and Feminist Theology" in Journal of Feminist Studies in Religion (Scholar's Press, Fall 1986).

11.   For more on homophobia see Beverly Wildung Harrison, "Misogyny and Homophobia" in Making the Connections: Essays in Feminist Social Ethics, ed. Carol Robb (Boston: Beacon Press, 1985), pp. 135-151.

12.   Helmut Thielicke, The Ethics of Sex (New York: Harper and Row, 1964), p. vi.

13.   Ibid., p. 19.

14.   Ibid., pp. 21-24.

15.   Ibid., p. 23.

16.   By this he meant a connection between two human beings which has personal character. This was a term he used to refer to other aspects of human relationships in addition to the exclusively sexual (genital) aspects.

17.   Thielicke, p. 26 ff. Here Thielicke grounds his use of the term "eros" in Platonic philosophy.

18.   Ibid., p. 26. I have purposely left Thielicke's sexist language intact here. I find it more than a little amusing that for one who is so heterosexist, he refers to his sexual partner with male pronouns!

19.   Ibid., p. 27.

20.   Ibid., pp. 28 ff.

21. Ibid., pp. 49-50.

22. Thielicke, p. 51.

23. Ibid., p. 58.

24. Ibid., pp. 84-85.

25. Ibid., pp. 282-285.

26. D.S. Bailey, Common Sense About Sexual Ethics: A Christian View (New York: The MacMillan Company, 1962), p. 8.

27. Ibid., p. 81.

28. Specifically, the second creation account in Genesis, with rabbinical collaboration, and I Cor. 11:2. "...Neither is the woman without the man, nor the man without the woman, in the Lord."

29. Ibid., p. 82.

30. Ibid., p. 87.

31. Ibid., pp. 89-90.

32. Ibid., p. 96.

33. Ibid., p. 127.

34. Bailey, Sexual Relation in Christian Thought (New York: Harper and Brothers, 1959), p. 286.

35. Conversation with Tom F. Driver, April 1988, Union Theological Seminary, New York City.

36. Bailey, Homosexuality and the Western Christian Tradition (London: Longmans, Green & Co., 1955), p. 155.

37. Ibid., p. 166.

38. Ibid.

39. For the record, let me state that I am not arguing against life-long, monogamous, heterosexual marriage. I am only arguing against that which stipulates such relationships as the only option for Christian people.

40. Excerpt from the Interim Report to the House of Bishops of the Protestant Episcopal Church in America by the Commission on Human Affairs and Health, September 30, 1987. To be presented to General Convention, July 1988. The exclamation point is theirs.

41. Episcopal House of Bishops resolution, 1986, in San Antonio.

42. Episcopal House of Bishops Statement on homosexual unions, 1977.

43. The Book of Common Prayer, pp. 517, 532, 544. "Every ordinand is expected to lead a life which is a wholesome example to all people."

44. There are a handful of dioceses in which this is an exception. Unfortunately, they are becoming fewer and further between.

45. The Presiding Bishop, Edmond Browning, originally signed the statement when he was Bishop of the Diocese of Hawaii. Since becoming Presiding Bishop he no longer endorses that statement, at least not publicly.

46. Dissenting Statement formulated by bishops opposed to the General Convention Resolution, 1979.

47. Statement by the Presiding Bishop and Council of Advice, February 20, 1990.

48. On December 16, 1989, Robert Williams was ordained to the priesthood by Bishop Spong in Hoboken, NJ. Contrary to the media reports at the time, he was not the first openly gay man ordained to the priesthood. Due to the publicity surrounding this ordination, ecclesiastical authorities opposed to lesbians/gay ordination are agitated and are intent on clamping down on Robert Williams and Bishop Spong in particular, and self-affirming lesbians and gay men who seek ordination in general.

49. Statement by the Presiding Bishop, et al., pp. 2-3.

50. Frederic Maurice, ed., The Life of Frederic Denison Maurice, Vol 11 (New York: 1884), p. 137.

51. Many people have offered me feedback in the development of these roots. I particularly wish to acknowledge Katie Geneva Cannon, Alison Cheek, Tom F. Driver, Robin Gorsline, Beverly Wildung Harrison, Carter Heyward, Joy Mills, Larry Rasmussen, Nancy Richardson, Elisabeth Schussler Fiorenza, Owen Thomas, and Wilma Wake.

52. See Juan Luis Segundo, The Liberation of Theology, trans. John Drury (Maryknoll, NY: Orbis Books, 1976). See also, Elisabeth Schussler Fiorenza, In Memory of Her: A Feminist Theological Reconstruction of Christian Origins (New York: Crossroad Press, 1983).

53. I am greatly indebted to the work of Carter Heyward on this topic. See especially, The Redemption of God: A Theology of Mutual Relation (Lanham, MD: University Press of America, 1982).

54. The question here is not whether those who do not profess a belief in God can love their neighbors. The answer is obviously affirmative. Rather, the point is that for people of faith, love of neighbor as self is also the love of God. Conversation with Robin Gorsline, Cambridge, MA, 1985.

55. Foundational feminist works on the erotic include Carter Heyward, Touching Our Strength, op. cit., and Audre Lorde, "Uses of the Erotic: The Erotic as Power" in Sister Outsider (Trumansburg, NY: The Crossing Press, 1984); and Rita Nakashima Brock, Journeys By Heart: A Christology of Erotic Power (New York: Crossroad Press, 1988).

56. Here I am indebted to the work of Beverly Wildung Harrison, especially her book Making the Connections: Essays in Feminist Social Ethics, op. cit.

57. Holly Near, "Unity," recorded on Speed of Light, by Redwood Records, Oakland, California, 1982.

58. Note that I am not against monogamy per se. Rather, I see it as a relational choice arrived at by the people in the relationship and not mandated by church authorities.

COMING OUT AND RELATIONAL EMPOWERMENT[1]

Carter Heyward

The words of Audre Lorde, Black lesbian feminist poet and theorist, spoken in the context of her struggle with cancer:

> Of what have I ever been afraid? To question or to speak as I believed could have meant pain, or death. But we all hurt in so many different ways, all the time, and pain will either change or end. Death, on the other hand, is the final silence. And that might be coming quickly, now, without regard for whether I had ever spoken what needed to be said, or had only betrayed myself...while I planned someday to speak, or waited for someone else's words. 'And I began to recognize a source of power within myself that comes from the knowledge that, while it is most desirable not to be afraid, learning to put fear into a perspective gives me great strength.
>
> I was going to die, if not sooner than later, whether or not I had ever spoken myself. My silences had not protected me. Your silence will not protect you.[2]

Lynn, a 36-year-old student, and I sat and shared memories of having crept furtively out of our seminary dorms fifteen years apart -- I in 1971, Lynn in 1986 -- to find our ways, alone, to meetings of the Daughters of Bilitis and, once there, of having slipped in as invisibly as possible, taken seats as close to the door as possible, and tried as hard as possible to convince ourselves that we couldn't possibly be one of "them" -- those lesbians.

Winding our way out of isolation can be a touching and empowering process. Lynn said, "Coming out has been for me learning to experience myself as a woman who receives energy from other women. Coming out has helped me establish my identity as a relational person." She noted, "I couldn't have done it alone," though she was quick to add that she spent her whole first year in seminary avoiding the very people she wanted most to be around. She and Patricia, a lesbian priest currently working in New York, confessed that, for the first year or two they were in seminary, they would cross to the other side of the campus to avoid running into me as I walked from my home to my office.

Diane, formerly a chaplain at Brandeis, tells me that some fifteen years ago she freaked out when she came upon the essay on lesbianism in the first edition of <u>Our Bodies, Ourselves</u>. The article was called, "In Amerika, They Call Us Dykes," and, at age 16, Diane wasn't ready for this.

Coming out as lesbians -- recognizing and naming ourselves as women whose primary erotic energy is generated in relation to women -- is, in heterosexist society, a process laden with risk: emotional, physical, relational and professional. It can be also a revolutionary, empowering and, from a theological perspective, profoundly sacred process.

Appreciating connections between us in our work

I want to acknowledge here the courageous, pioneering work of the Stone Center. I want to thank especially my good friend and colleague, Jan Surrey. I thank also a woman who has been for so long an inspiration to many of us -- Jean Baker Miller, a remarkable resource of a clear and gentle wisdom. I recognize the contributions of Nanette Gartrell and Lennie Kleinberg's work on "lesbian identity disclosure."[3]   And I am grateful to my perceptive colleague and friend, Peg Huff, a pastoral psychologist who introduced me to Jan Surrey and to the Stone Center's work, and who herself is attempting to integrate basic presuppositions of feminist liberation theology and the Stone Center's self-in-relation approach to psychology.

Our limits

Before moving into the body of my paper, I want to say a word about the limits of what I am attempting to do. An important tenet of feminist liberation theory is that we recognize that our knowledge is limited by the particularities of who we are. White women, for example, cannot construct theory "for" or "about" women of color. Or we can construct it, but, in a racist society, it lacks intellectual credibility and the power of moral persuasion for and among most women of color and for those white women who catch the deceptive nuances of white racism in our own work. The best we can do is to speak for ourselves -- of our own lives and work and commitments and learnings -- and listen carefully to others.

To acknowledge that there are limits to what a white, southern, Christian lesbian can know about "relational empowerment" in no way diminishes the value of what I can contribute to this ongoing study. It serves simply to ground and secure my words.   Such an acknowledgement does not render me "separate" from people of color, northerners, Jews or heterosexual women. Rather, it may help strengthen our awareness of our differences and our commonalities as we struggle together toward realizing our power as women...as humans...as earth creatures.

*****

This presentation has four parts: First, I shall discuss heterosexism as a structure of alienated power, for coming out cannot be understood as an empowering relational movement unless we recognize the alienation out of which lesbians and gay men, especially lesbians, are coming. Second, in order to establish further the context of coming out, I shall speak of the erotic power which enables us to come out as a sacred resource available to all. Third, I shall reflect on some ambiguities and tensions in the coming out process, drawing from my own experience. Finally, I shall comment briefly on what I see to be some critical implications of the coming out process for healing in women's lives and, in particular, for the relationship between women healers and women who seek our help, and between us, when we need help, and those women to whom we turn. Until the closing section of this paper, my primary focus will be on lesbian lives and movement. But everything I am saying involves us all.

Heterosexism, power and lesbian women

Heterosexism is the basic structure of gay/lesbian oppression in this and other societies. Heterosexism is to homophobia what sexism is to misogyny and what racism is to racial bigotry and hatred. Heterosexism is the historical social organization of our life together in which is generated fear and uneasiness toward dykes and queers -- toward ourselves if we are lesbian or gay. Dialectically, these feelings serve to hold the structure in place, thereby strengthening not only such traditional patriarchal religious institutions as Christianity, which have done much to set heterosexism in place, but also more deeply personal institutions such as the self-loathing of homosexual youths and the hatred of such youths by their peers.

A "structure" is a pattern of relational transaction which gives a society its shape. Consider the analogy of a house: If there is a structural problem, we don't solve it by changing the wallpaper or rearranging the floor space. We cannot solve the structural problems of class elitism, racism, heterosexism or any other ideology simply by rearranging our lives, institutions and professions to accommodate those who historically have been left out. To solve structural problems, we have to dig into the foundations of our common life in order to discover the rot. Only then can we begin to reconstruct our life together in such a way as to provide adequate, trustworthy space for us all. Let's dig, then, for a few minutes, into the foundations of heterosexism: We are digging toward the realization that our problem is one of alienated -- abusive, nonmutual -- power relations.

Alienated power

In a profit-consumed economic order, the value of persons is diminished. The accumulation of capital on the part of the wealthy and the hope for wealth on the part of the rest of us are designed to take precedence over the essentially nonmonetary value of human beings and other earth creatures as valuable simply because we are who we are. In this context, the capacity to love and respect our bodies, enjoy a strong sense of self-esteem, take real pleasure in our work, and respect and enjoy others, is a weakened capacity. In a literal sense, we have lost ourselves -- ourselves as a people in solidarity with one another and other creatures.

This loss of ourselves and one another is what Karl Marx meant by "alienation."[4]   It forms the basis for what Jean Baker Miller names as our "disconnections" -- the "intensely confounded opposites of the 'good things' that flow from growth-enhancing, mutually empowering connections."[5] In an alienated situation, no one relates as humanely as she or he might desire. It is not that we do not want to be caring people, nor that we do not want to experience and share the "good things" that flow from mutually-empowering relationships. It is, rather, that largely unbeknownst to us in the course of our daily lives, we became alienated from ourselves, from our feelings and our values. In this situation of alienation from ourselves and one another, power has come to mean power over others as well as over our own base "natures." Power has come to mean the domination, however benign, by a few over the lives and deaths of many. I am referring to the real, daily control of all human and other natural resources: the food we eat, the air we breathe, the energy we burn, the love we make, even the dreams we nurture -- all are controlled to a large extent by the structural configurations of power which have been shaped by the interests of affluent white males who usually fail to see the exploitative character of their own lives.

The alienation in our life together is so pervasive that we assume that it is "natural" and "normal." Thus we assume that it is only natural to want to come out on top...to pull ourselves up by our own boot straps...to distinguish ourselves as better than, other than, separate from... We learn to live over/against one another, out of touch with the sacred value of that which is, in fact, most fully human -- common -- among us. It's important that we see the extent to which our acceptance of alienation as "just the way it is" characterizes our common life in the United States in the late twentieth century. This resignation generates a sense of powerlessness among us in which we are largely out of touch with our power as a people to create, to change and to hope. For, while alienated power is not shared, alienated powerlessness is -- and it moves us toward our undoing as a people and a planet.

In the context of alienation, our eroticism -- the deepest stirrings of our relationality, our need and desire to connect -- is infused with dynamics of alienated power. As mirrors of the world, our bodyselves reflect the violence intrinsic to alienation. What we know, what we feel and what we believe to be possible are mediated by images and acts of domination and control. We learn to associate survival, how we control our future, with symbols and acts of coercion and submission. Whether at home or elsewhere, children and adults learn that whether or not might makes right, it shows who's in charge: a whipping, a war movie, a rock video about gang rape, Rambo, the gung-ho carryings on by the President and all his men about the so-called "freedom fighters" in Nicaragua... These are lessons unforgettable in the most embodied sense, by which we learn to experience our most personal world as fraught with tensions of being more, or less, in control of our lives.

The dynamics of alienated power shape our eroticism as surely as they do the Pentagon budget. Ours is a sadomasochistic society, literally, in that we are taught to lie back and enjoy the fruits of control and compliance. Alienated power, for most people, becomes synonymous with relational power.

Heterosexism: structure of alienated power

Sexism is a structure of alienated power between men and women. It refers to the historical complex of practices and attitudes essential to men's control of women's bodies and, thereby, women's lives. Heterosexism is a logical and necessary extension of sexism. It is cemented in the assumption that in order to secure sexism in the social order, men must be forced, if need be, to stay in control of women's bodies. Thus, penetrating to the core of sexism, heterosexism heralds the recognition that, in order to keep women down, men's sexual activity must be imposed upon women. Without male control of female bodies, patriarchal power relations would not prevail: things would fall apart -- "romantic love" between men and women, the ideal of lifelong monogamous marriage and the nuclear family, "traditional values," and "freedom" of the nation...all that is predicated upon privileged men staying in control of the world as we know it.

Insofar as we recognize that heterosexism is the fundamental means of enforcing sexism, we will realize that we cannot separate an analysis of gender relations from an analysis of sexual relations in our efforts to develop feminist psychologies, theologies, or theories of moral reasoning.

"Closet" as instrument of control

We cannot simply up and leave heterosexism behind until we leave this world via death. Coming out refers not to leaving behind us the structures of oppression, but rather exiting from "closets" of psychospiritual, physical and political bondage. A closet is a lonely, cramped place in which to hide... a place of disconnection and disembodiment in which, because we are out of touch with one another, we are out of touch with ourselves.

The closet is also the only culturally acceptable place for lesbians and gay men to live in this culture of gender and sexual alienation. For only insofar as we are closeted will the prevailing power relations be held in place. That's why most of the liberal Protestant churches, for example, have decreed that openly gay men and lesbians who are sexually active cannot be ordained. The issue is not simply sex, but power -- the fundamental organization of social, economic and political power in heterosexist patriarchy. In this context the closet serves as a masterful device of control.

To come out, then, is not merely a step in personal authenticity. It is a step also into a posture of social and political deviance and resistance. In both senses, as movement in authenticity and as act of political dissidence, coming out can become a remarkable process of relational empowerment. It can reflect a "direction of growth"[6] in which the lesbian is seeking more, not less, authentic connection with friends and loved ones and, in so doing, is signalling an investment (however small or unaware) in helping to shape unalienated -- mutual, honest -- power relations in society.

Coming out is a process in which a lesbian's "differentiation" from the relational norms of heterosexist patriarchy becomes clarified, and in which the differentiation happens within the context of her efforts toward making authentic connection with others.[7] Thus, the coming out process is not, fundamentally, a way of separating from parents or others in the lesbian's past or present, but rather of inviting -- implicitly or explicitly -- others to "foster, adapt, and change" with her experience of herself in relation to them.[8] The fact that the lesbian's self-disclosure often precipitates rejection by family, employer and others in her life should not be interpreted as the lesbian's way of disconnecting from others. To the contrary, as Lennie Kleinberg suggests, the act of disclosure is often "an act of love."[9] The high incidence of rejection of openly lesbian women signals the pervasive extent of heterosexism in our lives together.

Erotic as sacred power

Openly lesbian women are dangerous to heterosexist patriarchy because, whether or not it is our intention, our visibility signals an erotic energy that has gotten out of control -- out of men's control. Historically, we have learned that this erotic power is not good -- for us, for others, for the world or for God. Operating on the basis of an interpretive principle of suspicion in relation to heterosexist patriarchal religious and social teachings, feminist liberation theologians in Christianity and Judaism have begun to suspect that our erotic power -- this object of such massive fear among ruling class men, from generation to generation -- is, in fact, our most creative, liberating power -- that is to say, our sacred power, that which many of us call our God or Goddess. And she is indeed dangerous to a culture of alienation and abuse because she signals a better way. She sparks our vision, stirs our imagination and evokes our yearning for liberation. In the image of old wise women, dark and sensual, she calls us forth and invites us to share her life, which is our own, in right, mutual relation. From a theological perspective, coming out as lesbians -- icons of erotic power -- is not only a significant psychological process. It is also a spiritual journey, a movement of profoundly moral meaning and value, in which we struggle, more and more publicly, to embrace our sisters, our friends and ourselves as bearers of sacred power. Let me say a bit more about eros as sacred power.

Christian theology, which has shaped the prevailing relational norms of European and American cultures, traditionally has held that eros (sexual love) and philia ("brotherly" love, or friendship), are, at best, merely derivative from agape (God's love for us, and ours for God and our neighbor -- "neighbor" being interpreted usually as those who are hardest to love: humankind in general, our enemies, those who aren't like us...). The moral distinctions among the three forms of love has been fastened in the classical Christian dualisms between spiritual and material reality and between self and other and, moreover, in the assumption that it is more difficult -- therefore, better -- to express God's (spiritual) love of enemies and strangers than to love our friends and sexual partners.

These distinctions represent a radical misapprehension of love. They fail to reflect, as godly and sacred, the embodied human experience of love among friends and sexual partners because they are steeped in the assumption that erotic power -- or, in patriarchal, androcentric culture, women's power -- is dangerous and bad and therefore always in need of spiritual justification.

To this, feminist liberation theologians say "No." To the contrary, the erotic is our most fully embodied experience of the love of God. It is the source of our capacity for transcendence, or the "crossing over" among ourselves, making connections between and among ourselves. The erotic is the divine Spirit's yearning, through us, toward mutually empowering relation which becomes our most fully embodied experience of God as love.

And how do we know this? We know this by living life, by experiencing the power in mutuality. We know this by having learned to trust our own voices, not in isolation, but in relation to the voices of those whose lives we have learned to trust - prophets, poets, people in our past and present, known personally to us or only by reputation, those whose ways of being in the world, and in history, draw us more fully into mutual connection with one another.

Mutuality is not a matter simply of give and take. It is not, Margaret Huff notes, mere reciprocity.[10] Nor is it equality. Mutuality is not a static place to be. It is movement into a way of being in a relation in which both or all parties are empowered with one another to be more fully themselves: mutually, we come to life.

In the context of mutually empowering relationship, we come to realize that our shared experience of our power in mutual relations is sacred: that by which we are called forth more fully into becoming who we are -- whole persons, whose integrity is formed in our connection with one another. And our shared power, this sacred resource of creation and liberation, is powerfully erotic.

Audre Lorde speaks of erotic power as

> an assertion of the life force of woman; of that creative energy empowered, the knowledge and use of which we are now reclaiming in our language, our history, our dancing, our loving, our work, our lives.[11]

She associates the erotic with wisdom -- "the nurturer or nursemaid of all our deepest knowledge," (p. 56) and, again, with creativity -- "There is, for me, no difference between writing a good poem and moving into sunlight against the body of a woman I love" (p. 58).

Recognizing the fear-laden conditions of our lives in a culture of alienation and isolation, Lorde warns that

> we have been raised to fear the yes within   ourselves, our deepest cravings. The fear of our desires keeps them suspect and indiscriminately powerful, for to suppress any truth is to give it strength beyond endurance. The fear that we cannot grow beyond whatever distortions we may find within ourselves keeps us docile and loyal and obedient, externally defined.[12]

Even our inner voices, which we may call "conscience" or "God" or "ethics" or "intuition," are trained to speak to us in the spirit of homage to a force invisible to us because it is our fear of our YES to our own life force. We fear this life force, our erotic power, because, if celebrated rather than denied, it would "force us to evaluate [all aspects of our existence] in terms of their relative meaning within our lives."[13] Nothing would remain the same. For, as Lorde affirms,

> Once we begin to feel deeply all the aspects of our lives, we begin to demand from ourselves and from our life pursuits that they feel in accordance with that joy which we know ourselves to be capable of.[14]

The capacity to begin moving through fear towards this joy is the beginning of healing. It is erotic power at work among us. It is the spiritual context in which lesbians are coming out, rearranging ourselves in relation to friends, families, love, work and the world itself.

Coming out: A lesbian feminist perspective

Though the lesbian cannot determine by herself the effects of her self-disclosure on others, her desire to come out is, at root, a desire to connect authentically with others. Coming out, we lesbians seek to participate in relationships in which, as Jean Baker Miller suggests, at least five "good things" happen (and I paraphrase):

> We feel a greater sense of "zest"... We feel more able to act and we do act... We have a more accurate picture of ourselves and others; we feel a greater sense of worth; and we feel more connected to others and a greater motivation for connection with others beyond those in (our immediate realm of family and friends).[15]

This description of "growth-fostering relationship" characterizes beautifully the effects of how, in coming out, we experience ourselves in relation to those who meet us in this relational movement.

To look at several particular aspects of the coming out process may help clarify in what ways our integrity, as lesbians, is formed in a relational matrix of creative (often difficult, painful) tension between ourselves and others; between the explicitly sexual dimension of our lives and the rest of our lives; between how much of ourselves we reveal and how much we conceal; between acting for the immediate present and acting for the long haul; between clarity and confusion about what we are doing; and between letting go, erotically and otherwise, and maintaining a sense of control over our bodyselves and our lives.

Self and others

We cannot come out in such a way as to do justice to anyone, ourselves or others, if we cannot discern connections between our own sense of well-being and happiness and that of others. We cannot come out "perfectly." We cannot make everyone feel good about what we are doing. We cannot make everyone agree with us that our sexuality is good or that our relationships are good or that our divorce is good or whatever. We can be aware, however, that everything we say, do, choose or refuse to choose, affects us and others. Our words do, and our silence does. We can use words and silence in the spirit of profound respect for ourselves and others, including those who remain captive to their own fears. In this tension between self and others, we can learn with others gradually how to embody both an active indignation with injustice and a sense of patience with those who may be, in this particular moment, more frightened than we are. We learn, with one another's help, to experience anger and compassion, not as opposites or contradictions, but as essential dimensions of love.

The sexual dimension and the rest of who we are

When I came out, many people asked, "Why put limits on how you're going to be perceived? Why box yourself in? Don't you know that folks are going to think this is all you are -- a lesbian -- and that all lesbians do is fool around together under the sheets? What about your interest in Latin America? In the work of Elie Wiesel? In christology? Why do you want people to think that sexuality is all you can talk about?"

I knew, when I came out, that I was still interested in Elie Wiesel and in El Salvador and in working against racism and in jogging and walking my dogs. Maybe because I was already reasonably "well established" as a dissonant voice within my professional circles, as priest and theologian, I have not experienced myself as being perceived by most people solely on the basis of my lesbian sexuality.

Still, I would be lying or foolish to suggest that a lesbian who comes out can continue business as usual. She cannot. We cannot. But then, why would we want to? Do we not come out in order to disrupt business as usual?

When I came out publicly (by way of two published essays) in 1979, I knew, to some extent, that my coming out was an act of resistance to unjust power relations, unjust gender relations in particular. I did not realize at the time, however, how fundamentally these power relations are interstructured into our lives on the basis of gender, sexual preference, race, religion, age, able-bodyism, culture, ethnicity, nationality, etc. It has been far easier for me to be "out" as a lesbian since I began to understand, through my own life as well as the lives of others, that the ways in which sexual power is used and abused among us are connected to the ways in which religious, economic, racial and other forms of power-over are exercised. I see now what I saw, but not as clearly, a decade ago: that the same motive which urged me out of the closet is that which drew my attention to what's happening in Nicaragua. It's the same motive that invites me to do feminist liberation christology and sparks my interest in Elie Wiesel's work. The motive is to cast my lot with those who resist unjust -- nonmutual -- power relations wherever in our lives we experience them -- in our most intimate relationships and in our professional lives, as well as in the more explicitly public and political arenas of our lives together.

In relation to her Jewish roots, Adrienne Rich writes,"I had never been taught about resistance, only about passing."[16]   In 1979, I still wanted in some ways to pass. I suspect that, in some remnant ways, I still do. But I am clear today that I do not pass in relation to the norms of dominant political, theological or psychological cultures. Slowly, I am learning to live not in disappointment, but rather gladly, at the margins. Coming out pushes me further, a day at a time, into a realization that I don't want to pass, not really. This has been the most liberating, creative and painful lesson of my life -- learned in an educational matrix shaped by friends and lovers and enemies, by students and teachers and therapists and compañeras and all sorts and conditions of other earth creatures. I have been learning to trust the authority of those voices, my own and those of others, which call us more fully into mutually empowering relationships.

Revelation and concealment

A difficult tension for me has been between revelation and concealment of myself. I was raised to "tell the truth." This little moralism has served me well, by and large, such as in my decision to live openly as a lesbian. Today, however, I see how little I knew, when I came out, about taking care of myself emotionally, spiritually and physically. It is possible, I am learning, both to take care of ourselves and to take public stands. Possible and very hard.

There is profound theological wisdom in the tension between revelation and concealment. The Sacred reveals herself to us when we are ready to see her -- which is to see more clearly ourselves in relation. As T.S. Eliot noted, humankind cannot bear much reality, at least not in large doses. Hence the presence of the Spirit of Life is often concealed from us: that is, we do not realize what is good for us until we are ready to help generate the conditions for it. Yet this sacred knowledge can be called forth. It is available to us whenever we are ready to use it. Revelation -- of the divine, of the fully human -- is a matter of timing, of seasoning our capacities to risk seeing, and showing forth, our goodness when we are ready to embrace what we see and who we are. And in the hidden places of our lives, preparations can be made even now toward enabling us to respond to those moments in which the time will be right for us to open ourselves more fully to one another and to the larger world. Like bread, we are being prepared to rise.

We should remember, in coming out, that the light we are shedding critically on our society shines no less upon us, and we are likely to find ourselves feeling exposed and vulnerable. Like everyone in this society, we too are frightened of homosexuality: it's called "internalized homophobia." Moreover, if we have good sense, we are frightened of heterosexism -- of being rejected, hated, wounded or killed. We also do not know, none of us, the full implications of living publicly as happy faggots or dykes in the world. In this situation, some purposeful concealment and carefully refracted light is often wise.

The immediate present and the long haul

The tension between revelation and concealment can be illuminated by recasting it as a pull between taking a stand here and now and sustaining the longer-term, ongoing process of coming out. Coming out, we are attempting to live in both "places" at once -- and we can, provided we are able to keep faith in our interrelatedness and in the power of our relation. To do so gives us confidence that, for example, even if I can't say what I want to now, or be where I feel like I need to be now, then perhaps I can be later; or if I can't do it, someone else can represent me, just as I am representing others now. This is radically relational faith. It enables us simultaneously to take a stand here and now and to wait with one another on the Spirit to move us together into a future that is beyond our control as individuals, yet which we are helping to shape.

Clarity and confusion

There is tension also between our clarity and our confusion about coming out, about our sexualities, about ourselves in general. This very real pull in us is unavoidable. By "confusion," I mean that which is still unclear, cloudy, unable to be seen well at this time. It is a form of concealment. Among lesbians and gay men, confusion is bred in our experience of alienated power relations. Heterosexist expectations, after all, have shaped us in their image. Coming out of them, we are bound to be mystified. For we literally are coming out of long-standing senses of who we are. In a very real sense, we are changing identities, as we come out of ideological assumptions that have made us believe that we were either mad or bad.

Every healthy lesbian and gay man, like every woman or person of color who is aware of the pernicious effects of sexism or racism, at one time or another has been profoundly confused about his or her sense of sanity or worth in our society. The process of coming out tends, at first, I believe, to exacerbate our confusion and, as we live into the process, to resolve it more and more. We need to honor our own and others' confusion and let it be in order to move with one another, gradually, through it. For women to be able to sort these things out together, to "clear the air" with one another's help, is a rich relational blessing.

Letting go and maintaining control

There is also tension throughout our lives between the desire to express sexually our yearning for mutuality and our efforts to stay in control of our bodies/ourselves. Coming out often involves being stretched between these urges -- coming into a wild, erotic ecstasy, a full celebration of our bodyselves and those of others and, at the same time, a need to hold on to ourselves, to keep the lid on lest we feel as if we are disintegrating in the midst of a culture already hostile to our well-being.

We must be gentle with ourselves and one another. We ought not push too far ahead of ourselves, nor act too fast. But when we do, we need to be patient, tender, with one another and with ourselves, as we try again and again to find relational rhythms that are good for us and others. Coming out is, in heterosexist patriarchy, a lifetime project. It requires that we give ourselves lots of time and space to feel and appreciate the radical significance of our lives as openly lesbian women.

Sexual orgasm can be literally a high point, a climax in our capacity to know, ecstatically for a moment, the coming together of self and other; sexuality and other dimensions of our lives; desire for control and an equally strong desire to let go; sense of self and other as both revealing and concealing; the simultaneity of clarity and confusion about who we are; and tension between the immediacy of vitality and pleasure and a pervasive awareness, even in moments of erotic excitement, that the basis of our connection is the ongoing relational movement -- the friendship -- that brings us into this pleasure and releases us into the rest of our lives, including the rest of the particular relationship.

There is remarkable sacred power in these tensions. To stretch and pull, with one another, is to come out more and more into a fullness of ourselves in relation, in which the Sacred is born among us.

Implications for healing relationship

In closing, I shall comment briefly on how the coming out process might inform the relationship between women healers and those who seek our help. My focus, finally, is not on lesbians per se, but on women healing with women. As affirmation of our erotic power, as movement in relational authenticity and as resistance to alienated, nonmutual power relations, the coming out process is a paradigm, I believe, for healing.

Therapists, priests, pastors and other healers should not underestimate the extent to which, like Freud, we remain fearfully preoccupied with the dangers inherent to embodied intimacy: the "libidinal" dangers of erotic power. Moreover, we should not fail to remember the origins of this fear of eros: we are heirs of long-standing religious and civil traditions in which eros and women, and especially erotic women, are perceived as a threat to the prevailing social order.

Rather than realizing our erotic power as power for healing, we are torn apart from ourselves in right relation, alienated from our most creative power. We have become frightened of one another -- and of ourselves -- when we are most deeply in touch. This fear of eros, of intimacy, of one another, and of ourselves with one another, becomes an enormous impediment to the healing process and badly distorts the healing relationship.

One of the primary effects of the fear of our erotic power is to keep the healer "in the closet" as it were -- hiding her own authentic presence, her real life and values, from those who seek her help. It is deeply troubling to me that most therapists, who presumably are aware of the destructive effects of nonmutual, withholding relationships in their patients' lives, and in their own lives outside the clinical setting, do not see the damaging character, however benign, of nonmutual relationships within therapy -- damaging to both therapist and patient.

Becoming real together: movement in mutuality

From an ethical perspective, we must be suspicious of any transaction in which one person's becoming increasingly authentic and self-revealing is predicated upon another's self-concealment. Outside the clinical situation, most of us are able to recognize such a dynamic as the emotional root of sadomasochism, but inside we have learned to accept it as a condition for healing. Audre Lorde characterizes such a relationship as emotionally abusive. She suggests that, whether professional or personal, such a relationship borders on the pornographic and the obscene. Surely there is a connection between the fear of erotic power, the withholding of honest presence, the veiling of real feelings and the obsessive, eruptive sexual violation of patients by therapists.

Our fear of intimacy and of being in touch with one another generates a perverse misapprehension that the more "self-possessed" and less relationally vulnerable we are, the more helpful we can be to others. The truth is: **nothing is as profoundly healing as real, mutual presence.**

Our lives have deep, decadent roots in obscene power relations which, in countless ways, obscure our capacities even to believe in the possibility of mutuality. All of our lives are implicated. All of us are involved. Feminist professionals, especially perhaps those of us in religion or psychology, need to help one another come out of the structures of nonmutual power relations which, literally, have secured our professions, shaped our psyches and still do. Despite our commitments to justice and compassion in our work, we have a hard time loving one another very well. And, my sisters and brothers, this is not our fault as individuals. We must be gentle with ourselves and one another, realizing that we have enormous power to heal with one another or to hurt ourselves and one another very badly.

We all experience relationships in which for a time mutuality is not fully realizable. Therapy is a good example. The mutuality in such a relationship may be limited temporarily, as perhaps it must be, by purpose and function. If, however, the limitation is static and unchanging -- that is, if the dynamics of a one-way dependency are fixed permanently, which they are assumed to be in all patriarchal relational configurations, including the psychotherapeutic tradition -- the relationship will be emotionally and spiritually distorted regardless of how well-meaning and skillful the persons in it may be. **Individual goodwill, personal integrity and professional competence cannot solve systemically abusive power structures. Any relationship which does not contain seeds of movement toward the possibility of becoming a fully mutual relationship is intrinsically abusive.** In such relationships, healing can happen, and often does, in spite of, or even by way of, the abusive dynamics. But the harm done by the lack of mutually authentic participation, at the very least, diminishes the power of healing.

As healers, and as women seeking healing, we have an opportunity to bring one another out of the "closets" in which is hidden the fullness of our creative, liberating relational power. And we know this sacred power, our erotic power, as we actually experience and/or long to experience it. Yet, as Audre Lorde writes, "We have been taught to fear the YES within ourselves,

our deepest cravings. "[17]   Our challenge, as women in the healing process, is
to encourage one another to embrace this YES together.[18]

NOTES

1.   This is a revision of a lecture in the Colloquium Series of The Stone Center for Developmental Services and Studies at Wellesley College, in Massachusetts, March 1, 1989. Part of the lecture was adapted from Touching Our Strength: The Erotic as Power and the Love of God by Carter Heyward. Used with permission of Harper and Row Publishers, Inc., San Francisco.

2.   Audre Lorde, Sister Outsider: Essays & Speeches (Trumansburg, New York: Crossing Press, 1984), p. 41.

3.   Lennie Kleinberg, "Coming Home to Self, Going Home to Parents: Lesbian Identity Disclosure," Works in Progress No. 24 (Wellesley, MA: Stone Center, 1986).

4.   Eric Fromm, Mark's Concept of Man (New York: Frederick Ungar, 1961).

5.   Jean Baker Miller, "Connections, Disconnections and Violations," Works in Progress No. 33 (Wellesley, MA: Stone Center, 1988).

6.   Janet L. Surrey, "Self-in-Relation: A Theory of Womens' Development," Works in Progress No. 30 (Wellesley, MA: Stone Center, 1985).

7.   Ibid.

8.   See Surrey, "Self in Relation," and Kleinberg, "Coming Home to Self."

9.   Kleinberg, p. 10.

10.   Margaret C. Huff, "The Interdependent Self: An Integrated Concept from Feminist Theology and Feminist Psychology," in Philosophy and Theology, No. 2, pp. 160-172.

11.   Lorde, p. 55.

12.   Ibid., pp. 57-58.

13.   Ibid., p. 57.

14.   Ibid.

15.   Jean Baker Miller, "What Do We Mean By Relationship?", Works in Progress No. 22 (Wellesley, MA: Stone Center, 1986).

16.   Adrienne Rich, "Split at the Root," in Nice Jewish Girls: A Lesbian Anthology, E. T. Beck, ed. (Watertown, MA: Persephone, 1982), p. 72.

17.   Lorde, p. 55.

18.   Special thanks to those people who, in discussing with me specific parts of this paper, helped sharpen basic perceptions: Susan DeMattos, Beverly Harrison, Peg Huff, Karl Laubenstein, Diane Moore, Jan Surrey, Will Thompson and Ann Wetherilt.

FACING OURSELVES:
MAKING THE CONNECTIONS BETWEEN INCEST AND WHITE CHRISTOLOGIES

Corine Johnson[*]

I am the daughter of a minister. I come from a long line of ministers, missionaries, bible college professors, elders, deacons and their wives. I am the third of four girls -- all of my sisters are heterosexual, as are my parents. Both of my parents are white. My father comes from a working class family, and my mother from an educated middle class family.

This is a presentation about how I have made connections, in my life, between incest and white Christologies. I choose to talk about white Christologies even though I understand that there are many Christologies in white churches in the United States. Examples are Christus Victor, the historical Jesus, Jesus as brother, and the Christology in which my parents believe, Christ-the-blesser-of-middle-class-values. Under this christological model, I was taught that if I love Jesus or the Christ, if I live a good Christian life, get a good job, save money, and buy a house, Jesus will bless me and increase my physical and financial comfort. I know I am making a sweeping statement when I talk about white Christologies, but because enough white women recognize some or all of my experience, I am led to believe there are throughlines in many white Christologies.

I also want to define incest. Incest is the sexual violation of a person, usually a minor, by a perpetrator who holds power over the violated one and who is trusted by the violated one.

This is a presentation about how Christology helped me make sense out of my incest and how the incest helped me make sense of Christology. I cannot give irrefutable evidence that incest and white Christologies are scientifically connected, but I will present the theological connections as I have discovered them in my life. I take this approach because when I have made similar presentations in academic papers, classes, meetings, and in other places, my experience has been met with the criticism, "That's not what it (it meaning scripture, liturgy, Jesus, God, etc.) really means. What it really means is..." My experience is dismantled and my interpretation of my experience is dismissed. I begin to think I am crazy. And so, until there is a large body of

---

[*] This essay was originally presented as part of a forum on Christology sponsored by the Feminist Liberation Theology and Ministry Program at the Episcopal Divinity School in 1990. Corine Johnson is a pseudonym employed by the author to protect her identity.

literature that concurs with my interpretation, and until the knowledge and the language we use is shaped by that body of literature, I will contend that what the connection between incest and white Christologies "really means" is how it gets played out in my life and in our lives.

Patriarchy, as a system of organizing people, commerce, agriculture, religion and ideas, requires a hierarchy. This hierarchy must be maintained in a patriarchal system or the system collapses. Systemically and systematically, people, animals and land are controlled and annihilated in order to maintain this hierarchy. Often, the white church provides the sense, the "logic,"[1] for this annihilation. Time and time again the white church, its doctrine, and its ministers have condoned the violence necessary to maintain the hierarchy. I cite as examples, justification for racial violence in the U.S. and U.S. imperialism and the occupation of parts of Central America, South Korea and other places on the earth where "Godless Communism" threatens. In my case, it is violence against me, my sisters and my mothers, and sometimes brothers -- the children of the patriarchs.

I was raped by my Sunday School teacher when I was eight years old. The Sunday before he raped me, he had told my Sunday School class about how Mary, the mother of Jesus, had become pregnant. Since I did not yet know how women became pregnant, I pressed the teacher for details. That afternoon, my father reprimanded me for "disrupting" his Sunday School class. The following Saturday, the teacher raped me in the basement of the church and told me the Holy Spirit had done it to Mary and so he could do it to me. I understood the rape as painful punishment for my bad behavior in Sunday School, as my duty as a girl, the duty that girls do for God/Jesus.

This story of incest is not just my story. There are too many stories: the violence is prevalent. Perpetrators, who are overwhelmingly heterosexual men, but sometimes women, sexually abuse one out of every three women, and one out of every 10 men in the United States.

I grew up with two models of Jesus; Jesus as rapist and Jesus as model survivor. I have always thought of Jesus as the rapist. My father and my grandfather are both ministers. They taught me that as ministers of the church (regardless of the Protestant rhetoric) they are Christ's representatives on earth. And both my father and grandfather hurt me in ways that are indescribable. For me, my father and grandfather were so mixed up in and with the church that when as a child I saw a baptism, the rite of initiating someone into the family of Christ, I would mumble under by breath, "Don't do it, don't do it." Baptism was the last surrender, atonement, the final acquiescence.

Rita Nakashima Brock in her book Journeys by Heart, writes,

> The shadow of omnipotence haunts atonement. The ghost of the punitive father lurks in the corners. He never disappears even as he is transformed into an image of forgiving grace... Such doctrines of salvation reflect by analogy,...images of the neglect of children or even child abuse, making it acceptable as divine behavior -- cosmic child abuse, as it were.[2]

The father demands perfection of the child. Of course, perfection is never possible because the definition of perfection lies in the omniscient head of the father. When the child fails to be perfect, the father gives the child up for punishment/sacrifice, as a kind of love. And the child goes willingly to the punishment, convinced of her own unworthiness. Because she is so worn and "split out" from the threats of punishment/sacrifice, she is unable to make judgements concerning her own worthiness.

In her book Sexism and God-talk[3], Rosemary Radford Ruether writes about the imagery of Christ as the Bridegroom and the church as the Bride. The relationship between Christ and Christ's church is often described in sexual terms. The following Christian Reformed hymn is a case in point:

> He plays with us, he goes in and out of us. He plants within us his own life as a tree. He is with us, he takes us for his bride, and all that we are is given to us from him.[4]

It is clear from the christological model I was taught that I am the bride and must accept this sexual relationship as Mary did. This relationship is both the reward and the threat of piety. A good Christian girl or woman must both want and accept this relationship. If she does not want it, she will get it anyway or go to hell/purgatory.

There is a parable that Jesus tells of the 10 virgins and a bridegroom. We are to understand that the Bridegroom is Jesus. The 10 virgins are assigned to wait at the house of the bridegroom, lamp in hand in order to greet the awaited bridegroom with light. Their job is to wait and watch. Five of the virgins, called "foolish" in Matthew's gospel, bring no spare oil. Having waited a long time for the bridegroom's arrival, the five foolish virgins must go for more oil. While away purchasing more oil, the bridegroom arrives. The five wise virgins go in with Jesus to the marriage feast.

It is the story of me and my three sisters. All of our lives we have stood outside the door of our father, the bridegroom with our lamps and oil. We

await his arrival. We are ever vigilant for his coming, hoping never to run out
of oil. Because if we do not attend to his coming, if we are not prepared with
enough oil, enough devotion, enough of everything, he will hurt us. But it
never matters if we run out of oil or not, we will still be hurt. It doesn't
matter, but we must always be prepared. We will only leave our vigil outside
the door of our father, the bridegroom, to get more oil, then hurry back. This
is the last line of the parable, "Watch therefore, for you know neither the day
nor the hour." We never know when he will come and he will never release us
to live our own lives.

The picture is this: Christ, the absent and elusive, but all-powerful
bridegroom/husband, must be complimented by the always attending but passive
bride/wife. And if she, the bride, "splits out" and leaves her body, she is
rewarded as a mystic.

The other message that we receive is that Jesus is the model survivor.
If Jesus can hang on the cross and suffer and die to atone for the sins of others,
why can't you, why can't I? If Jesus' father gave him over to suffer, and God
is the model father, can I not be the model child?

This family of Jesus sounds just like my family. The abuse of Jesus was
not for his benefit, though it was said to be (you will sit at the right hand of the
Father in glory). Jesus was unable to resist the abuse ("Let this cup pass from
me... Not my will, but thine be done.") Mary was not the father's equal and
was unable to protect Jesus from his father. And Jesus' father was well thought
of and had a powerful place in the community.

I will conclude with two more pieces of the connection between incest
and white christologies. The first is that we have been taught that what we
experience is not what is real. The statement, "Oh, that's not what it really
means" does its work of keeping us guessing what means what. It keeps us off
center and confused. We must trust what we KNOW. We must find sisters and
brothers who will validate our realities. We must do our own naming. For
example, I went to the store and bought The Courage to Heal: A Guide for
Women Survivors of Child Sexual Abuse. I bought this book because denial is
a large part of the way I survived. For a long time I denied what happened.
I had no memories.

I was reading the first chapter entitled, "Effects: Recognizing the
Damage" and there was a long list of questions such as "Do you feel that you
were bad, dirty or ashamed? Do you feel powerless? Do you feel different
from other people? Do you feel that something is wrong with you deep down
inside?"[5], etc. I immediately recognized that I could answer "yes" to the

questions because I understood that this is how Christians, white Christian women in particular, are <u>supposed</u> to feel. I wondered if Christianity taught me how to be a victim and then I wondered if being a victim taught me how to be a Christian. In the next months I began to refuse to sing all the old hymns that I have loved since I was a child; such songs as, "I am thine, O Lord,"[6] "Faith of Our Fathers,"[7] "Take my life and let it be consecrated Lord to thee..."[8] and "Have thine own way, Lord. Have thine own way. Thou are the potter, I am the clay. Mold me and make me after thy will while I am waiting yielding and still."[9] Naming our experience is a matter of life and it is a political and theological act. If, in fact, white Christologies teach us to be victims, will we not tell our daughters and loved ones? A friend says there are two kinds of survivors' stories. There are the kind that are too horrible to tell, and there are the kind that are, when compared to the horrible stories, too trivial to tell. Either way, we don't tell our stories. Either way, we continue to believe that what happened to us was our individual fault rather than what happened to us happens systematically to one in three women and one in 10 men in the United States.

The second and last piece is this: we MUST do more than tell our stories. We must act, resist, do analysis. But I believe, if we are white, it is not good enough to act, resist, and do analysis only in our own communities. Without universalizing our experience onto other communities, we must make connections in other communities. For example, many white lesbians already understand the white churches' contribution to the logic of heterosexism. If as survivors and "pro-survivors" we resist the violence in our white homes and point to the source of the logic that condones domestic violence, we may also be pointing to the source of the "logic" that holds racism in place.

NOTES

1.   Dr. Katie G. Cannon is an Associate Professor of Christian Ethics at the Episcopal Divinity School in Cambridge, MA.   She teaches a class entitled "The Genealogy of Race, Sex, and Class Oppression."   In this course Professor Cannon argues that logic must be applied to the practices of racism, sexism, and classism.   This logic is used to justify racism, sexism, and classism. To illustrate this "logic", I cite an example I heard repeatedly growing up. Scientists of the nineteenth and twentieth centuries have shown that Black people have smaller cranial cavities than white people.   Black people have smaller brains than white people, therefore white people are intellectually superior to Black people.   Since God created both Blacks and whites, Black people were created inferior by God.   Racial discrimination therefore does not exist because the superiority of whites is natural, inevitable and God-given, God-made.

2.   Rita Nakashima Brock, Journeys By Heart: A Christology of Erotic Power (New York: Crossroads, 1988), p. 56.

3.   Rosemary Radford Ruether, Sexism and God-Talk (Boston: Beacon Press, 1982).   See especially chapters 5 and 6.

4.   I do not know the author of this hymn or where it has been published.   I heard it sung by Dutch Roman Catholic friends.   Translation done by Marian Groot.

5.   Ellen Bass and Laura Davis, The Courage to Heal: A Guide For Women Survivors of Child Sexual Abuse (San Francisco: Harper and Row, 1988), p. 35.

6.   From "Draw Me Nearer," lyrics by Fannie Crosby, music by William H. Doane.

7.   Lyrics by Fredrick W. Faber, music by Henri F. Hemy.

8.   From "Take My Life And Let It Be," lyrics by Frances A. Havergal, music by Henri A. Cesar Malan.

9.   From "Have Thine Own Way," lyrics by Adelaide A. Pollard, music by George C. Stebbins.

PART FOUR

CELEBRATING THE LIFE AND WORK OF BILL WOLF

An Autobiographical Reflection:
Looking Back And Forward[*]

William J. Wolf

I wrote my doctoral thesis at Union Theological Seminary (1934-45) on "Alienation and Reconciliation in the Writings of Soren Kierkegaard." At that time there was little commentary on Kierkegaard in English since, some of his basic books and Journal were still untranslated. I had to learn Danish, commuting on the subway, on the order of Paul Tillich, although my doctoral committee, with Tillich present, had agreed the previous year that in view of the availability of French and German translations, it would not be necessary for me to learn Danish. At the suggestion of some members of my committee, I intended to revise the dissertation for publication, but I could not find the time because of rapidly developing events.

In 1945, when Dean Angus Dun left his faculty post at my alma mater, the Episcopal Theological School, to become bishop of Washington, Reinhold Niebuhr and Paul Tillich recommended that I be invited to fill this position. As it turned out, after two others had turned the position down, I was called as a lecturer for a trial period of six months. At issue was not only my youth, but also a fear among the "old liberals," faculty and alumni, of what they feared was my "neo-orthodoxy." Years later, I realized that I had left any trace of presumed neo-orthodoxy far behind me through my graduate studies. But my training in both the crisis (neo-orthodox) and liberal theology prepared me to be the only teacher of Systematic Theology at the Episcopal Theological School for some years.

Soon after my return to EDS as a member of its faculty, and having been "conscienticized" on the ordination of women by Ursula Niebuhr and Mrs. Drown, I preached in chapel on the subject, supporting Bishop Hall of Hong Kong who had, as a war emergency, ordained a woman to the priesthood for Macao, but was later forced by the Lambeth Conference of 1948 to cease and desist. There was a chill silence in the faculty room after the sermon, broken only by Dean Taylor's comment that while he agreed theoretically with this theology, the ordination of women was "light-years away." Most students felt it was a great joke or a "deficiency in catholic substance." One drew a cartoon on the blackboard in the theological classroom of me ministering in "Gracie's" Church, since I had been a curate at Grace Church, New York before my return to Cambridge.

---

[*] Eds. note: Bill wrote this autobiographical piece at our request. He did so in the third person, perhaps out of modesty or, as a classically trained theologian, out of habit. Bill died before we could discuss this with him. We have changed the tense to the first person.

With lectures and new courses started, I hoped to get to writing, the universal requirement for tenure. More constructively, I also had in mind a study of our knowledge of God, or "revelation," to use the technical theological term. The diocese of Massachusetts, however, responded to a petition from lay persons in Sudbury where there was an unused chapel built by Ralph Adams Cram and willed to a monastery, but with no congregation. Archdeacon Phinney persuaded me to start a mission there. I became weekend vicar of St. Elizabeth's, Sudbury from 1948-1951, resigning when I thought the congregation was ready for a full-time priest.

At that time I also accepted an invitation from the World Council of Churches to become temporary director of its Institute for the Laity at Bossey, near Geneva, while its official director, Hendrik Kraemer, attended the Buffalo Laity Conference and lectured in Canada and the United States. Although I found it painful, as did my wife Eleanor, for me to leave her with our three young boys in Cambridge for a semester and summer (1951-52), this appointment was a meaningful one for me. I was particularly inspired at Bossey by the Bible study of Susanne de Dietrich, encouraged by visiting the European Centers of Renewal, and was made aware of voices for renewal and ecumenism in the Roman Catholic Church at a closed conference at Chevetogne. The secret meeting was organized by Paul Albrecht of the World Council and its proceedings taped for the Curia and for review by Pope Pius XII.

The faculty in 1951 voted me tenure without my having yet produced a book, perhaps as insurance against my leaving for another position as a result of my experience with the World Council of Churches. In 1954, they voted me the recently created chair of Howard Chandler Robbins Professor to celebrate the numerous benefactions to the School of its alumnus Dean Robbins, a friend of mine and a summer resident of Heath.

The teaching of theology at the school had been strengthened by the coming of Frederich W. Dillistone from England in 1947, for a stay of five years. "Dilli," as he was known by all, taught a course on the Atonement and another on church and ministry. He would later write important books on these subjects. In order to be sure that all students were exposed to Dilli in the day of required courses, Dean Taylor insisted that the basic one-year course for middlers be divided so that Dilly would teach the first half and I would continue to teach the second half. Dilli much preferred his seminar type of teaching. After I had presented the Dillistone's oldest son David for confirmation at St. Elizabeth's, I asked Dilli what he thought of the service, held before an altar with six huge Jesuit candle sticks and with the celebrant wearing a heavy historic Spanish chasuble obtained somehow from Mexico by Ralph Adams Cram. Dilli replied at once: "Geneva facing Rome."

Joseph Fletcher, although primarily responsible for ethics, taught courses in the theology of William Temple and the thought of Bonhoeffer. Owen Thomas came in 1952, to replace Dilli who returned that year to England. With his doctorate in William Temple, Owen took over my course in the philosophy of religion and that part of the middler course in theology which Dilli had taught. Then, after 1968, Owen taught the basic course. Owen's distinguished teaching and writing are well known. After the merger with the Philadelphia Divinity School in 1974, John Skinner offered an alternative approach for beginners and a course in A.N. Whitehead and process theology, the only offering on this subject by the schools of the Boston Theological Institute. The arrival during the following year of two of the newly ordained women priests, Suzanne Hiatt in Pastoral Theology and Carter Heyward in Systematic Theology, meant the arrival of feminist theology and later, through Carter's interest in Latin America, of liberation theological studies.

First Writing Period (1955-1960)

My first book, Man's Knowledge of God, embarrasses me today for its sexist title. I had wanted even then to call it Our Knowledge of God, but that title had already been used by the Scottish theologian John Baillie.

Doubleday had persuaded Reinhold Niebuhr to become the editor of their Christian Faith series and I accepted their invitation to write an introduction on revelation. The book wrestled with the related poles of historical fact and of faith trying to reconcile the distinctive faith of a community with a modern scientific world view. The problem is still with us, though today nearly all theologians accept a scientific world view. Within this context, we seek to perceive the reality of transcendence.

The influence of Richard Niebuhr is clear throughout, especially his Meaning of Revelation. I had taken a course at the Episcopal Theological School on the problems of church and state, which Richard Niebuhr commuted up from Yale to teach. I regard myself as lucky to have had the Niebuhr brothers as teachers and later as friends. I felt that some theological discussion never advanced beyond the tribal cry, "My Richard is better than your Reinhold" or vice versa. My answer to such analysis was that neither Reinhold nor Richard would have been the persons they were nor would they have held the theological conceptions they did without each other. My friend John Porter and I had talked of retirement in Heath to write a book establishing this basic dialogue between the Niebuhr brothers, but cancer carried off both John and his wife Nelle before this project could be more than started.

My first book showed my centering in the Bible through continued use of Kittel's Theological Wordbook to the New Testament. I accepted C.H. Dodd's emphasis on the preaching message (kerygma) of the early church as behind later creedal affirmations. The influence of Martin Buber's I and Thou was also obvious in my work.

Then too I was responding to Kierkegaard's expectation that the "paradox" was the most "rational" approach to the truths of religion, when it was understood that the real proof of the existence of God was the tortured activity of denying God, whether in personal life or in historical movements of atheism such as Marxism. I sensed an ally in Erich Frank's classic Philosophical Understanding and Religious Truth and quoted from him. "For the existence of God infinitely transcends our thought, or will, and even our belief. And it is precisely in this transcendence that God and his existence can be grasped by us."[1]

My own special emphasis, however, was to have claimed that the blackboard equation, in which revelation equalled historical fact plus believing interpretation, was too simple a formula. Each term in the dichotomy already had a dimension of the other in it. Part of the problem lay in ambiguities in the notion of history. Some historians had wanted so desperately to be considered "scientific" in their discipline and methods that they impoverished the conception of "fact", but there is no fact that has not already had more than merely quantitative things done to it. Why have certain so-called "facts" been "selected" for analysis rather than others?

I had long admired Samuel Eliot Morison as a historian. In treating the subject of clipper ships, Morison might have listed their components "scientifically," the amount of wood, rope and cordage, sheeting and blocks. But who could have described this means of transportation even as a "fact" more movingly than he did? He addressed the clipper ship Flying Cloud as a living being with its relics invested with sacramental significance. This is not "objective" history, whatever that might mean beyond a list of constituent parts. It is a deeper and more meaningful history because it is also the testimony of a faith:

> O Flying Cloud, what eulogy and admiration you had in your lifetime; what joyous hours have been spent by armchair sailors, gloating over your records and the spare journals of your voyages; what delight is given today even by models, prints, and paintings, imperfect images of you in your splendor as you logged your eighteen knots in the trade winds, studding sails aloft and alow...[2]

This maritime illustration of the mutual interpenetration of fact and believing interpretation in Flying Cloud seemed to touch a chord in reviewers and letter writers alike. History, commonly thought a secular discipline, could be analyzed to show the element of believing interpretation in the historian and, by analogy, in the problem of revelation itself. This seeing of transcendence in immanence established a basic pattern for my theology for the future, even though its pantheistic implications for theism and of process-thought as a useful tool for its exposition were still in the future. An English reviewer thought the use of the secular to explain the holy might have influenced the English publisher Victor Gollancz to venture into more religious themes than he had hitherto explored. Man's Knowledge of God was published in England in 1956.[3]

No Cross, No Crown: A Study of The Atonement (1957) was the first book I initiated.[4] It remains my most basic theological writing. It was ultimately responsible for my being asked to write on "Atonement" for the recent Encyclopedia of Religion (Mircea Eliade, Editor-in-chief).[5] Yet the book has also been used in some Southern Baptist seminaries, quoted by Billy Graham, and recommended for seminary libraries in the third world by a special commission set up by the American Association of Theological Schools. Originally published by Doubleday, it has been reprinted by Archon Books and by Seabury Press, which carelessly forgot to include an updated preface relating its views on atonement with developments from the Second Vatican Council.

My method has been to show that atonement in the Bible and beyond has been described by metaphors and comparisons. What God did at the Cross was like a triumphant battle over the forces of evil (classical theories), like proceedings in a law court with a surprise ending (Paul, Anselm and Reformation types), like the infliction of punishment, like a payment of redemption money for a slave's freedom, and like a moral act of forgiveness and love ready to be followed (Abelard and moral influence theories). Often underlying them was the comparison to a sacrifice at the altar (sacrificial theories in Roman Catholic liturgical change and Anglican Prayerbook revision).

People have often been puzzled by an overdevelopment through Chalcedon and beyond of official dogmas of the incarnation and a corresponding underdevelopment or chaos in theories of the atonement. The contrast, however, can be exaggerated, since the official Church's criterion for christological decision was usually how the proposed understanding of Christ's person would effect the salvation of humanity and the world. It is necessary to integrate the work and the person of Christ, Christ does what he is and is what he does.

The understanding of atonement is the Christian attempt to answer questions about ignorance, suffering, death and sin that are being asked by the history and comparison of religions, but always for Christianity the alienation caused by sin is considered more basic than ignorance, suffering, or death. Christ "has broken down the dividing wall of hostility...so making peace and (reconciling) us both to God in one body through the cross...(Ephesians 2:14-16)."

When asked what I would change if I were to revise No Cross, No Crown, I recall that when I wrote it I had every intention to discuss atonement more fully in terms of the resurrection of Christ, but that I literally wrote myself out of space and time. The title itself, No Cross, No Crown, suggests this unfulfilled dimension. At the time I profited by the painstaking analysis of Vincent Taylor in his trilogy Jesus and His Sacrifice (1937), The Atonement in New Testament Teaching (1946), and Forgiveness and Reconciliation (1952). If there had existed then any comparable New Testament studies of resurrection in such depth, a development which I have not yet seen, I would have wanted to use such material.

Ragnar Leivestad, in Christ the Conqueror: Ideas of Conflict and Victory in the New Testament, through his analysis of demons and healing, supplemented and strengthened the direction of Aulen's classic theory with its conviction that Anselmian and moral influence types were destined to become its satellites. I also feel that, in Reinhold Niebuhr's Gifford Lectures, there are suggestions of the social and historical effects of atonement that remain undeveloped. Such a way forward might be helped by Dorothee Soelle's Christ the Representative, built creatively on Bonhoeffer's christological title "the man (person) for us."

Speculating upon these suggestions, I closed the article in Eliade's Encyclopedia with a prediction. "Perhaps the next development lies with a reformulation of the sacrificial theory, which, fortified by the use of liturgy and having come abreast of new understandings of sacrifice in the comparative history of religions, may for a time become a new primary center in its own right." [6]

In 1959, I wrote The Almost Chosen People: A Study of the Religion of Abraham Lincoln.[7] Stimulated as a college undergraduate by sermons of Fosdick and Reinhold Niebuhr with their references to Lincoln as a profound biblical thinker, I wanted to see how other strands of testimony to Lincoln as the village atheist or opportunistic user of religion could be reconciled. The question was timely because Benjamin Thomas' splendid biography had appeared in 1952, and the eight volumes of Lincoln's Collected Works by the Rutgers Press in the following year. For the first time bogus Lincoln materials had been winnowed away, leaving an interpreter free to concentrate on an accepted body of writings without losing momentum by having to argue regularly the case about authenticity.

"The Almost Chosen People" was a phrase used by president-elect Lincoln before the New Jersey Senate on his trip to Washington. It revealed two sides of Lincoln, his use of the Bible and his humorous or ironic disclaimers. It has been my most popular book. My Doubleday editor, Clement Alexandre, phoned to say that it had been tentatively chosen for the Book-of-the-Month Club subject to veto by their marketing department. The veto was, however, cast and friends kidded me about "The Almost Chosen Book-of-the-Month Club Selection." It did become a selection of the Religious Book Club. It was chosen by President Kennedy's Commission on the White House Library as "an example of the American experience." It has been widely used in colleges with Departments of American Studies.

I proceeded in chronological order trying, to comment on all the significant material and not concentrating on some special theme. More attention was always paid to Lincoln's own words than to the testimony of others. Reinhold Niebuhr described the book as "a real masterpiece of scholarship and religious insight...(It covers) every aspect of (Lincoln's) religious development and his heterodox but profoundly moving biblical faith. It makes all the previous books about Lincoln's religion passe... Lincoln has always been my hero in religion and in statecraft (and this book) does full justice to the many facets of his religious life."

I believed that the Second Inaugural was "one of the most astute pieces of Christian theology ever written. It was also a charter of Christian ethics. It may seem strange to call Lincoln a theologian, for he was obviously not one in any technical sense. There are many profundities in the Christian religion which he never did illuminate, but in the area of this vision he saw more keenly than anyone since the inspired writers of the Bible. He knew he stood under the living God of history... Lincoln could detach himself from his own interested participation in events and submit all, including himself as judging, to higher judgment."[8]

I had expected that many would take exception to this high evaluation of Lincoln. Instead I received many letters from zealous denominationalists claiming that Lincoln, in spite of his statement that he was not a member of any church, was really a member of their group, or a secret member or about to become such. I added a new appendix to the next edition dealing with this subject. In a sense, I returned to this problem by request from the larger perspective of "Abraham Lincoln and Calvinism" when I accepted the Woodrow

Wilson Lectureship. My lecture became a chapter in Calvinism and Political Order edited by George Hunt and John T. McNeil in 1965.[9]

During this period I joined with Professor Ehrenstrom of the Boston University School of Theology and Professor Dunstan of Andover-Newton to start the Joint Boston Ecumenical Seminar. The Harvard Divinity School soon joined the enterprise. In the opening under Pope John XXIII, Cardinal Cushing delegated Father Charles van Euw of St. John's Seminary to participate. The Greek Orthodox Seminary also sent a representative. It was from this example of ecumenical cooperation between seminaries that the Boston Theological Institute would be later formed, largely at the suggestion and under the initial guidance of Dean John Coburn.

Concentration on Ecumenics (1960-1972)

In the next period my writing derived its themes largely from my ecumenical responsibilities, which caused me to be called by many "the ecumenical work horse of the Episcopal Church." There was almost no post I did not hold at some time in bilateral talks with other churches, or on national multilateral commissions or with international groups such as the Orthodox Churches and the Roman Catholic Church.

I was appointed to the Consultation on Church Union (COCU) shortly after its inception. In 1965, I published Plan of Church Union: Catholic, Evangelical, Reformed,[10] largely a digest of the Constitutions of Union Churches abroad. It has been widely used in third world countries. At its centennial in 1967, the Episcopal Theological School was host to the annual meeting of the Consultation on Church Union (COCU) and some months thereafter to a Consultation of Seminarians at Cambridge on COCU.

In 1970, I was appointed Dudleian Lecturer at Harvard University with a request that my subject be the 1970 Plan of Union for the Church of Christ Uniting. While the Plan of Union was the work of a special commission (the secretariat and an editorial committee at St. Louis), it has been reported that I originally drafted more than half of it. I was the first to suggest its name: "The Church of Christ Uniting."

In 1972, Paul Crow and William Boney brought out Church Union at Midpoint, a symposium on COCU. I was asked to write the chapter on "Catholicity and 'A Plan of Union.'" In it I analyzed, usually with agreement, the document Consultation on Church Union: A Catholic Perspective by Bishop William Baum, one of the official Roman Catholic observers to the Consultation, who wrote: "COCU's treatment of sacraments and liturgy illustrates the amazing degree of convergence which has already been achieved thanks to contemporary biblical-theological development and to the Liturgical Movement. It is especially hoped that Catholics will become familiar with the COCU statements on Baptism and the Eucharist."[11] It is especially interesting that Cardinal Baum, now in the Curia, is in charge of Catholic education throughout the world.

The Archbishop of Canterbury appointed me to be an official Anglican Observer at Vatican II. Delighted by the evidence of Catholic reform of liturgy, theology, and the evaluation of the "Church in the Modern World," I edited, in 1964, a symposium entitled Protestant Churches and Reform Today. My purpose was to ask the non-Roman Churches what they perceived to be in need of reform and renewal in their own churches.

As one of eight contributors to a symposium by Anglican Observers edited by Bernard Pawley, the first representative of the Archbishops of Canterbury and York in Rome, I was assigned the task of following the "Declaration on Religious Liberty" through what might be described as "the perils of Pauline" in the four sessions of the Council. My critique and evaluation of this schema is especially interesting in the light of current developments.

"While the Declaration is presumably directed to religious liberty as a civil right, and while conservatives have denied that it had to do with 'liberty within the Church,' this is a point fraught with great potential hopefulness ecumenically for the future. There are overtones here of 'liberty' as a principle of an authentically responsible life. This evaluation may in time revolutionize the internal forum of the Roman Catholic Church... As it stands now without a specific application of 'liberty' within the Church, and with the emphasis on human dignity as a civil right within the state's sphere of influence, the question could be raised: What happens to human dignity when one becomes a believer? or, What happens to human dignity when one becomes a priest?"[12]

Alas! Far from revolutionizing "the internal forum of the Roman Catholic Church," Pope John Paul II has shown himself a reactionary against much of Vatican II, harassing scholars and theologians, opposing the ordination of women and the marriage of priests, and filling the episcopate with docile appointments. In short, he has destroyed the picture of an ecumenically responsible exercise of the papal office by his immediate predecessors.

I joined with Professor Michael Fahey, S.J., of the Weston School of Theology in teaching a joint course on Anglican-Roman Catholic relations. At the invitation of Cardinal Cushing, I taught "Protestant Theology" for a time at St. John's Diocesan Seminary. Again at the request of Cardinal Cushing, I accepted appointment as a voting member of the Archdiocesan Ecumenical Commission.

I designed an ecumenical course entitled "Theological Interpretations of the Human Situation" by comparing and contrasting a Protestant and a Roman Catholic theologian. The first pair was Reinhold Niebuhr and Teilhard de Chardin. Then came Bonhoeffer and Teilhard. What seemed to be emerging in the 1960s was a high student interest in theologians who began their analysis with the human situation instead of systematics, and also who suffered for their convictions, whether from the world or the church or a combination of the two. When Vatican II ended the persecution of theologians and Teilhard seemed increasingly dated, I substituted Hans Kung.

Kung's Council and Reunion (1961) was a prophetic work that rallied liberals but deeply offended conservatives, who made threats of condemnation. That persecution, however, had to await John Paul II. It turned out that Bonhoeffer the martyr was ideal pedagogically in his progression from conservative theological opinions (Ethics) to exciting new perspectives in Letters and Papers from Prison (1953), interpreted in Bethge's superb biography (1967). Some students called the course: "Applied Theology 101: How to Terminate your Fuhrer."

There is a fragment of Bonhoeffer's, dating apparently from 1942, which I used to claim as a forerunner of the Theology of Liberation and Black liberation theology. "There remains an experience of incomparable value. We have for once learnt to see the great events of world history from below, from the perspective of the outcast, the suspects, the maltreated, the powerless, the oppressed, the reviled -- in short, from the perspective of those who suffer." [13]

Maurice As A Theological Influence

An important element in my thought has not been mentioned up to this point, partly because it was a relatively late development. One might have expected to hear something about the influence of Frederick Denison Maurice on my work, especially since the Episcopal Theological School was founded by a first generation of teachers most of whom might be described as Mauricians. I had heard this fact when I was an undergraduate at the Episcopal Theological School, but, curiously, it never motivated me to read Maurice, nor did it cause any of my teachers to recommend that I read Maurice. It is somewhat ironic that I heard about Maurice as an important voice from non-Anglicans at Union Theological Seminary during my graduate years there. To their recommenda-tion should be added as a contagious influence Richard Niebuhr, who, in his

Christ and Culture, opted for my fifth and last way of relating Christ to culture, namely, Christ as the transformer of culture, with F.D. Maurice as the classic illustration.

I once asked my old theological teacher, Bishop Angus Dun, why he had never mentioned Maurice in class, especially since so many of his own points were Maurician. Dun laughed and said that his own generation in theology sought to free themselves from the influence of Maurice on their older colleagues. Dun said he had never really read Maurice and, if I thought his theological positions were Maurician, it must have been due to the fact that his own theological mentor, Henry Sylvester Nash, had been devoted to Maurice. I hope sometime to read enough of the books produced by the early faculty to be able to document this situation and perhaps to relate it to the debates among its lay founders about whether or not the School should be located in Cambridge next to Harvard University.

My late plunge into Maurice was occasioned by a request of the editors of A Handbook of Christian Theologians for an article on Maurice. I might have written at once on Kierkegaard, where my special competence lay, but I resolved to read the basic Maurice books, helped in selecting them by Alec Vidler's Witness to the Light: F.D. Maurice's Message for Today (1948). Vidler is the person most responsible for the renewed interest in England in Maurice, as Richard Niebuhr must be considered the comparable figure in America. To the discomfort of my editors, I kept delaying the writing of the article until I had read just one more of Maurice's books.

John Porter had chosen to write his doctorate at Union on The Place of Christ in the Thought of F.D. Maurice. Further collaboration between Porter and myself, facilitated by spending our summers in Heath, led to our joint anthology of Maurice's letters published as Toward the Recovery of Unity: The Thought of F.D. Maurice (1964).[14] I also used my part of the Hale Lecture-ship at Seabury-Western Seminary in 1973, to deliver "Maurice and Our Understanding of 'Ecumenical.'"

My desire to make Maurice's classic Kingdom of Christ (two volumes) both more accessible and less burdened by much Victorian material largely irrelevant today led me to publish, through the University Press of America in 1983, An Abridgment of Maurice's Kingdom of Christ.[15] Beginning in 1957, I had developed a course in Anglican Theology that had units on Richard Hooker, F.D. Maurice, William Temple, and some current controversial Anglican book, often one by Bishop J.A.T. Robinson. I was delighted to see the relevance of Maurice to later generations (once I was liberated from my

Victorianism and male chauvinism) when I participated in Carter Heyward's Maurice seminar.

***

I recently reread the Alumni Sermon I delivered in 1969. The dominant theological voice in it was Bonhoeffer, whose words were frequently redirected at the War in Vietnam. The American Church was praised for its leadership in the civil rights movement, but faulted for its ineffectiveness in dealing with Vietnam and with the military-industrial complex. The biblical basis was Luke's record of the sermon at Nazareth on liberation.

"My sermon presupposes the need for what many call a theology of revolution, but I much prefer not to use that phrase because it sounds too ideological. The truth is still more primary than any theology. The Gospel itself is revolution, a revolutionary change in the person and in society. One cannot be played against the other. There is no individual without the society to which he belongs; there is no society except for the individuals who compose it. If we are true to the Gospel our parish churches will cease to be, in Bonhoeffer's phrase, 'mere religious associations.' We shall then be able with God's help to confront the Vietnam war and the military-industrial-legislative-religious complex in this nation."

Second Writing Period (1972-1983)

After more than ten years "the ecumenical work horse" needed to find time to write again. While I had been an outdoorsperson from my youth, took my family regularly on canoe and mountain trips particularly in the Katahdin region of Maine, led theological students on day trips up Mt. Chocorua, and had read Thoreau avidly since my college days, my interest in the world of nature up to that time might best be described as mainly recreational and aesthetic rather than self-consciously ecological or theological. All of my outdoors activity began to take on a new dimension in the light of the growing environmental crisis.

One of my students, Brendan Whittaker, with a degree in forestry and work experience in that area, wrote his senior thesis in search of a theological foundation for ecology. I worked with him, exploring Brendan's bibliography in what became a significant learning experience for me. Brendan has since served as the Secretary of the Environment for the State of Vermont.

The next related event was Earth Day in 1970, with its widespread student participation. As a result, a student petition was organized requesting

Professor George Williams of the Harvard Divinity School and me to offer a joint Boston Theological Institute course in ecological theology. Williams was to concentrate on the historical background and I on its theological interpretation. A generous foundation grant made it possible to import lecturers of national significance in their fields. Afterwards, I developed a course on Theology and Ecology which I taught for a number of years.

I was eager to spend a full year sabbatical in Heath that would allow me to experience our earth cycle in full while I would be writing on theology and ecology. What emerged was Thoreau: Mystic, Prophet, Ecologist (1974).[16] Writing on Thoreau seemed to fill a deep need to try to answer such questions as what Thoreau really believed about God, considering his devastating assault on organized religion. How did he reconcile, if he did, his nature mysticism (Walden and the Journal) with his concerns for social justice (Civil Disobedience and A Plea for Captain John Brown)? How were his religion and ecology related to each other? Having written on Lincoln's religion, I was fascinated by Odell Shepard's preface to this Heart of Thoreau's Journals: "They bring back alive a man who, with all his extravagances, perversities, and fierce denunciations of much that America now stands for, is as quintessentially American as Abraham Lincoln. He comes, moreover, as great men are wont to do, in a time of great need."[17]

The Thoreau project was a family affair. Eleanor wanted to type the manuscript and our three sons, Edwin, John, and Stephen kept sending needed books and articles from their college and university libraries. The place chosen to write was our "summer place," nearly two thousand feet high in Western Massachusetts, where winter winds from the northwest blast the hill from which can be seen four of Thoreau's mountains: Greylock, Hoosac, Monadnock, and Wachusett.

Thoreau and Lincoln were both dependent on American Christianity to a greater degree than they realized. This suggests that some of the most profound religious thinking has been done in America quite apart from the vast numbers of competing denominations through an inherited common tradition of biblical wisdom. This biblical wisdom remains after the institutional element in church organization is largely discredited by the self-contradictions inherent in the denominations. I believe that there is still a reservoir of biblical wisdom, although less than in Lincoln's and Thoreau's day, of a lay and ecumenical respect for biblical reality that is struggling to find expression through literature, education, art, and other facets of culture rather than in the institutional churches.

While Thoreau had an aversion for metaphysics, he still had clear, although not completely harmonized, ideas of that environmental complex which has been diagramed as GOD (Nature, Self, Other People, History). Thoreau already has been recognized as one of America's greatest literary artists. He deserves recognition also as one of America's major religious thinkers. Whether in the categories of this study as mystic, prophet, and ecologist, or in his own terms as "mystic, transcendentalist, and natural philosopher, to boot," he is remarkable for the range of his perception of the interrelated aspects of reality, and even more for his courageous consistency in molding a life-style to express them. Robert Windsor, Cox Fellow at St. Paul's Cathedral, Boston, and I have a long term project for a joint book on Wilderness and Spirituality.

My second book of this period was Freedom's Holy Light: American Identity and the Future of Theology (1977).[18] Its nucleus was a pamphlet "Our Declaration of Independence and the Liberating God" printed in 1976, as part of the celebration of the nation's Bicentennial and requested by a special committee of the Episcopal Church for that purpose. The book consisted also of three chapters delivered originally in 1976, for the Kellogg Lectureship at the Episcopal Divinity School as a theological interpretation of the nation's Bicentennial. Considerable use was made of Erickson's categories of "identity-identification," but its basic purpose was to examine the Declaration despite its limitations and its subsequent impact upon American consciousness as, in part, an exercise in liberation theology. "Too often the religion of the founders has been dismissed as 'deism.' Rather, it should be analyzed in sufficient depth to reveal the biblical story of the Liberating God behind many of the deistic phrases. The figure of Jefferson necessarily looms large in these considerations."[19] I had been gathering books of Jefferson preparatory to a study of his religion, but shortly after this time a good study appeared on this subject, making it doubtful that another book was needed.

The second chapter of Freedom's Holy Light examined the process of secularization of the Puritan concept of "the chosen people" into that of "manifest destiny." Sydney Mead has aptly characterized America as "the nation with the soul of a church." The next chapter analyzed the protracted and murky debate over civil religion in America. Lincoln has emerged by all odds as the classic public theologian of the American experience. He is, therefore, critical for any attempt to define civil religion, an entity for which, interestingly enough, he himself showed almost no concern whatever. The following chapter analyzed Thoreau and ended with suggestions for the redoing of theology in an ecological context.

The last chapter surveyed the course of American theology for the past forty years, relating its findings to an evolving consciousness of American identity that might lead to two alternative paths forward. One path would be that of increased secularization as developed by Langdon Gilkey and related to current movements in liberation theology. Added to this would be a critical Nieburian evaluation of the degree to which power corrupts the agents of historical revolutions as well as the oppressors. The second option would be the further development of a process theology along the lines of Whitehead considerably heightened in intensity by the ecological crisis. This product in the current atmosphere of pluralism will inevitably confront ecological theology with the necessity of becoming a political theology with all the needed Niebuhrian restraints on power.

I acknowledge the impact of my mentor on my thought and politics through a friendship symbolized by the Niebuhrs making Heath their summer home with the Robert Browns, the John Porters, and the Bill Wolfs close by. It is interesting that my first writing for publication was an essay on Reinhold Niebuhr's conception of the human situation (the "doctrine of Man," as it was then naively called) in Kegley's and Bretall's Reinhold Niebuhr: His Religious, Social and Political Thought (1956).[20] That symposium signaled three fields in which Niebuhr would continue to make contributions: (1) politics (Arthur Schlesinger, Jr. and Kenneth Thompson), (2) evolving relations with Roman Catholicism (Gustave Weigel, S.J.) and (3) Judaism (Abraham Heschel and Alexander Bernstein). Contributions also by Daniel Day Williams and Henry Nelson Wieman might be said to symbolize an uneasy interest of process theologians in Niebuhr's work. The present Niebuhr revival and the possibility of yoking him with developments in Whiteheadian thought may not be so fantastic after all. Niebuhr's Moral Man and Immoral Society, which he had doubts about allowing to be republished, has proved by its sales his most popular work. Departments of political science and of government have been chiefly responsible for this.

Ordination of Women

In one of my earliest sermons in the chapel, I advocated the ordination of women. In 1974, I joined with a group to plan and carry out the Philadelphia Ordinations. I presented a deacon, Betty Bone Schiess, for ordination as priest to the ordaining bishops. John Allin, who had been elected the new Presiding Bishop by a conservative backlash, summoned a meeting of the Bishops in Chicago at which, given poor theological advice, they denied the validity of the ordinations. I was assigned the task of defending the validity of the ordinations. My argument was that, although the service was "irregular," it was not therefore "invalid," using the Official Catholic terminology of orders. My basic argument, however, was that it was a long overdue act of justice and the Gospel necessitated by a sound Christian theology. Charles Willie, head of the Lay Deputies and myself, the senior presbyter on the Joint Commission for Ecumenical Relations, resigned until the Episcopal Church acted affirmatively on the subject of women's ordination. Bishop Allin saw to it that I was not appointed to any responsibility for the remainder of his pontificate.

There is much more to be done in our advocacy of feminism and of inclusive language. Racism still needs continuous attention. I believe, however, that gayness and lesbianism now need the church's strongest support. For a number of reasons, the Episcopal Church probably has more homosexuals closeted within it than any other mainline church. The blessing of same sex unions as a support for monogamous fidelity in practicing homosexuals is the best way a liturgically oriented communion can initially face up to its responsibilities. The struggle will not be easy, and the price may be high, because of reactionary movements that build on the public's alarm over AIDS and a politics of retreat from responsibility that has increasingly characterized the past decade in episcopate, priesthood, and laity. There has been tremendous criticism of liberation theology among conventionally minded people over its phrase "a preferential option for the poor." The phrase needs expansion to include those unjustly discriminated against on grounds of sexuality.

Later Projects

After writing on Lincoln in Freedom's Holy Light and deciding not to pursue Jefferson further, I began to read once again the nine volumes of Lincoln's Collected Works. When Professor James Fowler taught his course at Harvard on the five or six stages of moral development, he often asked me to discuss my Lincoln book with a class that had just read it.

I was led to begin writing on Lincoln's own moral development in a book to be entitled Lincoln's Moral Development and His Politics, but I discovered that there just was not enough empirical evidence from Lincoln's younger years to match up with the Harvard developmental schema. I had reached a blind alley and saw the need to recast my project. Three terms continued to be used in confusing configurations: politics, morality and religion. While it might be impossible to trace these terms developmentally in Lincoln from his infancy to his maturity, an analysis of how Lincoln distinguished them as an adult and then put them together with great effectiveness might be a useful piece of research. I had just begun with an introductory chapter when I put the project on the back burner in order to join in producing two books by the faculty. There have been useful partial studies of Lincoln's politics, morality and religion, but no one has persuasively put all three of them together or accounted for Lincoln's masterful touch.

The Spirit of Anglicanism, which I edited in 1979, brought together a chapter by John Booty on Richard Hooker, one on William Temple by Owen Thomas, and a third which I wrote on F.D. Maurice.[21] Each of the writers read the contribution of his colleagues at least twice and made criticisms and suggestions and received in kind. I remember drafting a Preface five times before all three could sign it jointly. Its popularity has surprised the contributors. The appearance of the new Prayer Book may have had something to do with its acceptance as the communion faced new problems of identity.

In 1980, I put together Selections from Thomas Traherne's "Centuries of Meditations"[22] with an introductory essay. I had long found that Traherne spoke to me and typified many of the features of Anglicanism I had been trying to define. There is something of the romantic also in the finding of Traherne's Centuries in an English book stall at the beginning of this century and in the literary detective work that finally yielded the author's name from the seventeenth century.

I edited Anglican Spirituality in 1982. It was meant to be a faculty project with a number of planning sessions to design the chapters and to assign topics or to accept offerings if they were appropriate. The interest of so many of the faculty in spirituality surprised some readers, but was a testimony to the widespread concern with spirituality in a seminary not previously noted for it.

In the first chapter, Harvey Guthrie describes Anglican spirituality and examines such issues as its liturgical setting, spiritual direction, and the Book of Common Prayer as a genre comparable to the Rule of St. Benedict or to Bonhoeffer's Life Together. David Siegenthaler discusses some of "The Literature of Anglican Spirituality" in chapter two, with special attention to spiritual tracts, devotional manuals, poetry, diaries and the biographies of saints. In chapter three John Booty studies contrition in Hooker, Donne and Herbert, showing us that we have lost their understanding of contrition as the work of God's love in our current minimizing of the penitential note in public in favor of a happier atmosphere. In the fourth chapter, I bring together biography, theology, ethics, poetry, mysticism and saintliness to describe "The Spirituality of Thomas Traherne." In chapter five, John Booty presents a historical and theological survey of "Anglican Spirituality from Wilberforce to Temple" with special emphasis on participation, the law of sacrifice, the Incarnation and the dichotomy between this world and the next. Daniel Stevick, in chapter six, entitled "The Spirituality of the Book of Common Prayer," analyzes six of its major characteristics, underlines again the importance of the liturgical orientation of Anglicanism, and suggests that, while there is one authorized Book of Common Prayer, there might and should be many spiritualities. Alastair Cassels-Brown in chapter seven describes "Music as an

Expression of Anglican Spirituality" and concludes that music is an unofficial sacrament of the church. In chapter eight, "An Incarnational Spirituality," John Skinner describes a spirituality responsive to the Incarnation using the process philosophy of Whitehead as a conceptual foundation, thus continuing work in this area already started by William Temple, Lionel Thornton, Norman Pittenger and others. An Afterword locates the consensus among the authors chiefly in the liturgical orientation of Anglican spirituality and to the "comprehensiveness" of Anglicanism.

In the 1982 Commencement Address, before my retirement at the end of the following term, I spoke of a "social spirituality:" "We have seen that our text commends an ecumenism that goes well beyond mere 'churchiness.' In the New Testament the word 'ecumene' is used not for churchly activities, but simply as meaning 'the whole inhabited earth.' Only the oneness of Christians can make credible the message of oneness to the world. Beyond religious ecumenism we are summoned to human ecumenism. We ask with all the world's people: What does it mean to be human? How can the world be made more humane? What is distinctive about the Christian form of humanism?

"The electronic preachers have gotten it wrong when they attack 'secular' humanism! The parables of Jesus are a case in point. Hans Kung reminds us that Christianity is, as he calls it, 'radical humanism.' We cannot speak of the Gospel without speaking of the world. Nor can we really speak of the world without speaking of the Gospel.

"The mission, evangelism, and social action of the church are not separate activities of those who make holy hobbies out of one or two, but they are three interrelated and essential components of the Gospel -- all supported by a spirituality that sees increasing oneness among human beings as enabled by the very life of God. (I in them and Thou in me). In other words, we need a social spirituality and not merely a personal one."

Following this project, I turned my attention to lighter fare. For the Bicentennial celebration, in 1985, of Heath, Massachusetts, a town committee was formed on which I served as vice-chair. It produced, among other things, a ski race, an Edwardian reception, a beard contest, and a special town fair, and a publication, The Book of Heath. I wrote a chapter, "In Search of the Mohawk Trail," which allowed me to draw on hiking, interest in old maps, talk with old-timers, and some field exploration. Another chapter, "Why the Town Was Named for General Heath," described the militia general who commanded on the Day of Lexington and Concord (April 19, 1775) and would have been the first hung by the British if they had won. Washington later showed his confidence in Heath by entrusting to him the command of West Point following Benedict Arnold's treason.

A second book, The Heath Bicentennial 1985, was also published a few years later. The neighboring town of Rowe, where Richard Niebuhr had had a summer place until his death there, was also celebrating its Bicentennial. The churches of the two communities, with official participation by members of the Jewish community, organized an Ecumenical Service at which I was asked to speak. I adapted his "Declaration of Independence and the Liberating God" to the situation in 1785, when the U.S. Constitution did not yet exist and when the Declaration was the only common document in the two towns that related religion and politics.

Benedict Arnold: A Novel

From my high-school days, when I read the historical novels of Kenneth Roberts, I had been intrigued by Benedict Arnold, the friend of Washington and the most active General of the Revolution who yet became America's greatest traitor. I had guided canoe trips over parts of Arnold's Kennebec route to Quebec and collected copies of the journals of participants. I researched Arnold's years after his treason in Canada, the West Indies, and England since no novelist had really included this period in their writings. For most Americans, the treason seemed to mean his death, but there was life after treason. I had written on Lincoln and Thoreau, two impressive "good guys" of American history. Why not write on Benedict Arnold, the notorious "bad guy"? I determined that because of the condition of the sources, only a novel could do justice to Arnold. Not wanting to write a novel on "company time," I made it my first writing project after my retirement.

The aim was not to write a "theological" novel, but to tell an exciting story that would compel the reader to finish it. There were surprises in it for me. It ultimately took more than twice the time I had spent on any of my previous writings. Most of my previous books had been requested by editors or agreed to in advance. I deliberately wrote the novel without promise of publication and without deadlines -- to reduce stress, I thought. In my naivete, I discovered that editors were so suspicious of a retired theological professor writing his first novel that they would not even allow the manuscript or parts of it to be sent to them for reading. This was a stressful situation. One editor whom I knew personally explained that editors wanted (when they wanted novelists at all) young people who had a prospect of many years and much profit before them. Finally two fine editors of Paideia Press came forward who were actually pleased to publish it and made the process a pleasure.

When asked why a theologian should be interested in writing a novel, I usually reply that Benedict Arnold's is our story, the story of the good, the bad, and the ugly in each of us, in those around us, and in the history of nations. Arnold still remains a mystery for me, but so does the reality of evil and suffering. The Arnold I now know and want to share with my readers is both a better person than I realized when I began the project and also a much more evil one than I knew. The contradictions are deepened in Arnold who appears more and more like a tragic figure (cf. Shakespeare's Coriolanus) who does not know how to forgive an enemy or to find forgiveness himself. The religious dimension has asserted itself from the narrative of Arnold's life itself, not as a moralistic overlay by the author. W.H. Auden throws light on this mystery: "If, when we finish reading Billy Budd, we are left with questions which we feel have been raised, but not answered...this is due not to any lack of talent on Melville's part, but to the insolubility of the religious paradox in aesthetic terms."[23]

In 1987, the Episcopal Divinity School discovered very late that their desired Kellogg Lecturer could not come. The selection committee turned to me who, at their urging, hastily chose some passages to read from my novel and led a discussion on "Benedict Arnold: A Study in Good and Evil" (with subtitle: "The Novel as a Vehicle for Theological Reflection"). Even if I could not produce some systematic theology on command, the novel allowed me to appear as a narrative theologian in the latest style. I still have hopes, however, of reaching a wider audience.

NOTES

1. William J. Wolf, Man's Knowledge of God (Garden City: Doubleday & Co, Inc., 1955), p. 167.

2. Samuel Eliot Morison, By Land & By Sea: Essays & Addresses by Samuel Eliot Morison (New York: Alfred A. Knopf, 1953), p. 44.

3. Ibid.

4. William J. Wolf, No Cross, No Crown: A Study of the Atonement (Garden City: Doubleday & Co, Inc., 1957).

5. William J. Wolf, "The Atonement: Christian Concepts" in The Encyclopedia of Religion, edited by Mircea Eliade (New York: Macmillan Pub., 1987), Vol. I.

6. Ibid., p. 498.

7. William J. Wolf, The Almost Chosen People: A Study of the Religion of Abraham Lincoln (Garden City: Doubleday & Co., 1959).

8. Ibid., p. 186.

9. William J. Wolf, "Abraham Lincoln & Calvinism" in Calvinism & Political Order, George Hunt & John McNeil, eds. (Philadelphia: Westminster Press, 1966).

10. William J. Wolf, "Plan of Church Union: Catholic, Evangelical, Reformed," pamphlet (Cambridge, Massachusetts: ETS, 1965).

11. Paul Crow, Jr., "The Church: A New Beginning" in Church Union at Midpoint. (New York: Association Press, 1972), p. 23.

12. William J. Wolf, "Religious Liberty" in The Second Vatican Council: Studies by Eight Anglican Observers ed. Bernard C. Pawley (London: Oxford University Press, 1987), pp. 198-199.

13. Bethge, Eberhard et al., Glaube und Weitlichkeit bei Dietrich Bonhoeffer (Stuttgard: Colwer Verlag, 1969), p. 12.

14. William J. Wolf and John F. Porter, Toward The Recovery of Unity: The Thought of F.D. Maurice (New York: Seabury Press, 1964).

15. William J. Wolf, Abridgement of Maurice's Kingdom of Christ: The Original Two Volumes Abridged into One Based on the 1842 Edition Emended with an Introduction (New York: University Press of America, 1983).

16. William J. Wolf, Thoreau: Mystic, Prophet, Ecologist (Philadelphia: Pilgrim Press, 1974).

17. Odell Shephard, ed. The Heart of Thoreau's Journals (New York: Dover Publishers, Inc., 1961).

18. William J. Wolf, Freedom's Holy Light: American Identity and the Future of Theology (Wakefield, MA: Parameter Press, Inc., 1972).

19. Ibid., p. vii.

20. William J. Wolf, "Reinhold Niebuhr's Doctrine of Man" in Reinhold Niebuhr: His Religious, Social, and Political Thought, Charles W. Kegley and Robert W. Bretall, eds. (New York: Macmillan, 1956).

21. William J. Wolf, ed. The Spirit of Anglicanism: Hooker, Maurice, Temple (Wilton, Conn.: Morehouse-Barlow Co. Inc., 1979).

22. William J. Wolf, Selections from Thomas Traherne's 'Centuries of Meditations' (Cincinnati: Forward Movement Press, 1980).

23. W.H. Auden, The Enchafed Flood (London: Faber and Faber, 1951), p. 119.

BILL WOLF: THEOLOGIAN, NEIGHBOR, FRIEND
Robert McAfee Brown

Although Bill Wolf was officially called a systematic theologian, he fit the category loosely at best, which is taken here as a plus. Readers may remember that Bill wrote his doctoral dissertation on Soren Kierkegaard, whose major polemic was directed against "the system" in general and George Wilhelm Friedrich Hegel, systematizer par excellence, in particular.

Unpredictability is a chief characteristic of a thinker relatively unconcerned with systematizing. Bill's life, as well as his thought, exemplified this admirable trait. To be sure, he did spend his entire teaching career in one place. But consider: this man also has been a licensed Maine guide, a wartime aerial photographer, an arranger of trysting places for courting couples, a veteran barker at an annual New England town fair, a frustrated but determined novelist, a plumber-carpenter-electrician-house painter-"water witch" who bought a decrepit abandoned farm house and made out of it a thing of beauty, a raconteur without parallel, and an accomplished ornithologist.

Bill had all the gifts to be a scholar-recluse: a vast array of ancient and modern languages, an almost inordinate love of history, and a bent for the excitement of research and the lure of ancient texts. He did become a scholar -- as books on the doctrines of revelation, atonement, F.D. Maurice, and Abraham Lincoln attest. However, he never became a recluse -- as his activities on behalf of women's ordination, and later the rights of gays and lesbians, similarly attest. He was a wonderful burr under Episcopal saddles.

Bill Wolf and I met at the opening of the second semester at Union Theological Seminary in New York City in 1943. Although he was a Th.D. candidate and I a mere B.D. candidate, we were the newest guys on the block, having entered at midyear. We were surrounded by people who were already well into the Union ambiance. I had graduated from Amherst College on the last day of January, taken the night train to New York, and become an enrollee of Part V of Paul Tillich's "Systematic Theology" course the next morning. This was baptism by fire, and I needed a sponsor to help me affirm the world, the flesh and the demonic. I don't know whether Bill felt such displacement as I did, but fresh from my humanistic college training, I at least felt that I was contra mundum, as Athanasius said so well (even though at the time I had never heard of Athanasius). Bill was a "Niebuhrian" already, I discovered, and I needed him in that arena as well, since I had come to Union partly to test my then pacifist convictions against Niebuhr's.

Bill, fresh from Trinity College and the Episcopal Theological School, had "Anglican" stamped all over him, but a "Niebuhrian Anglican" was something else! And I learned a few more things about his Anglicanism the very first evening, when we went to chapel together. I discovered that Bill was an ecumenical Anglican, since he didn't leave or even snort at the very free church Baptist-inspired service we attended. I also discovered he could not carry a tune with enough accuracy to celebrate a "high church" Anglican mass.

Fresh from my Amherst education, which was long on John Dewey and short on Jonathan Edwards, I needed a lot of help in those first weeks, when it was Tillich at 9 and Niebuhr at 12 with Van Dusen in between. Stern stuff; and who better to explain existential dialectics to me than a man immersing himself in Kierkegaard? So I was helped into the world of "impossible possibilities," heteronomy, the shortcomings of the said John, faith as gnosis, the merits and demerits of Schleiermacher, and a host of other holy mysteries.

I think the seeds were even then being sown for Bill to escape the clutches of too systematic a way of thinking. I know that they bore fruit in the future; when lecturing years later on Nicolai Berdyaev, Bill engaged in an enthusiastic gesture that deposited his lecture notes on the floor. After retrieving them and trying vainly to restore them in proper sequence, Bill finally gave up the effort and finished the class ex tempore, commenting, "Actually, with Berdyaev, it doesn't matter too much how you number the pages."

* * *

My longest sustained time with Bill, aside from summers in Heath, Massachusetts, was at the second session of the Vatican Council in the Fall of 1963. We were both official "observers," he from the Anglican Communion and I from the World Alliance of Reformed and Presbyterian Churches. Because we both summered in the farming community of Heath, we soon established the fact that Heath, Massachusetts, had a greater per capita representation of inhabitants at the Vatican Council than any other population center in the entire oikoumene.

Back in our Union days, Bill and I had been pretty hard-nosed about institutional Roman Catholicism, from our respective vantage points of Canterbury and Geneva, by virtue of the fact that we received much of our theological education in Cardinal Spellman's archdiocese. However, by the early sixties, we had mellowed sufficiently to cheer the Council on rather than hope it would fall ignominiously on its face. Bill also had been softened up by living his post-student years back in Cardinal Cushing's archdiocese. Cushing was a good-hearted ecumenist who cornered Bill one day in the coffee bar at St. Peter's to inquire, "Wolf, what language are they speaking out there?"

Bill was extraordinarily helpful to me at the Council, both officially and unofficially. Unofficially, he saved the honor of the World Alliance of Reformed and Presbyterian Churches on the morning of the opening of session two, a formal affair at which we fratres seiuncti ("separated brethren" as Vatican lingo described us) were supposed to wear our emblems of ecclesiastical office. I had dutifully brought my Geneva gown and tabs to wear, just as John Calvin had prescribed, but for some reason I had arrived with a clerical collar that was too small. Bill came through with an appropriately sized collar from his amply-stocked Anglican wardrobe, and I was thus able to enter St. Peter's with the proper accoutrements of office. We both took covert satisfaction in the fact that the borrowed collar was called "Pontiff."

Bill's official help was guiding me through the Council's Latin texts -- which were almost as difficult for me as for Cardinal Cushing -- by translating them into English. Such knowledge was mandatory if we were to reflect sensibly on the discussion of the texts in our observers' meetings, and in sessions with expert Roman Catholic theologians. Not even a summer immersed in Scanlon and Scanlon, "offering the full vocabulary of the mass in 20 lessons for priests making a late vocation," prepared me to make sense out of the council documents without Bill's scholarly assistance.

* * *

There have been references to Heath, Massachusetts, and here is where the "neighbor" and "friend" part of the title comes to focus. After finishing his Th.D. at Union, Bill, in an extraordinary burst of efficiency, acquired a job, a house, a car, and a fiancée, within the space, as I remember it, of about eight days. He had been asked to return to the Episcopal Theological School to teach systematic theology and on the strength of that offer bought a decrepit farm house in Heath, and, further, persuaded Eleanor Dun, niece of Dean Angus Dun of E.T.S., to marry him and share the Heath home.

Part of Heath's attraction for Bill was that he had come to know the residents as summer pastor of the Heath Evangelical Community Church. Another sign of the ecumenical generosity of his Anglicanism is that he learned to say -- without choking -- "debts" instead of "trespasses" in public recital of the Lord's Prayer. It was a congregation that, in addition to the local farmers and their families, included such summer residents as Reinhold and Ursula Niebuhr, Felix Frankfurter, Bishop Gilbert of New York, the aforementioned Angus Dun (later Bishop of Washington), Dean Howard Chandler Robbins of the Cathedral of St. John the Divine in New York City, and various other (mostly Anglican) luminaries.

* * *

Three years out of seminary I decided to return to graduate school and work for a Columbia University-Union Seminary Ph.D. Sydney had just delivered our first child, we were going off salary for two years at least, and our one fiscal surety was the G.I. Bill with its $90 per month living allowance. At this point Bill and Eleanor approached us, offering to sell us fifty acres of Heath woodland, an offer we couldn't refuse but also couldn't afford. The idea was as attractive as the timing was impossible. However, we visited the Wolfs at their freshly painted home, were captivated by the land and the view, and proposed spreading our payments over a period of six years. Deal closed. A windfall to the Wolfs in the next year was shared with us and the land was paid off in three years!

My first teaching job was in Minnesota, so we delayed the development of the land. Two years later, however, we were unexpectedly on the Union faculty and faced with the prospect of raising a family on the asphalt-covered environs of Broadway and 122nd Street. Heath, just four hours away, was ideal for reassuring our kids of the reality of fields and forest. I don't know whether there is an Anglican word for all that, but there is a Presbyterian one: Providence.

* * *

Freed, in writing about a non-systematic theologian, to be non-systematic myself, I now take the liberty of recounting even earlier Wolfian contributions to the Browns' lives. After Sydney Thomson (a woman I very much wanted to marry) graduated from Smith College in 1943, she took a summer job caring for the Niebuhr children in Heath. I had to go to summer school as a condition of remaining a wartime seminarian, but summer school ended on August 15. I was certain I did not wish the full month before the Fall semester to pass without pursuing my cause with Sydney.

I wrote to my friend, the summer minister of the Heath Evangelical Community Church, for pastoral help. My very specific query to him: was there a farm in Heath that would gamble on a city-bred, inexperienced "chore boy" who would work for a pittance from dawn to dusk in exchange for free evenings? Bill engaged in a search that netted a willing family, the forever-to-be-blessed Oscar Landtroms, who lived a mere 2.9 miles from the Niebuhr's stone cottage. What is 2.9 miles (each way) to a man in love? Bill also furnished "Ye Olde Lover's Mappe," a paradigm of cartographic expertise -- this man had been an aerial photographer, after all -- that indicated a variety of

trysting sites along the trail (including the pre-eminent South Heath Cemetery!).
Less than one year later we were married.

* * *

The result of these events, in which Providence has been aided by acts
of human intervention, is that the four Brown children and the three Wolf boys,
along with their respective parents, have spent all their subsequent summers
within several hundred yards of each other. This has created bucolic memories
for all of us, though more recently they have been tinged with unutterable
sadness: the youngest Wolf, Steve, had an increasingly troubled adult life from
which his early death was almost a release; and John, the middle son, happily
married and the father of two lovely daughters, unaccountably and unpredictably
collapsed and died at age 36 while jogging.

However, the memories of dozens of earlier summers remain intact, the
more precious from recognizing the fragility of life. The memories range from
building tree houses to learning to drive a tractor, from playing Little League
to swimming in a pond almost every summer afternoon. More recently, eldest
Brown child Peter asked Ned Wolf, "my oldest friend," to stand with him at his
Heath wedding.

All these things the Browns owe to the Wolf's initial invitation to share
summers on a beautiful hillside. Peter, who is a professional photographer, had
a show in Houston, Texas, coincident with his wedding, that was composed
exclusively of shots of Heath summers. In his explanatory note for the show,
he said it best:

> This show is by no means a portrait of the town of Heath, which is a
> small but complex mix of farmers, academicians and workers. It is more
> the beginnings of a collective portrait of the people I grew up with --
> their children, their summertime activities, their spirit, energy and
> humor. In essence the show is a collection of photographs of personal
> moments with people I live in a place I care for very deeply...
>
> If this a sunny and fun-filled show, it is because Heath in the summer is
> a genuinely sunny and light-filled place.

* * *

One cannot conclude an account of Bill Wolf's activities without
mentioning his gift as a storyteller. The spoken word cannot be transferred
easily to the written page, and I will not try. Far better that those who wished

the true flavor of a Wolf narration to have approached Bill with a request such as, "Tell us about the time you took Mrs. Drown and her two elderly friends on an automobile tour in New England..."

So, maybe the stories acquired a little embellishment with the passing of time. They nevertheless remain anchored in history, and became truer to type as they became less obsessed with fact. Their power to entertain, to enlighten, and even to instruct, was enhanced with each repetition. "Let no piddling pedant," as Kierkegaard said on another occasion, "lay a hand to these words, but let them stand as they are."

Bill Wolf did not vegetate at Heath. Books were written, fields cleared, children and grandchildren raised, papers written for the Heath Historical Society, and the Benedict Arnold story crafted into a potential prize winner. Of course, events of the outer world always impinged. I remember particularly the summer plans were being made for the first ordination of Episcopal women -- an event without, shall we say, the collaboration of the ecclesiastical establishment which was even in its planning scandalizing many among the faithful. The Browns shared a party line with the Wolfs in those days, and I recall how difficult it was to get access to the phone as one after another of the Anglican principalities and powers importuned Bill to withdraw his support for the allegedly scandalous scheme. And when there were no incoming calls of protest, Bill was calling out messages of renewed support for the beleaguered few planning the ordination service.

* * *

It is for others to describe Bill at the Episcopal Theological School and it successor institution, the Episcopal Divinity School, Bill within the life of the Anglican communion, and Bill as a citizen of Cambridge, Massachusetts. However, those who knew him best as a clear lecturer, a patient counselor, an involved churchman, and a leftist voter, need also to be aware that the man they so admired once faced the following test for certification as a Maine guide. He was given a pail of water in which a small log had been immersed for 24 hours, a hatchet, and two matches. He was told that by using the wet wood and no other wood, he must build a fire that would boil the water in the pail.

The expert on Soren Kierkegaard, F.D. Maurice, the Thirty-Nine Articles, and Vatican II, passed the test with ease.

EULOGY FOR BILL WOLF[*]

Pamela Porter

I want to say a few words for those of us who first knew Bill as children. Many of the thoughts and memories I have to share are personal and I am aware that what I have to say of Bill represents only a small portion of the life he shared so extravagantly with Heath, with ETS and EDS and, in his teaching and writing, with the whole world.

Extravagant is not the first word that comes to mind, thinking of how Bill lived. He lived simply with few indulgences. But thinking of his interest in the world, his energy and generosity, extravagant seems a fair term.

Bill's faith took the form of an abiding and compassionate interest in the world. He was a model for us of Yankee citizenship, devoted to the issues of his communities and times. He was also a model of faithfulness, true to his family and friends through illness and tragedy.

"Life is worth living," he said to me after the death of his and Eleanor's son, Stephen, "Never give up on it."

Bill was born again in his granddaughters, Emily and Catherine. He took a special interest and delight in them. Careful always to let them know he loved them both equally, he hung not one but two swings in the trees near the house, one in the moraine locust and one in the huge old maple. He named the inflatable boat he provided the Emmie-Cat. During their summer visits he was at his granddaughters' pleasure giving tractor rides, reading bedtime stories and entering into their world of make-believe without reservation. He attended endless tea parties and helped transform the old milk house that had once been his study into the Mayberry Cottage. It is a beautifully furnished and magical retreat.

He was a great story teller. Stories of Mrs. Drown and Daddy Hatch, of Heath and seminary life were full of humor and appreciation for human character with all its peculiarities and greatness.

Bill was our introduction to the natural world. Being a Maine Guide, he led us up and down Pocumtuck, Monadnock, Greylock and Haystack with equal confidence whether he knew just where we were or not. He taught us to keep our eyes open for wild animals, was always interested to hear what we had seen,

---

[*] This homily was given at Bill Wolf's funeral at the Evangelical Community Church in Heath, Massachusetts, on June 9, 1990.

always excited to share what he had seen. A few summers ago, when a moose appeared at his pond, Bill rushed to make a plaster cast of its foot prints, for proof. He was one of the few Heath residents ever to have seen a wolverine.

He welcomed with an embracing interest anyone who came to his door. He engaged young and old, stranger and friend, great and humble with the same eager attention. He never let theology stand in the way of neighborliness. You couldn't help but feel bigger when you were with him and important even while he himself seemed larger than life; a mountain of a man. For many of us he was a kind of second father or grandfather.

Bill was a model of generosity. He gave of himself unstintingly to the town of Heath, through the Church, the Historical Society, the Bicentennial Committee and the Fair, to name a few. And how many of us have walked through his and Eleanor's yard to swim in the pond, all welcomed, except beavers. How many of us have hunted or planted gardens in his fields? How many stored our possessions in his garage, including even the Heath Public Library which operated for a time from there during renovations to the Town Hall.

For many of us Bill has been a model of saintliness. It was not at all that he was perfect. It was rather that he was finally and ultimately faithful. He persevered to overcome personal short-comings such as plague us all, the contradictions of his times and the tragedies of his life, of which there were more than his share, without giving in to self-centered apathy, bitterness or despair. He remained true: true to life, true to his faith, true to the lives of his family, friends and neighbors.

He taught us, finally, about holding fast to what is good: the beauty of the earth, the blessing of children and grandchildren, the company of friends, generosity of spirit, an animating faith in God's goodness and justice, and a good story, well told. He lived life with the same interest and devotion right up to the moment of his death.

It is odd that although it was known by most of us that his health was failing, none of us was prepared to hear of his death. We were still planning the news we would share with him, questions and topics we would discuss, the pleasure of watching with him one more season come and go, and he was gone. He was not one to linger over good-byes.

There used to be a saucer-shaped pool in the Wolf's backyard and I remember Bill and Bob Brown and my father, John Porter, sitting on the far rim of it, belly deep in water, discussing the intricacies of faith and sad contradictions of politics, while we children swam together around them and became friends. In many ways the friendship of those three shaped the world as we first knew it and has provided a context for us ever since. In that friendship we have known the action of providence. Sitting together on the shore of the pond watching our children, their grandchildren, swim together and become friends we catch a glimpse of it; indiscriminate blessing, raining down on us from generation to generation.

BIBLIOGRAPHY OF WORKS BY WILLIAM J. WOLF

BOOKS AUTHORED

Man's Knowledge of God (Garden City, NY: Doubleday, 1955)

No Cross, No Crown: A Study of the Atonement (Garden City, NY: Doubleday, 1957)

The Religion of Abraham Lincoln (NY: Seabury Press, 1963), a reprint of The Almost Chosen People: A Study of the Religion of Abraham Lincoln (Garden City, NY: Doubleday, 1959)

A Plan of Church Union: Catholic, Evangelical, and Reformed (Cambridge, MA: Episcopal Theological School, 1966)

Thoreau: Mystic, Prophet, Ecologist (Philadelphia: United Church Press, 1974)

Freedom's Holy Light: American Identity and the Future of Theology (Wakefield, MA: Parameter Press, 1977)

An Abridgement of Maurice's Kingdom of Christ (Lanham, MD: University Press of America, 1983)

Benedict Arnold: A Novel (Boston: Paideia, 1990)

BOOKS EDITED

Protestant Churches and Reform Today (New York: Seabury Press, 1964)

Toward the Recovery of Unity: The Thought of Frederick Denison Maurice, with John F. Porter, (New York: Seabury Press, 1964)

The Spirit of Anglicanism: Hooker, Maurice, Temple (Wilton, Conn: Morehouse-Barlow, 1979)

Anglican Spirituality (Wilton, Conn: Morehouse-Barlow, 1982)

ARTICLES

"How Barth has Influenced Me." Theology Today, 13 (1956), 372-373.

"The Ordained Ministry in Uniting Churches." 1964, unpublished.

"Abraham Lincoln and Calvinism." In Calvinism and the Political Order. Ed. George L. Hunt and John T. McNeill (Philadelphia: Westminster, 1965), 140-156.

"Curriculum Revision at the Episcopal Theological School and Some Dynamics of its Acceptance." In Horizons of Theological Education. Ed. John B. Coburn, Walter D. Wagoner, and Jesse H. Ziegler (Dayton, OH: American Association of Theological Schools, 1966)

"Ecumenism and Women Episcopal Priests." Journal of Ecumenical Studies, 9 (1972), 229-235.

"Maurice and our Understanding of 'Ecumenical'." Anglican Theological Review, 54 (1972), 273-290.

"The Theological Landscape 1936-1974: An Address." In Theology and Culture. Ed. W. Taylor Stanley (Evanston, IL: Anglican Theological Review Supplementary Series, No. 7, 1976)

"Anglicanism and its Spirit." In The Spirit of Anglicanism: Hooker, Maurice, Temple. Ed. William J. Wolf (Wilton, CN: Morehouse-Barlow, 1979), 137-188.

"Frederick Denison Maurice." In The Spirit of Anglicanism: Hooker, Maurice, Temple. Ed. William J. Wolf (Wilton, CN: Morehouse-Barlow, 1979), 49-100.

"Selections from Thomas Traherne's Centuries of Meditations." (Cincinnati: Forward Movement Press, 1980), pamphlet.

"The Spirituality of Thomas Traherne." In Anglican Spirituality. Ed. William J. Wolf (Wilton, CN: Morehouse-Barlow, 1982)

CONTRIBUTORS

Susan Adams became a priest in the Diocese of Auckland in the Anglican Church of the Province of New Zealand in 1979. She was the first person to receive a Doctor of Ministry in Feminist Liberation Theology from the Episcopal Divinity School. She co-authored, with partner John Salmon, Being Just Where You Are and Women, Culture and Theology. She is presently Co-ordinator of Ministry Education for the Diocese of Auckland, with responsibility for the selection and training of priests and for post-ordination and lay ministry education. She lives in Auckland, Aotearoa-New Zealand.

John Booty, Professor Emeritus of Church History at the Episcopal Divinity School, is a former Dean of the School of Theology at Sewanee. He is the author of 18 books, including The Christ We Know and The Episcopal Church in Crisis.

Robert McAfee Brown is Professor Emeritus of Theology and Ethics at the Pacific School of Religion in Berkeley, California. Dr. Brown received his Ph.D. from Columbia University. His latest books include Gustavo Gutierrez: An Introduction to Liberation Theology, and Spirituality and Liberation: Overcoming the Great Fallacy.

Anne E. Gilson is currently finishing her Ph.D. in theology at Union Theological Seminary. She is a graduate of the Episcopal Divinity School. Anne's work is centered around the construction of a theo-ethic of sexuality from a feminist liberation theological perspective. She was co-editor of Revolutionary Forgiveness.

David McI. Gracie, an Episcopal priest, David is the former Episcopal Chaplain at Temple University and Urban Missioner for the Episcopal Diocese of Pennsylvania.

Barbara C. Harris is Suffragan Bishop of the Diocese of Massachusetts. She was ordained to the Episcopal priesthood in 1980, and consecrated Bishop in 1989. A former executive with the Sun Oil Company, Bishop Harris currently writes and preaches on a wide variety of social justice issues.

Carter Heyward is currently Professor of Theology at the Episcopal Divinity School. Her latest books include Speaking of Christ: A Lesbian Feminist Voice and Touching Our Strength: The Erotic as Power and the Love of God. She was ordained a priest with 10 other women in Philadephia in 1974.

Suzanne R. Hiatt is Professor of Pastoral Theology at the Episcopal Divinity School. Bill Wolf preached at her ordination to the diaconate in 1971, calling for the immediate ordination of women to the priesthood. She was ordained a priest in Philadelphia in 1974.

Margaret Craddock Huff received her Ph.D. in Pastoral Psychology and Counseling from Boston University in 1987. She is an adjunct instructor at Northeastern University in the Department of Religion and Philosophy. She is also in private practice as a consultant in pastoral psychology.

Corine Johnson (a pseudonym) is a musician/ethicist who could not have lived without music or without trying to make sense of what is right and what is wrong. She is a lesbian graduate of the Episcopal Divinity School. Corine's shortest sermon is "Sisters hold up the sisters."

Joanna Kadi is a Lebanese-Canadian writer and activist. She received her undergraduate degree in Women's Studies from the University of Toronto and an M.A. in feminist ethics from the Episcopal Divinity School. Joanna receives her greatest inspiration from her cats, Orlando and Fury.

Sue Phillips is an ethicist and political activist. She received her Master of Divinity, concentrating in feminist ethics and theology, from the Episcopal Divinity School. She currently resides in Washington, DC.

Pamela Porter is currently a nursery school teacher in Heath, Massachusetts. She is a graduate of the University of Michigan and received her Master of Divinity from the Episcopal Divinity School.

J. Antonio Ramos, former Anglican Bishop of Costa Rica, is presently Regional Coordinator for the South American Project of the Christian Children's Fund in Richmond, Virginia. He is former Chair of the Board and contributing editor of The Witness.

Diana F. Scholl is a freelance writer and Doctor of Ministry student at the Episcopal Divinity School. She is writing on the topic of spirituality as a resource for healing, especially for women with AIDS. She received her Master of Divinity from Duke University and worked for five years at the Chapel of the Cross in Chapel Hill, North Carolina.

Owen Thomas is currently the Francis Lathrop Fiske Professor of Systematic Theology at the Episcopal Divinity School. A graduate of the Episcopal Theological School, he received his Ph.D. from Columbia University. He is the